A GENERAL JURISPRUDENCE
OF LAW AND SOCIETY

BRIAN Z. TAMANAHA

OXFORD
UNIVERSITY PRESS

OXFORD

UNIVERSITY PRESS

Great Clarendon Street, Oxford OX2 6DP

Oxford University Press is a department of the University of Oxford.
It furthers the University's objective of excellence in research, scholarship,
and education by publishing worldwide in

Oxford New York

Athens Auckland Bangkok Bogotá Buenos Aires Cape Town
Chennai Dar es Salaam Delhi Florence Hong Kong Istanbul Karachi
Kolkata Kuala Lumpur Madrid Melbourne Mexico City Mumbai
Nairobi Paris São Paulo Shanghai Singapore Taipei Tokyo Toronto Warsaw

and associated companies in Berlin Ibadan

Oxford is a registered trade mark of Oxford University Press
in the UK and in certain other countries

Published in the United States
by Oxford University Press Inc., New York

© B. Tamanaha 2001

The moral rights of the author have been asserted

Database right Oxford University Press (maker)

First published 2001

British Library Cataloguing in Publication Data

Data available

Library of Congress Cataloging in Publication Data

Tamanaha, Brian Z.
A general jurisprudence of law and society/Brian Z. Tamanaha.
p. cm.
Includes bibliographical references and index.
1. Sociological jurisprudence. 2. Law—Philosophy. I. Title.
K370.T358   2001   340′.115—dc21   2001034063

ISBN 0-19-924466-9
ISBN 0-19-924467-7 (pbk.)

1 3 5 7 9 10 8 6 4 2

Typeset in Baskerville
by Hope Services (Abingdon) Ltd.
Printed and Bound in Great Britain by
Biddles Ltd., Guildford and King's Lynn

For Jolijt and Kats

General Editor's Introduction

Brian Tamanaha's book challenges some widely-held assumptions about the relationship between law and society. It builds on his earlier work *Realistic Socio-Legal Theory* to explore and take issue with central organizing ideas in contemporary scholarship. It challenges what the author calls the 'mirror thesis', that is, the view of law as a reflection of society. It takes on the assumption that law has an ordering function: that law maintains order by establishing and enforcing rules, and by resolving disputes. It questions the idea, one which has long had a strong hold on our thinking, that law reflects the customs and morality of society and in doing so maintains social order.

Professor Tamanaha breaks away from this orthodox view, which he regards as based on a mistaken assumption about the nature of law in Western societies. This view is not simply inaccurate with respect to Western legal systems, he argues, it also fails to address the implications of globalization, on the one hand, and the spread of local legal forms, on the other. His task is to produce a general theoretical framework which can embrace this complexity. In starting this project, Brian Tamanaha draws not only from legal theory, but also from social and political theory, sociology, and anthropology.

This is a bold and ambitious book. To some it will seem controversial and provocative. But there is no denying its importance, for it speaks to some of the fundamental questions in socio-legal studies.

Keith Hawkins

Contents

Preface   xi

1. The Law–Society Framework   1
2. Law and Society in Western Legal Theory   11
3. Loosening the Hold of the Mirror Thesis   51
4. Fundamental Shifts in the Law–Society Relationship   77
5. Against the Mirror Thesis   107
6. A Socio-Legal Positivist Approach to Law   133
7. A Non-Essentialist Legal Pluralism   171
8. Elements of a General Jurisprudence   206

Bibliography   243
Index   259

Preface

Despite the theoretical nature of this work, my motivations for attempting to construct a general jurisprudence are far from theoretical—they derive from my experience working as a lawyer in Micronesia. Law in Micronesia was remarkably unlike what I had learned law was, and should be, in the course of my legal training. I was taught—legal theory instructs us—that law is a mirror of society that functions to maintain social order. In this standard understanding, the norms of law are derived from and reflect the customs and morality of society. The problem with these theories is that they emphatically made no sense as an explanation or description of law in Micronesia. Micronesian law was transplanted in its entirety from the United States; even the majority of the legal actors, like myself, were American expatriates.

Their customs and values could hardly have been more different from the legal system and its norms. To cite a few examples, from Yap in particular: they had a thriving caste system, yet the law prohibited discrimination; their culture was consensual in orientation, but the law was based upon the adversary model; their understanding of criminal offences required a response by the community itself (literally), but the state insisted that it has a monopoly on the application of force, and any community reaction is illegal vigilantism; property ownership was a complex mixture of possession rights, use rights, consultation over use and possession, and community ownership simultaneous with chief ownership, whereas the property system and the mortgage laws were based upon common law notions of fee simple, life estate, and remainders; their political system was democratic, but for most elections candidates stood unopposed because the approval of traditional leaders was de facto required of anyone who wished to run; the law was written in English legal language, while many people had a rudimentary command of English, and others could not speak it at all (never mind the far more complex and inaccessible legal language); court decisions were filled with arguments based upon US common law and constitutional analysis which simply had no parallel or grounding in Micronesian society; many people were ignorant of the law, and feared or avoided it; state law was a marginal force in the maintenance of social order (see Tamanaha 1993b). The law in Micronesia was like an alien presence in their midst, mostly irrelevant, taking care of tasks related primarily to the operation of the

government, occasionally intruding into their social lives in various un-
welcome ways.

Following this experience, after returning to the academy, I learned
that what I had thought was a unique situation is not that unusual after
all. Legal transplantation, either through colonial imposition or voluntary borrowing, is a widespread phenomenon. What I encountered in
Micronesia is one manifestation of a multitude of such situations around
the world, each unique in its own way, yet alike in their inconsistency
with standard theories about the relationship between law and society. It
might be tempting to dismiss this as an aberrant situation not worthy of
attention, since the most extreme examples exist in non-Western countries. However, the West constitutes a relatively small proportion of the
world both geographically and demographically.

No existing theory of law accounts for this situation in any satisfactory
way; indeed it is all but ignored by theories about law. The explanation
for this gap is plain: legal theories have been produced by Western
theorists who see law much as I did, through the lens provided by our
assumed view of the law in our own societies.

With further probing, however, it becomes evident that this standard
theoretical understanding of law is inadequate even with regard to the
Western contexts in which it has been produced, as would be evident following an examination of the immigrant communities, or the sweatshops, or the blighted pockets of impoverished, lawless anarchy which are
located in many major Western cities. This inadequacy is heightened
when the implications of globalization, and the apparent proliferation of
legal forms at the local and transnational levels, are taken into consideration. Other fields of study such as legal sociology and legal anthropology
have observed aspects of these phenomena, yet they have largely failed to
engage legal theory, and they have failed to produce any viable theories
of their own to account for this situation. Meanwhile, legal theory continues to repeat the soothing bromide that law is a mirror of society that
maintains social order, blind to the messy reality, assuming away counter
examples as insignificant exceptions or variations.

The question—the challenge—is whether there is some way to wrestle
all of this complexity and variety onto a single framework. Without one,
there is no hope of understanding law in situations like those in
Micronesia, together with those in West, as well as everywhere in-
between, and no hope of comparing these situations in ways that will be
fruitful for all. That is the promise of a general jurisprudence. There is no
reason to believe that there must be one basic theory of law for the West,

and no theory, or a multitude of separate theories, for all of the rest. In the absence of a general jurisprudence, that is what we are left with.

Characteristics of a General Jurisprudence and its Problems

'General jurisprudence' is the study of law *as such*. It is based on the belief that 'Law is [a] . . . social institution found in all societies and exhibiting a core of similar features' (Gavison 1987: 28). The fundamental idea is that there are certain elements and concepts common to all legal systems, as a function and consequence of what it means to constitute a legal system, and the task of a general jurisprudence is to identify and analyse these elements and concepts. A general jurisprudence was thought to be essential for the understanding of, comparison of, and improvement of law around the world. The project to construct a general jurisprudence, initially placed on the agenda about two centuries ago by legal positivists Jeremy Bentham and John Austin, was taken up by a diverse group, including scholars who worked under the banner of legal science, comparative law scholars, and by legal theorists generally. Despite the efforts dedicated towards the completion of this task, however, a general jurisprudence was not successfully accomplished, and for a number of generations the project had all but expired.[1]

With the notable exception of H. L. A. Hart, and more recently William Twining, few recent legal theorists have embraced the challenge of constructing a general jurisprudence. 'In the English-speaking world traditional positivism, normative legal philosophy, critical legal studies, post-modernism, and even economic analysis of law seem to have been going through a somewhat parochial or inward-looking phase, although there are some notable exceptions' (Twining 1996: 119). A factor contributing to this self-obsession is that the quest for a universal or general jurisprudence, traditionally indulged in by Western jurisprudence scholars, has embarrassingly imperialist, old-fashioned overtones. Currently popular notions of cultural relativism and postmodernism privilege the local, suggest that nothing is universal, and challenge the very ability to construct generally applicable standards. 'The authority of "grand theory" styles seems suspended for the moment in favor of a close consideration of such issues as contextuality' (Marcus and Fischer 1986: 8). Postmodernism, in particular, counsels strongly against even making the attempt:

---

[1] An excellent discussion of the history and key aspects of a general jurisprudence can be found in Twining (2000: chap. 2).

Grand theories and universal overviews cannot be sustained without producing empirical falsification and intellectual authoritarianism. To assert general truths is to impose a spurious dogma on the chaos of phenomena. Respect for contingency and discontinuity limits knowledge to the local and specific. Any alleged comprehensive, coherent outlook is at best no more than a temporarily useful fiction masking chaos, at worst an oppressive fiction masking relationships of power, violence and subordination. (Tarnas 1991: 401)

Another inhibiting factor is that it is difficult to imagine how to go about constructing a general jurisprudence given the existing multiplicity of legal theories, as well as of social theories and social sciences, each with their own presuppositions, concepts, terminology, and objectives. So accustomed have we become to this rampant profligacy of theories that any claims of overarching singularity appear foolishly ambitious or naive.

There is, however, a cost to forgoing the attempt at general theory. Without such theory it is difficult to formulate a sense of the whole, to spot patterns and relationships across contexts, to observe large-scale or parallel developments. As we are confronted with confusing and possibly contradictory changes—like the globalization of law on the world level, simultaneous with an apparent profusion of legal pluralism on the local level—more than ever there is a need to put it all together in a single framework, if possible.

A brief exploration of past attempts at a general jurisprudence, and the objections raised against them, will provide the point of departure for my own approach. Here are descriptions of the project written by its two most influential early and recent proponents, respectively, Austin and Hart:

I mean, then, by 'General Jurisprudence,' the science concerned with the exposition of the principles, notions, and distinctions which are common to systems of law: understanding by systems of law, the ampler and maturer systems which, by reason of their amplitude and maturity, are pre-eminently pregnant with instruction. (Austin 1954: 367)

My aim in this book was to provide a theory of what law is which is both general and descriptive. It is *general* in the sense that it is not tied to any particular legal system or legal culture, but seeks to give an explanatory and clarifying account of law as a complex social and political institution with a rule-governed (and in that sense 'normative') aspect. . . . My account is *descriptive* in that it is morally neutral and has no justificatory aims: it does not seek to justify or commend on moral or other grounds the forms and structures which appear in my general account of law, though a clear understanding of these is, I think, an important preliminary to any useful moral criticism of law. (Hart 1994: 239–41)

These two quotes contain the key characteristics of what has been thought of as a general jurisprudence. The first characteristic is that they looked at law at two different levels: at the level of what law is (at the nature of law), and at the level of legal concepts, with a greater emphasis on the latter. The second characteristic is that their focus was not on any particular legal system, but on many and perhaps all legal systems, on law as such, which is what qualifies it as a general or universal jurisprudence. The third characteristic, which is often identified with the second, but is separable therefrom, is that they looked exclusively at common elements. The fourth characteristic is that they—with the exception of Bentham— assumed a stance of evaluative or moral neutrality. These characteristics, separately or in combination, have generated a series of core criticisms of the enterprise of a general jurisprudence.

Serious questions have been raised about whether we can come up with a concept to identify what law is, and, separately, whether the elements identified by such a concept can be said to exist everywhere (or at least in every manifestation of law) (see Bix 1999a: chap. 2; M. Moore 1992). 'In its main contemporary versions, general jurisprudence assumes that there is something called "law" which has a set of features that are more or less characteristic of all possible legal systems' (Burton 1989: 751–2). This assumption invokes several of the most complex un- resolved puzzles in legal theory (see Raz 1998).

Doubts have also been raised about whether English legal concepts can be translated into legal concepts in other languages and legal sys- tems (see Barberis 1996). A different objection is that the focus on com- mon concepts results in a relatively short list of both concepts and qualifying systems. Austin's version was virtually an immediate non- starter for this reason. He based his jurisprudence on a list of what he deemed to be necessary legal concepts, including right, duty, liberty, injury, redress, contractual obligations, and sovereignty. In the end he concluded that only the 'maturer' legal systems qualified for inclusion, limiting its application to the Western civil law and common law sys- tems of his time, which rendered it more an extended particular jurisprudence than a universal one. Twining added a different object- ion: 'the generalists as well as the particularists in the analytical tradi- tion are equally open to the charge of "narrowness," insofar as they concentrated almost exclusively on legal concepts . . . that is on "law talk" to the almost total exclusion of "talk about law" ' (2000: 37). A focus on legal concepts leaves little room for sociological insights about law.

Whether looking at legal systems or at legal concepts, the requirement of commonality imposes a debilitating limitation. 'If general jurisprudence is confined to describing the features that are common to all or nearly all legal systems, the descriptions will almost certainly be rather thin because in fact legal systems are quite diverse and the interest of a legal system lies typically in its detail' (Twining 2000: 41). Jeremy Waldron (1995: 649) put a further objection: 'after a while, the payoffs would begin to evaporate in the heady realms of such abstraction, and we would be overwhelmed by the distortions introduced by a theory that insisted one size fits all.'

The final characteristic that has generated serious objections is the claim that a general jurisprudence can or should be evaluatively neutral. Joseph Raz (1994: 219–21) observed that when picking out the key features of law for the purposes of study one makes an evaluative (though not necessarily moral) judgement about which social structures are important. John Finnis (1995: 469) raised the penetrating criticism that a descriptive analysis of law as an instrument 'cannot proceed without evaluating the diverse purposes and uses' to which it is put. Law has an inherently purposive, normative character, according to Finnis, of bringing about a morally good human order. Any attempt to describe and understand law must therefore involve evaluations of it relative to its purpose.

All of the above objections and questions are formidable. Learning from past failures, the general jurisprudence I construct will strive to avoid most of the problems that stumped earlier versions, though not all can be circumvented. The issues regarding the concept of law must be met directly. Chapters 6 and 7 will engage these issues, taking a different tack from prevailing approaches to the concept of law in a manner which advances the discussion and facilitates the achievement of a general jurisprudence.

The general jurisprudence I construct eschews completely the attempt to build a general jurisprudence upon a corpus of common legal concepts. Even if it is true that more and more legal systems in the modern world share a set of basic concepts, as is arguably the case, this focus leaves out too much of significance and interest. Instead, this general jurisprudence will focus on the relationship between law and society. Owing to this expanded subject-matter, in lieu of the traditional positivist emphasis on conceptual analysis, the approach elaborated here will call upon various perspectives and fields of thought for insights, including social theory, political theory, sociology, anthropology, and legal theory. This subject-matter, and the interdisciplinary approach taken to it, results in a general jurisprudence that will be situated at the intersection of four different branches of academic legal thought—legal theory, socio-legal studies, comparative law, and law and development—drawing from and contributing to all.

This general jurisprudence also rejects the traditional focus on common features. Not only are there too few such features, much information of consequence and interest is to be found in the differences as well as the similarities. Accordingly, the general jurisprudence I construct will be designed to identify similarities and differences against a common standard, for the purposes of understanding, comparison, and evaluation. This approach will straddle the gap between the general and the particular by using studies of particular contexts to fill in the details of the general standard, and by comparing particular situations against the general standard.

Finally, this general jurisprudence will consist of both evaluative and descriptive aspects. The general jurisprudence framework has been constructed to illuminate key features of the law–society relationship, which involves choosing (evaluatively) certain features over others. In addition, the framework is designed to test central claims made in legal theory about this relationship. In this respect it puts legal theory directly to the test, which is an avowedly evaluative aim with respect to legal theory. I expect that the findings of the general jurisprudence will have evaluative implications (as Hart did of his version), in the further sense that any framework that helps clarify and uncover aspects of law can be used to improve law and its relationship with society. However, the general jurisprudence I construct is, like Hart's, non-evaluative in the sense that it takes no stance on whether law is moral or immoral. It observes the many claims made on behalf of law to having a moral connection and value, and it subjects these claims to sustained scrutiny. Furthermore, this general jurisprudence is descriptive in the important sense that the guiding attitude to be applied when compiling information for the general jurisprudence should be the social scientific one of getting the facts of the matter right.

While I have departed in significant respects from traditional strategies, the objective I pursue remains true to the original aim of developing a single theoretical framework that can be applied to all systems and situations. Against those opponents who assert that a general jurisprudence cannot or should not be done, either or owing to its supposed impossibility, or its imperialist bent, or its negligible use value, I submit that the test will be whether there is value in what is produced by this effort.

Outline of the Book and Acknowledgements

Chapter 1 will set out a framework for the law–society relationship, built around a basic set of core ideas, including what I call the mirror thesis and the social order function of law, and the relationship between positive law, customs, consent, morality, and reason. The remainder of the book will trace out the ideas set out in this framework.

Chapter 2 will survey seven basic categories of thought in Western social and legal theory on the relationship between law and society. The survey will be limited to an examination of the themes and elements contained in the organizing framework set out in Chapter 1. As with any survey of this kind, it will be spare in what is covered; but it will cover almost all of the major and most influential thinkers and theories on law and society.

Chapters 3 and 4 will present theoretical challenges to the portrait of the relationship between law and society presented in Chapter 2; and Chapter 5 will present empirical challenges to this portrait. The varied subjects covered in these three chapters will include evolutionary and social contract theories about law, the impact of legal professionals, the consequences of colonization and globalization, and fundamental changes in theoretical discussions of the law–society relationship. Chapters 3, 4, and 5 not only contest widely held assumptions about law and its relation to society; they also place into doubt the common understanding of the nature of 'law', and the notion of 'society' as an analytical concept.

Chapter 6 proposes a conventionalist approach to the concept of law, and comprehensively reconstructs legal positivism into what I call socio-legal positivism. This extensive discussion of legal positivism recognizes the heritage of general jurisprudence as a legal positivist enterprise, and it furthers a project I began in a previous book, *Realistic Socio-Legal Theory: Pragmatism and a Social Theory of Law*. One of the key themes in that book was to infuse legal theory with insights from social scientific approaches to law, and vice versa. What I call socio-legal positivism attempts to accomplish this in an integrated fashion.

Chapter 7 builds upon the conventionalist approach to law to develop a non-essentialist version of legal pluralism. The analysis proceeds largely in relation to sociological discussions of legal pluralism, thereby complementing the predominantly legal theory discussion of Chapter 6. Chapters 6 and 7 together present a new way of understanding the kinds of legal phenomena operative in society today, and of how they should be studied, in ways that depart from but are also continuous with legal positivism as well as sociological approaches to law.

Chapter 8 ties all of the strings of the preceding argument together to set out the basic elements of the general jurisprudence. It specifies a replacement for the notion of society. It lays outs a typology of sources of social order and a typology of kinds of law. It provides a unifying standard, and the core enquiries around which the general jurisprudence is constructed. And it provides a list of tentative hypotheses regarding the relationship between law and society, both to identify fruitful lines of research and to indicate the edifying potential of the general jurisprudence.

The argument is cumulative. It begins by building up the standard picture of the law and society relationship. Then it breaks the picture down, throwing into doubt common understandings. Then it constructs a new way of conceptualizing law and provides a framework for the general jurisprudence. Because so much of the text involves critique and reconstruction, it is an extended prolegomenon that lays a foundation for a general jurisprudence, rather than a fully completed version. Given the pervasive hold of problematic assumptions about the law–society relationship, and the problematic conceptual apparatus that inhibits us from perceiving and understanding this relationship more acutely, a general jurisprudence cannot be achieved without this groundwork.

I owe thanks to many institutions and people for this project. In particular, I am grateful to the Oxford Centre for Socio-Legal Studies and the Institute for Jurisprudence at the University of Tilburg for inviting me to present Public Lectures on earlier versions of this general jurisprudence. The feedback I received on these two occasions was especially helpful in working out the ideas in this book. I am also thankful for critical comments I received when presenting parts of this work to the faculties at Northwestern University School of Law, Emory Law School, Temple Law School, Rutgers Law School (Newark), the University of Indiana School of Law (Bloomington), and Western New England School of Law. For their very helpful comments on various parts of earlier drafts of this book, I owe thanks to John Eekelaar, Philip Thomas, James Lindgren, and Dr Bärbel Dorbeck-Jung. I thank Paul Kirgis for his penetrating criticisms, which forced me to work out a couple of serious analytical problems that I did not fully recognize without his assistance. I am especially indebted to William Twining, and to Brian Bix, for their close reading of the entire manuscript and for their detailed critical comments. I am grateful to St. John's University School of Law for allowing me to teach one less course in the Spring of 2000, which facilitated the completion of this project. I thank Laura Fraher for her outstanding research assistance. Although this book was written and conceived as a single continuous project, I was fortunate to have parts of the book published as separate articles in the *Oxford Journal of Legal Studies* and the *Journal of Law and Society*. I thank those journals for allowing me to reuse material from the articles, respectively, in Chapters 6 and 7 of this book. I should note, however, that both chapters contain key modifications from the respective articles, owing to the structure of the book and owing to further developments in the argument after the articles were completed. Finally, I thank my family for the many sacrifices they made during the writing of this book.

1 The Law–Society Framework

A formidable threshold task in the project to construct a general jurisprudence is to come up with a characterization of the law–society relationship. Whichever way one begins will give rise to a multitude of legitimate objections. This relationship is too complex and unruly to capture fully in any single formula, and can be approached from too many different perspectives, each offering a choice from among too many possible alternative aspects on which to focus. The only way to begin is through drastic simplification. What follows is a working framework for the relationship between law and society, pared down to two basic components. The first component consists of two core themes about the relationship between law and society—the idea that law is a mirror of society and the idea that the function of law is to maintain social order. The second component consists of a breakdown of the connections between three elements: custom/consent, morality/reason, and positive law. The discussion in this book will be organized around these two components. They have been selected owing to their centrality within theoretical discussions of the law–society relationship. Every theory about law and society encompasses one or another or both of these components. To provide guidance for the upcoming exploration, this chapter will outline these two components.

The Mirror Thesis and the Social Order Function of Law

A large number and bewildering variety of theories about law have shaped the course of Western legal theory, from classical Greek theories about law, to natural law, to legal positivism, to evolutionary, historical, Marxist, sociological, and instrumental theories about law. Among their many differences, they offer contesting accounts of how law should be defined, the form that it takes, the criteria for its existence and validity, its relation to morality, whether it represents coercion or consensus, whether it need or need not be attached to the state, and so forth. Amidst this profusion of theories, however, a common presupposition can be found, that is: *law is a mirror of society, which functions to maintain social order*. This widely shared presupposition consists of two separate but intimately connected ideas.

The first idea is that law is a reflection—a 'mirror'—of society. So strong is the grip of this assumption that it is routinely asserted by social and legal theorists without supportive evidence or argument, with a sense of the self-evident. 'Every legal system stands in a close relationship to the ideas, aims and purposes of society. Law *reflects* the intellectual, social, economic, and political climate of its time' (Vago 1981: 3, emphasis added). 'Nowhere is the spirit of an age better *mirrored* than in the theory of law' (Ullmann 1969: p. vii, emphasis added). Indeed, the question of whether law does in fact mirror society is seldom seriously entertained by theorists. Legal philosopher Kent Greenawalt (1992: 165) exemplifies this in his rhetorical posing of the issue: 'Does law within a society reflect dominant cultural norms? In one sense, to ask this question is to answer it. Unless law is imposed from the outside by an alien power, a society's law will *reflect* its patterns of life and morality' (emphasis added). As H. L. A. Hart (1961: 199) sweepingly put it, 'The law of every modern state shows at a thousand points the influence of both the accepted social morality and wider moral ideas. . . . The further ways in which law *mirrors* morality are myriad, and still insufficiently studied . . .' (emphasis added). Or as legal historian and sociologist Lawrence Friedman (1996: 72) declared: 'Legal systems do not float in some cultural void, free of space and time and social context; necessarily, they *reflect* what is happening in their own societies. In the long run, they assume the shape of these societies, like a glove that molds itself to the shape of a person's hand' (emphasis added). Oliver Wendell Holmes (1962: 21) expressed it effusively: 'this abstraction called the Law, wherein, as in a magic *mirror*, we see reflected, not only our own lives, but the lives of all men that have been!' (emphasis added). This first idea will be referred to as the mirror thesis. The mirror is one of the most powerful and pervasively applied metaphors of the last two thousand years, central in philosophy (see Rorty 1979), in literature and art (see Torti 1991; Grabes 1982), and in the social sciences (see Haglund 1996). In law, its predominant use has been to provide a reassuring representation of the place that law holds in society.

The second idea is that law maintains social order by establishing and enforcing the rules of social intercourse, and by resolving disputes (see Tamanaha 1995a; Akers and Hawkins 1975). The notion that law is essential to social order 'underlies all the important general theories of law which are in currency today' (Collins 1982: 10). Like the mirror thesis, there are innumerable assertions by social and legal theorists linking law with order. Hans Kelsen (1945: 19) believed that by its nature 'law is a coercive order'. According to Eugene Ehrlich (1975: 24), 'the law is an ordering.' David Dudley Field (1995: 713) opined that 'Where there is no law there can be no order, since order is but another name for regularity, or conformity to rule'. Benjamin Cardozo (1924: 140) held that 'Law is the expression of the principle of order to which men must conform in their conduct and relations as members of society.' Edgar Bodenheimer (1957: 195) asserted that 'It would be difficult to deny the close relationship which exists between the institution of law and man's perennial search for order, regularity and fixity in human relations. This intimate link between law and order becomes visible in many of the institutions and processes of collective living.' Even Aristotle (1988: 162) declared, 'For law is order.' In an extensive study of the notion that 'law is a principle of order', Iredell Jenkins (1980: 162), who endorses this assumption, observes: 'it is almost universally accepted as an unquestioned truism, and it has rarely, if ever, been systematically examined. One encounters this notion everywhere in the legal literature, and almost always it is stated as a self-evident fact that requires neither substantiation nor explanation.' Outside of legal theory, the necessary connection between law and order is also a fundamental precept of functional analysis, which pervades sociological thinking about law. 'Finally, the best of all evidence of the close association of these ideas is found in the fact that the expression *law and order* has virtually ceased to be a phrase for us and has become a single word' (p. 10). This second idea will be referred to as the social order function of law.

The first idea assumes law's identity with society; the second idea assumes its key function within society. These two ideas are linked—the fact that law is a reflection of society is what renders it effective in the maintenance of social order (Jenkins 1980). They are linked in another way—together they constitute complementary aspects of two comforting, almost childlike beliefs we hold and tell one another about law. The implied threat of disorder works on our primal fears to render law in heroic terms, as a saviour or protector; the metaphor of the mirror makes it *our* savior, *our* protector, a power to identify with, not fear.

In the course of this book, the mirror thesis and the social order function of law will be elaborated on, explored, and tested. One objective of this book is to subject these pervasively held assumptions about law and its relation to society to sustained scrutiny, to have them regarded with greater scepticism than is heretofore evident.

A Tripartite Representation of the Law–Society Relationship

The second component of the framework will be an outline of the law–society relationship. This scheme will be organized in terms of a tripartite set of basic elements: (A) custom/consent and (B) morality/reason; as they relate to (C) positive law. Almost all of the Western theories about the relation between law and society consist of some mix of these three elements, though with varying combinations and degrees of emphasis. Here is a visual representation of the scheme:

Law and Society

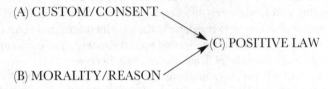

(A) CUSTOM/CONSENT

(C) POSITIVE LAW

(B) MORALITY/REASON

At the heart of this scheme are the relations between elements (A) and (C), and between (B) and (C), between custom/consent and positive law, and between morality/reason and positive law, respectively, although the relations between (A) and (B) are also significant. In addition, there are also interactions within element (A) and within element (B), between their two conjoined aspects. The content of these elements and their interrelations will be filled out in the course of the next three chapters. For the moment a brief sketch will suffice.

'Positive law', in general terms, refers to rules articulated and enforced by an institutionalized authority. The paradigmatic example of this is state law, though it has also been applied to other forms of publicly authorized, institutionalized enforcement of norms. Positive law (specifically, legal positivism) has often been characterized as the 'imperative' or 'will' theory of law, with an emphasis on the authoritative declaration of norms and on the use of force as the mechanism that obliges people to conform. What law is in a given context is a question of fact relating to the activities of legal officials and institutions. Standing alone, positive law represents power and authority; its degree of conformity to custom/consent and morality/reason is what confers legitimacy. It is the fact of such conformity that creates an obligation on the part of the people to abide by the dictates of positive law, in contrast to being forced or obliged to comply owing to the raw power of positive law (see Hart 1961: 80).

'Custom/consent' refers to the many theories that see a close connection between positive law and the customs, usages, habits, and practices of society. Several basic themes have emerged regarding the relationship between custom/consent and positive law: (1) as a historical matter, positive law evolved out of a social order controlled mostly by customs and habits; (2) the content of positive law norms are the products of, or derived from, customs and practices; (3) positive laws which are inconsistent with customs, usages or habits will be ineffectual[1] or illegitimate; and, at the extreme, (4) customs, habits, and usages *are* law. '[T]hat to which we give the name of Law always has been, still is, and will forever continue to be Custom' (Carter 1907). Custom is associated with consent because customs are seen to be the epitome of 'consent' by virtue of their long-standing, widespread, shared existence, and continued perpetuation (Pollock 1961: 145). Blackstone, for example, identified the common law as 'nothing else but custom, arising from the universal agreement of the whole community' (quoted in Boorstin 1996: 113). This view of the consensual nature of custom extends at least as far back as the Romans: 'Custom is the tacit consent of the people, deeply rooted through long usage' (Roman source, quoted in Watson 1985: 44). This view was also a staple of medieval thought. 'Almost without any exceptions, the Medieval jurists based the binding force of customary rules on the tacit consent of the people' (Ullmann 1969: 63). Positive law in harmony with custom is thus seen as obligatory, and more effective, because consensual. There comes a moment, however, when custom and consent are pried apart, with significant implications for law, as will be recounted in Chapter 4.

'Morality/reason' refers to the many theories that see a close connection between positive law and morality and reason, especially, but not limited to, natural law schools of thought. Again there are several basic accounts: (1) through institutionalization, positive law separates and emerges from a primordial state in which it is indistinguishably commingled with custom and morality; (2) the development of positive law is the mark of civilization, as a moral, reason-based way of ordering society;[2] (3) morality and reason are the sources of positive law norms

---

[1] Aristotle (1988: 39) asserted, 'For the law has no power to command obedience except that of habit.'

[2] '[O]ne can see from this perspective that the positivization of law and the accompanying differentiation between law and morality are the result of a rationalization process' (Habermas 1996: 71, see also 114).

(as has been claimed of the common law[3] and of civil codes);[4] (4) acting in conformity with the positive law is considered morally correct conduct (Ostwald 1986: 113); (5) positive laws which are inconsistent with reason and morality are illegitimate, invalid, and, according to certain schools of natural law, not law at all; (6) morality is an inseverable aspect of positive law;[5] and, at the extreme, (7) moral principles *are* law; or 'Law in general is human reason' (Montesquieu 1991: 7); 'The law is reason unaffected by desire' (Aristotle 1988: 78); 'Law is the highest reason' (Cicero 1998: 103). Positive law consistent with morality/reason is, by virtue of this fact, obligatory because it is just or right, or in accordance with God's will. Morality is paired with reason in the assertion that morality is available to us through reason. Like the preceding element, the relationship between morality and reason is altered at a later point, with significant implications for law, which will be elaborated in Chapter 4.

The roughly parallel nature of the relations between these two elements (A and B) and positive law is not accidental. Both have been called upon to serve the same purpose: to provide a standard with which to legitimize—and occasionally criticize—positive law in its relation to society. Medieval legal thought, for example, characteristically construed positive law legislation as 'concerned with the "finding" of a precept, whose binding force comes from "its supposed conformity to universal reason or to immemorial custom" ' (Ullmann 1969: 102). These parallel relations do not imply that the two elements are necessarily complementary. At the highest level of abstraction, they can be seen as competing ways of legitimation, representing the contrast between experience (local) and reason (universal). And reason and morality are sometimes enlisted to critique customs and habits. But usually they are discussed in a mutually reinforcing fashion with regard to one another and to positive law.

---

[3] Roscoe Pound (1912–13: 115 n. 5) cites the following view: 'For reason is the life of the law, nay the common law itselfe is nothing else but reason. The common law is the absolute perfection of reason; for nothing that is contrary to reason is consonant to law' (citation omitted).

[4] See e.g. K. Zweigert and H. Kotz (1992: 88), '[T]he Code civil is founded upon the creed of the Enlightenment and the law of reason that social life can be put into a rational order if only the rules of law are restructured according to a comprehensive plan'; Pound (1912–13: 115), '[P]ositive law came to be regarded as the application of reason to the civil relations of men, and on the Continent the *Corpus Iuris Civilis* stood as its exponent merely because of its inherent reasonableness.' Kelly (1992: 311) asserts that despite all the rhetoric about reason surrounding the drafting of the French Civil Code, in reality what mostly resulted was the codification of already existing rules.

[5] Ronald Dworkin (1986) is the most prominent current representative of this approach. Lon Fuller (1958, 1964) has also argued that law as a purpose activity cannot be sharply separated from morality.

Traditionally, for example, epitomized in the work of Blackstone, the common law was seen as *both* a reflection of customary practices[6] (which renders it consensual) and consistent with and derived from reason and morality:[7] an 'ancient collection of unwritten maxims and customs' and 'the perfection of reason' (quoting Blackstone, Postema 1986: 5, 11). A few legal theorists have asserted that natural law is the underlying inspiration for customary law (Kmiec 1995), or have taken widespread custom to be evidence of natural law, as Grotius did for international law. Reason and custom have been recognized as inseparable 'by the highest authorities' (Pollock 1961: 145–6). Western legal theory has for centuries associated or commingled custom with reason (Whitman 1991). Customs that survive the test of time represent the collective wisdom of the past (Boorstin 1996: 113–17). Under the conventionalist view, furthermore, morality itself is a kind of customary practice within a social group, as reflected in terms like 'ethical custom' and 'moral habits' (quoting, respectively, Weber and Vinogradoff, Pound 1959b: 273, 274). Austin (1913: 60–1) included both under the label 'positive morality'. Thus, while many Western theories about law emphasize one element over the other in their relationship with positive law, many also call upon both.

The relationship between these elements and positive law is not unidirectional, with custom/consent and morality/reason always dictating the terms for positive law. Since at least as far back as Plato's and Aristotle's view of the educational function of positive law, legal and social theorists of various stripes have also argued that law has a role in shaping customs and morality. Law has sometimes taken the lead in opposing or reforming prevailing customs or moral norms. Furthermore, as I will argue in Chapter 4, positive law or legality later comes to stake its own claim to legitimacy, apart from conformity with custom/consensus and morality/reason. Thus, each of these three elements, standing alone, represents a different theory as to the binding force of law (Pound 1938: 457).

Most often, however, the relations between these three elements have been painted in intimate terms. Many legal and social theorists, for

[6] Observed customs were considered 'as one of the foundations of English law; "these are the customs which are properly called the common law . . . and from those general customs, and other principles and maxims, the greatest part of the law of England arises" ' (quoting St Germain, early 16th-cent. English lawyer, Kelly 1992: 185). See also J. Austin (1913: 270–1), though Austin notes that not all of the common law is founded upon ancient custom.

[7] See e.g. Patterson (1940: 415) (Coke 'glorified the English common law as at once the common custom of the realm and the embodiment of reason'); Pollock (1961: 148) (the law merchant part of common law 'claimed an authority independent of any particular local jurisprudence, as being founded on general reason and usage approved as reasonable').

example, have postulated the existence of a pre-history period in social development when all three elements—specifically law, custom, and morality—coexisted in an undifferentiated state (see Pound 1959b: 218–19; Luhmann 1985: 81–3). 'Thus for a long time law and morals were merged with custom' (Durkheim 1993: 97). During this period, they were *one* in some sense, or at least did not have distinctly separate identities. According to this view, law/morality emerged out of habitual custom with the recognition of 'ought' or normativity; later, law separated from morality with the addition of institutionalized sanctions. '[F]or morality and law are only collective habits, constant patterns of action which come to be common to a whole society . . . it is like a crystallization of human behavior' (p. 67). 'Custom forms, generally speaking, the common and primitive "ancestor" of both law and morals' (Chroust 1944: 35).

Etymology provides further evidence of the intimacy of these elements. In Greek, *nomos* first referred to 'custom', then later to 'law' (as well as custom) (Ostwald 1986: 84–136). In fifth-century Athens, the '*nomoi* did not differentiate legal from moral concepts and therefore they encompassed customs and "a way of life" as well as actionable misdeeds which were, at the same time, moral misdeeds' (Janet Coleman 2000a: 24). Similarly, *ius* (Latin), *Recht* (German and Dutch), *Droit* (French), and *Diritto* (Italian) have all referred to both 'law' and 'ethically right' (Pound 1959b: 14–18). These ambiguous usages generate a sense of association or identity between these elements.

These three elements have also been characterized as functional equivalents. In various contexts to be elaborated on, all three have been given the label 'law', as in 'customary law' or 'natural law'. Likewise, they have all been considered types of normative orders or mechanisms of social control. Whichever way they are characterized—as types of law, norms, or mechanisms of social control—the equivalence is based upon their contribution to the maintenance of social order. In connection with this functional equivalence, there is also a kind of competitive tension between them, whereby proponents of each element suggest that their element is the most powerful, or legitimate, or significant.

Finally, each one of these three elements substantially matches up with one of the three great competing traditions in the history of Western legal theory. Custom/consent roughly matches the historical tradition, an approach especially prominent in the nineteenth century. Morality/reason aligns with the philosophical—particularly natural law—tradition, which has had several periods of dominance and revival, though held sway especially in the medieval period, and from the sixteenth through eighteenth centuries. Positive law is associated with the analytical tradition, which has had its greatest influence in parts of the nineteenth and twentieth centuries. The fact that these three traditions have been set out by way of contrast to one another partially explains the tension between the elements with which they are associated.

Running through the preceding articulation is an internal dynamic that should be drawn out. Theories about the relations between law and society have routinely identified a *close association* and multiple connections among these three elements. Beneath the surface, however, is also a *tension* among these three elements. These countervailing tendencies can be observed in connection with the issue of legitimation. The very fact that custom/consent and morality/reason serve as standards of legitimacy for positive law puts them in a position of potential conflict, and gives rise to the possibility of a contest for authority among the three when they diverge. However, theories about the relations between law and society tend historically to strongly emphasize the close association, with the tension remaining mostly submerged, erupting only occasionally.

To briefly summarize, as characterized by Western legal and social theory, the relations among these three elements are complex and far-ranging. They are thought to have a shared origin; they are thought to reflect one another, to feed or influence one another, and to determine the efficacy of one another. The relations between custom/consent and positive law, and between morality/reason and positive law, are parallel in many respects, especially with regard to the issue of legitimation. Coinciding with this general intimacy and with their mutually supporting relations, these three elements also exist in tension as competing sources of power and authority, overlapping one another in their reach, and each is championed by competing traditions of legal theory. The interrelations between these three elements will constitute the backdrop for this examination of the relations between law and society. The validity of this artificially narrowed focus will be demonstrated in the course of this study through its ability to illuminate.

In the next chapter I will survey the major views in Western legal and social theory about the relationship between law and society. While reading the survey, the two connected ideas of the common presupposition—law is a mirror of society, which functions to maintain order—should be kept in mind, for that is what I aim to explore. The tripartite scheme is a detailed rendering of the 'mirror' thesis: positive law reflects—is a mirror of—the customary practices and moral norms of the society to which it is attached. Law is effective in the maintenance of social order by virtue of this reflective quality. The pervasiveness of these ideas, and variations thereof, in legal and social theory is remarkable.

2 Law and Society in Western Legal Theory

Classical Legal Theory

This quick review of early Greek legal theory, as well as of the theories that follow, will be constrained in focus to aspects relevant to the framework just set out. Caution should be taken whenever projecting onto an earlier period an analytical framework based upon present understandings. It appears, however, that the Greeks conceived of positive (or 'written') law much as we do, in terms of authoritative declarations of the state (keeping in mind that theirs was primarily a city-state, not the nation state of today). According to Xenophon: 'Whatsoever the ruling power in the state, after deliberation, enacts and directs to be done is known as a law' (quoted in Cairns 1949: 34 n. 14). Law was presented in Greek legal thought as 'essentially a command or prohibition issued by a political authority' (Kelly 1992: 18). Plato (1980: 723a) identified law as a 'command' 'uttered by a legislature'. These views are forerunners of the command theory of law, given its definitive formulation by John Austin in the early nineteenth century.

Both Plato and Aristotle believed that the fundamental function of law is the maintenance of social order.[1] Aristotle (1988: 124) observed that 'In all well-balanced governments there is nothing which should be more jealously maintained than the spirit of obedience to law, more especially in small matters; for transgression creeps in unperceived and at last ruins the state, just as the constant recurrence of small expenses in time eats up a fortune.' Greek philosophers generally 'held that the end of law was an orderly maintenance of an idealized social *status quo*. The legal order was an ordering of men to keep each in his appointed place in the politically organized society of an ideal Greek city' (Pound 1959a: 29). Plato and Aristotle, however, desired that the order be a *good* order. They recognized that laws are often laid down to preserve the privileges of the ruling elite.[2] '[A]s the constitution reflects the distribution of power in

[1] For discussions of this position, see Aristotle (1988: 162); Cairns (1949: 43, 93–4); Jones (1956: 46, 73); Kelly (1992: 17).

[2] Indications of this recognition can be found in Plato (1980: 714c–e); Aristotle (1988:159); Jaeger (1944: 240–1); Kelly (1992: 19); Cairns (1949: 106–7). Although there are differences between Plato and Aristotle on this point, in this exposition I will focus on their similarities.

society, the laws follow the constitution in being shaped to serve the interests of the dominant group.'[3] Against this tendency, Plato (1980: 715b) argued that the laws should be 'for the sake of what is common to the whole city'. Aristotle (1988: 68–9) likewise suggested that a 'true government' must have just laws, and just laws are oriented towards the 'common interest'. He (p. 100) also proposed that, in the interest of stability, the law must favour the middle class.

Positive law and customs were seen by the classical Greeks as closely connected to one another. The historical connection was both etymological, as indicated in the previous chapter, and thought to be evolutionary. 'Among the Greeks, as among other peoples, the early words for law tend in the course of time to bring together two notions, that of something enunciated by some appropriate authority as a standard for men's conduct, and that of some long-standing or immemorial usage departure from which is viewed with general disfavour' (J. W. Jones 1956: 28). *Nomos* initially meant 'custom, usage, convention' (p. 34), and later came to refer to statutory law (Ostwald 1986: 85–93). The term has also been used to mean 'both custom and law without distinction' (Foster 1949: 116). Plato (1980: 680a) speculated that primitive societies were governed by habits and customs without the need for, or existence of, positive law. Positive law arose with writing, according to Plato, and with the expansion of society from families and clans to the joining of communities with differing customs; when more than one community comes together there must be lawmakers to articulate which of the customs are to govern all (681a–d). Plato believed that, following the emergence of positive law, law and custom constitute an essential combination. Unwritten customs 'are the bonds of every regime, linking all the things established in writing and laid down, with the things that will be set forth in the future . . .; if nobly established and made habitual, they provide a cloak of complete safety for the later written laws' (793b–d). They are 'vitally important', the 'ties that bind the state together' (Jaeger 1944: 248). Thus, while he thought that 'one shouldn't ordain these in law', they should not be left unmentioned (Plato 1980: 793b). 'Anyone who wants to construct a new city-state and bind it firmly together needs both elements [law and customs]' (Jaeger 1944: 248).

Aristotle described positive law and customary law as functional equivalents, though awarding priority to latter: 'Again, customary laws have more weight, and relate to more important matters, than written laws'

---

[3] Cohen (1995: 39) describing Aristotle's views.

(Aristotle 1988: 78–9). Aristotle also emphasized that obedience to law is primarily a function of habit (pp. 39, 175; see Cairns 1949: 98–100). Thus, he, like Plato, thought it essential that legislation train people in the habits of virtue and right action.

According to these views, positive law cannot, without risk to the survival of the regime, be substantially out of sync with the customs and habits of the society it purports to govern. This intimate relationship works in several ways and directions of influence. Habits and customs provide the supportive—and constraining—context within which positive law operates, while positive law likewise has a supportive and constraining effect on prevailing customs and habits; although for both Plato and Aristotle customs and habits de facto had more power than positive law. The Greeks were well aware that different societies had different *nomoi*, and, consistent with the mirror thesis, considered this an appropriate reflection of different habits, customs, and values (see Ostwald 1986: 250–66).

The connection between morality/reason and positive law was also significant in classical Greek legal theory. As indicated, Plato and Aristotle thought law essential to the maintenance of a good order. Morality and positive law are related in Plato's view that 'law may be understood as *the institutionalized judgment* of a community about proper pains and pleasures' (Cohen 1995: 46), and in his view that a significant role of legislation is to educate citizens in the proper virtues (Plato 1980: 874d–e, 722d; Jaeger 1944: 216–17). The classical Greeks also often identified positive law with reason and divine origin (Foster 1949: 116–17). As Anaximenes of Lampsacus phrased it, 'Law is reason defined in accordance with a common agreement of the state setting forth how men are to act in each matter' (quoted in Cairns 1949: 34 n. 14). Or as Demosthenes put it, 'The law is that which all men ought to obey for many reasons, but above all, because every law is an invention and gift of the gods, a tenet of wise men, a corrective of errors voluntary and involuntary, and a general covenant of the whole state in accordance with which all men in that state ought to regulate their lives' (ibid.). At the very outset of *The Laws*, Plato (624a) said credit for having laid down the law goes to the Gods. In later passages he identifies laws and legislation with reason (714a, 875c–d). Aristotle (1988: 78) asserted that 'he who bids the law rule may be deemed to bid God and Reason alone to rule, but he who bids man rule adds an element of the beast; for desire is a wild beast, and passion perverts the minds of rulers, even when they are the best of men. The law is reason unaffected by desire.'

Aristotle (1988: 175, 1985: 14. 2) thought it essential to a good order that the law enshrines the virtues and principles of justice, and habituates the young in these virtues.

The familiar feel of Greek legal theory in general, and of the views of Plato and Aristotle in particular, reflects our heritage in the Greek tradition and the extraordinary influence of these two thinkers. They produced the first influential accounts of the mirror thesis, articulating a tight relationship between custom/consent and positive law, and between morality/reason and positive law, despite expressing reservations about the extent to which these matches are achieved in practice. They were the first to emphasize the social order function of law. They also articulated precursors of social contract and evolutionary theories about the emergence of the law and state. One further respect in which they presaged later legal theory bears mention. Both were responding to the sceptical attacks of the Sophists, who characterized law as enacted in the interests of the strong, serving as a restraint on, against the interests and natural excellence of, the individual (Foster 1949: 45–50, 127–9; Ostwald 1986: 260–6). The 'effect of Sophistic doctrine was to strip the law of the state of all moral authority' (Foster 1949: 127). Plato and Aristotle sought to 'reestablish the moral authority of political laws' (ibid.). From this beginning, a predominantly legitimating orientation towards positive law has been a virtual constant of Western legal theory.

Before concluding the discussion of classical legal theory, I will briefly mention three aspects of the Roman legal tradition. First, the Romans had a strongly positivist, imperative conception of law. 'Law was to the Romans the object of a deliberate act of legislation. Law was the expression of the will of the Roman people, or the Emperor to whom the original power of the people had been transferred' (d'Entreves 1994: 66). Hence the Justinian Code contained the declaration 'Whatever pleases the sovereign has the force of law' (quoted in Aquinas 1993: 90. 1. obj 3). This emphasis is understandable considering the power of the state and the growth of legislation in Roman society. There appears to be a historical correspondence between periods of enhanced legislation and the popularity of the will theory of law (Pound 1912–13: 128–9, 145). Secondly, Roman law, in response to its conquest of foreign lands, came to recognize a distinction between the civil law, which applied only to Roman citizens, and the *ius gentium*, or law of nations, which applied to and was common to humankind, and facilitated international relations and transactions (dealing with trade, contracts, etc.) (see Stein 1999: 12–13; Janet Coleman 2000b: 105–6). Roman jurists added another category, the *ius naturale* (or natural law), which represents the precepts of nature. Roman jurist Ulpian distinguished these three bodies of law as follows: the *ius civile* are the particular codes of states; the *ius gentium* is the common law of mankind arising out of the necessity of transactions; and the *ius naturale* are the laws of nature (Fears 2000: 40).

The third aspect involves the contribution of Cicero, who was a bridge figure between Greek legal theory and the natural law tradition which was to arise during the Middle Ages, taken up next. Cicero drew upon Stoic philosophy for his views of natural law (Fears 2000: 21). He (Cicero 1998: 103) defined law as 'the highest reason, inherent in nature, which enjoins what ought to be done and forbids the opposite'. This law is not produced by human enactment, but by God; it is eternal and of universal application (pp. 68, 124). We have knowledge of this divine law through reason. 'Since, then, there is nothing better than reason, and reason is present in both man and God, there is a primordial relationship in reason between man and God. But those who share reason also share right reason; and since that is law, we must also be thought of as partners with the gods in law' (p. 105). 'For nature has created perceptions which we have in common, and has sketched them in our minds in such a way that we classify honourable things as virtues and dishonourable things as vices' (p. 112). Against his claim of a universal natural law accessible to reason, Cicero considered the obvious retort that there are a great variety of laws among communities. His response was threefold: that laws are made to fit the conditions of each community (pp. 64–5); that some of these laws are unjust; and that the wise man knows which are the true laws (pp. 125–6). Significantly, Cicero considered positive law to be subservient to divine law, and suggested that unjust laws are 'anything but laws' (p. 125). 'In a community a law of just any kind will not be a law, even if the people (in spite of its harmful character) have accepted it. Therefore law means drawing a distinction between just and unjust, formulated in accordance with that most ancient and most important of all things—nature' (p. 126). Unjust laws 'no more deserve to be called laws than the rules a band of robbers might pass in their assembly'(Cicero, quoted in Foster 1949: 190).

Before Cicero, Aristotle also made a distinction between natural law and positive law: 'What is natural is what has the same validity everywhere alike, independent of its seeming so or not. What is legal is what originally makes no difference [whether it is done] one way or another, but makes a difference whenever people have laid down the rule' (Aristotle 1985: 5. 74). He does not reconcile them, nor indicate whether one controls over the other in case of conflict.[4] Aristotle appeared to view the two as independent sources of law and justice. Cicero took a major further step when declaring the superiority of divine law. This step was potentially revolutionary, postulating a standard that each individual could discover and draw upon, through the application of reason, to render an evaluation of the positive law and determine whether it should be followed.

Natural Law Tradition

Summa Theologica, Treatise on Law (Questions 90–97), written by St Thomas Aquinas in the mid-thirteenth century, is the *locus classicus* of natural law theory. Aquinas (1993: 90. 4. c. 2) defined law as 'an ordinance of reason for the common good, made by him who has care of the community and promulgated'. His definition was intended to apply to all forms of law, which he then proceeds to distinguish in four varieties: Eternal Law (God's model for the entire Universe), Natural Law (law of creation, a reflection of God's reason, built into human nature), Divine Law (scripture revealed in Bible), and Human Law (positive law). Here we are concerned only with his views of human law, and its relation to natural law and to custom.

The purpose of human (or positive) law, according to Aquinas, is the preservation of social order through the maintenance of peace and the coordination of behaviour (see Finnis 1998: 222–8). He wrote: 'For human law's purpose is the temporal tranquility of the state, a purpose which the law attains by coercively prohibiting external acts to the extent that those are evils which can disturb the state's peaceful condition' (quoted in Finnis 1998: 224). Indeed, Aquinas (1993: 96. 4) asserted that one would be bound to abide by certain unjust laws if disobedience would lead to disorder, and he was not comfortable with the notion that individuals would decide for themselves which positive laws met the requirements of natural law.

Contrary to the impression that might be given by the frequently metaphysical orientation of natural law theory, for much of the history of this

---

[4] Stoic philosophy, according to John W. Jones (1956: 45), did address the conflict, though without much development: 'Human law was conceived as existing only in so far as this natural or divine law was understood and acknowledged by men, and no other kind of law had any authority.' In contrast to Jones, John Kelly (1992) asserts that Greek thought had no conception of the notion that a conflict with natural laws could invalidate positive law. I will leave this conflict to scholars in the field, with a note that in his discussion of Greek legal theory Kelly relies heavily on Jones's account.

tradition 'the natural lawyers saw the maintenance of social order as the crucial issue' (Schneewind 1998: 12). Grotius, the founder of modern natural law theory, declared that 'The maintenance of the social order . . . consonant with human intelligence is the source of law properly so called' (quoting Grotius, p. 72). Likewise, John Finnis (1980: 147–56, 266–70, 276–81), a leading current interpreter of Aquinas and exponent of natural law theory, defined both the positive law and the common good in terms of the coordination of the activities of individuals in groups and in society, thereby facilitating social order; and he defines 'Natural law' as 'the set of principles of practical reasonableness in ordering human life and human community' (p. 280).

Aquinas (1993: 90. 1. rep. 3) described positive law in terms of commands that are the will of the sovereign, and he recognized the necessity of coercion for the efficacy of law. 'This coercive power is vested in the whole people or in some public official to whom it belongs to inflict punishment. . . . Therefore, it belongs to him alone to make laws' (90. 3. rep. 2). People are subject to positive law rules in either of two ways, according to Aquinas: authority and coercion (96. 5). Coercion is necessary owing to the existence of the wicked. But authority is the primary source of obligation. Positive law possesses authority insofar as it is just and in accord with reason (90. 1. rep. 3). Through the diligent exercise of practical reason, the precepts of natural law are accessible to us because they are built into human nature through God's creation (see d'Entreves 1994: 43–4); positive law is, and should be, the product of this process of discovery (Aquinas 1993: 91. 3).

Unjust positive laws lack authority. Coercion may compel people to comply with the unjust law, but they are not under any obligation to do so (except in the case of impending disorder mentioned above). In this regard, Aquinas (96. 4. sec. 4) made an assertion which has ever since set legal positivists and natural law theorists at odds: 'And laws of this sort . . . are acts of violence rather than laws, as Augustine says . . ., "A law that is unjust seems *not to be a law*." ' 'Hence every human positive law has the nature of law to the extent that it is derived from the Natural law. If, however, in some point it conflicts with the law of nature it will no longer be law but rather a perversion of law' (95. 2). As indicated in a previous section, Cicero made a similar assertion.

Legal positivist John Austin's (1995: 158) response to this position is scathing: 'Now, to say that human laws which conflict with the Divine law are not binding, that is to say, are not laws, is to talk stark nonsense. The most pernicious laws, and therefore those which are most opposed to the will of God, have been and continually are enforced as laws by judicial tribunals.' Many legal positivists would concur that there is no *moral* obligation to follow an unjust law, but, Austin (1913: 73) insists, 'a law which exists *is a law*' (see Hart 1958). Legal positivists assert that because natural law scholars base their view of legal validity on conformity to (or delegation from) natural law, they fail to recognize that the grounds for legal validity differ from those for moral validity: 'They cannot say of a law that it is legally valid but morally wrong' (Raz 1974: 100).

John Finnis (1980: 20–5) replies that this is a mischaracterization of Aquinas's position and of natural law theorists generally. Finnis is adamant that, in *Summa Theologica*, Aquinas 'decisively affirms law's positivity' (Finnis 1996: 201), and recognizes that the existence and content of law does not rest upon conformity to moral principle (p. 204). Contrary to Finnis, however, Alexander d'Entreves (1994: 46), another leading natural law scholar, insisted that Aquinas' 'words must be taken literally'. He observed that there are different variations of natural law; the Thomist ontological version is the most extreme and does indeed deny that a positive law in contravention of natural law is a valid law (p. 177). Considering that Aquinas was not specifically concerned with the question of legal validity in our terms, it is difficult to know what he might have thought. Nevertheless, others in the natural law tradition have explicitly linked the validity of positive law to its conformity to natural law. Medieval jurists asserted that 'the validity of law depends upon its conformity to divine or natural law' (Ullmann 1969: 54). The great canon law scholar Gratian, about a century prior to Aquinas, wrote: 'Enactments, whether ecclesiastical or secular, if they are proved to be contrary to natural law, must be totally excluded' (quoted in Berman 1983: 147). Blackstone, who was Austin's (1995: 157–9) specific target, wrote in his Commentaries: 'This law of nature . . . is of course superior in obligation to any other. . . . [N]o human laws are of any validity, if contrary to this; and such of them as are valid derive all their force, and all their authority, mediately or immediately, from this original' (quoted in Boorstin 1996: 49). More recently, Lon Fuller (1969: 197) asserted in *The Morality of Law*, and in his famous debate with H. L. A. Hart, that there is a certain necessary minimum moral element to law, without which it is 'not simply bad law, but not law at all'.

The outcome of the debate over grounds of validity is less important than the fact of its persistence. It is evidence of a continuing tension between morality/reason and positive law. Positive law is characterized both as the product of morality/reason (descriptive) and subject to critique from the standpoint of morality/reason (prescriptive). The rhetorical priority given to natural law would appear to place greater emphasis on the critical aspect, but in practice it has 'been used to support almost any ideology' (Friedmann 1967: 96). Natural law principles and natural rights have all too often merely been derived from, and used to justify, the existing social order.

The account Aquinas (1993: 91. 3) provided of the relationship between custom/consent and positive law is similar to that of Plato: 'the beginning of law comes from nature; then certain things become customary because of their usefulness; afterwards, what had come from nature and was approved by custom was sanctioned by fear and reverence of the laws.' Aquinas (97. 2. rep. 1) also observed that 'laws obtain a very great force from custom . . . and therefore should not be easily changed'. 'For it is difficult to remove the custom of a people' (97. 3. rep. 2). Aquinas felt that customs often reflected the consensus or approval of the community (97. 3. rep. 3). Thus, Aquinas believed that 'both customary observance and deliberate enactment are valid modes of lawmaking. Human reason and will lie behind both; in the latter case expressed by words, in the former by actions' (Kelly 1992: 138). Aquinas suggested that 'custom is the primary source of law' (Postema 1986: 45). He accorded a kind of priority to custom: 'For if [the people] are free, and able to make their own laws, the consent of the whole people expressed by a custom counts far more in favour of a particular observance, than does the authority of the sovereign, who has not the power to frame laws, except as representing the people' (Aquinas 1993: 97. 3. obj. 3). Nonetheless, wicked customs exist, and should be 'overcome by law and reason' (ibid.). Like Plato and Aristotle, Aquinas (95. 1) believed that positive law played an important role in educating people towards virtuous conduct. As this description indicates, Aquinas (95. 3–4, 96. 1–2) also believed that positive law is and should be a reflection of the customs of the community to which it is attached.

Thus, according to Aquinas, positive law is in part derived from and obtains its force from customs; as a general matter it should not conflict substantially with customs; its de facto power and claim to legitimacy is sometimes less than that of custom; and it can and should be used to change those customs which are contrary to reason. With regard to the three elements, Aquinas in effect placed custom/consent on the same plane with positive law (each giving way to the other in certain contexts), and elevated morality/reason above them both, though all three held positions of respect. Gratian preceded Aquinas in setting up the same hierarchy (see Berman 1983: 145–7).

Recall, for a moment, the underlying thesis of this survey—a constant of Western legal theory is that positive law is a mirror of society that functions to maintain social order. There is one respect in which the natural law tradition appears to pull away from the intimate relation with society, at least in the local sense. Underlying natural law is a universalizing tendency (Friedmann 1967: 86). 'Natural law theorists would never have admitted that law is merely the expression of the standards of a particular group or society' (d'Entreves 1994: 79). Natural law theory requires that virtually all systems (allowing exceptions here and there, for the evil or deviant system) *throughout history* share a recognizable core of positive law (or customs) which reflect natural law principles. This is so because natural law arguments have been grounded in human nature and reason, both of which were thought to be universal (implanted by God). Hence natural law theorists have struggled with the burden of demonstrating this universal set of laws.[5] Even John Finnis, who anchors his position in self-evidence and practical reasonableness rather than human nature, nevertheless makes 'rather confident assertions' that the basic values he identifies—upon which positive law is constructed—are shared in 'all human societies' (Finnis 1980: 83).

John Locke took a different tack in his recognition of natural law. He (1990: 183–5) observed that the law of many societies sanctioned the worst kind of conduct, and that there was no uniformity to be found.

And so, were the consensus of mankind to be considered the rule of morals, there would either exist no law of nature, or this law would vary from place to place; one thing is considered virtuous in one place and vicious elsewhere. . . . For men have judged themselves not to have violated, but to have observed, the law of nature, since they have been guided by the then dominant opinion [and] have preferred one action or another in conformity with the custom of their race, actions which seem perhaps to others, and not without reason, vicious and impious.

Recognizing the great diversity of laws among different groups of people, many natural law theorists, including Locke, Aquinas, and Finnis, fall back on the argument that people are often deficient (as a consequence of the original sin or of succumbing to the passions) in their recognition of natural law; and that natural law principles are accessible only to the truly wise following the diligent application of reason (though it should not be forgotten, after all, that Aquinas defended the burning of heretics, believed in the inferiority of women, and had negative attitudes towards

---

[5] Yves Simon (1965) claims that this universality has been demonstrated by anthropologists. Kai Nielson (1959) argues to the contrary.

Jews (Janet Coleman 2000b: 83)). These theorists also accept that moral principles allow a range of choices among reasonable alternatives (Finnis 1996: 203). As natural law filters through particular circumstances and is made concrete in positive law and moral norms, it becomes variable, reflecting local customs and usages (Aquinas 1993: 95. 2. rep. 3; 95. 3. 1; 96. 2). Furthermore, natural law—indifferent to whether the law requires that we drive on the left or right side of the road—does not speak to all the details of social life, or on all subjects (Finnis 1980: 28). These are the factors, according to natural law theorists, which account for much of the observed variety amongst legal regimes (Finnis 1996: 202).

According to natural law theory, then, human societies—or at least those that have enjoyed the benefit of wise legislators—have certain universally shared aspects of positive law which are based upon reason and our common human nature, as well as many differences, reflecting different cultures, climates, geographies, and other surrounding circumstances. The mirror thesis, to draw the point for my purposes, is thus also adhered to in the natural law tradition.

I will conclude this discussion of the natural law tradition with a mention of the contribution of Grotius. Writing in the early seventeenth century, Grotius made the then daring suggestion that natural law is founded upon reason applied to human nature alone, independent of the existence and authority of God. The effect of his work was, in the words of Roscoe Pound (1912–13: 124), 'to emancipate jurisprudence from theology'. 'Accordingly, where the sixteenth-century jurist began with a theological disquisition, the seventeenth and eighteenth-century jurist begins with a discussion of the nature of man and the nature of human society' (p. 125 n. 45). Grotius re-grounded natural law theory in rationalism in a period of declining religious authority owing to theological controversy accompanied by the rise of science. This rationalist emphasis coincided with increased assertions of the value of the individual that followed from the Reformation: 'the break with authority which substituted private interpretation by the individual, each for himself, for authoritative universal interpretation by the church' (Pound 1959a: 476). The combination of these developments transformed traditional natural law theory with its orientation to the divine, into modern natural rights theory grounded in individuals and based upon the application of reason (see d'Entreves 1994: 53–62, 70–2). Grotius was by no means responsible for this shift, but his work helped begin the turn, and thus he is credited with being the father of modern natural law. Significantly, unlike natural law thought, natural rights thought characteristically has been sceptical about identifying substantive moral principles. Grotius began the trek down this path by dismissing the core focus of ancient moral and political thought on identifying the ultimate good (Schneewind 1998: 73). Natural rights is about abstract equality, freedom of will, and the liberty to pursue one's own vision of the good (whatever that may be). The implications of this development will be taken up in greater detail in Chapter 4.

For the purposes of this analysis, Grotius's work is also significant in that it provided the foundation of modern international law (Pollock 1961: 144–5), but in a manner which, in effect, drew upon the elements of custom/consent and morality/reason, to the *exclusion* of positive law. According to Grotius, essential to human nature is the desire to live in a peaceful society. The principles of human nature could be derived in either of two ways: a priori, by the application of reason to our social nature, or a posteriori, by observing the accepted usages of civilized nations (Friedmann 1967: 115). This has led to some disagreement about whether reason or custom is determinative of the law, but Pollock (1961: 145–6) argued that there is no inconsistency in Grotius's position: 'In fact, the elements of reason and custom have been recognized by the highest authorities as inseparable, and strengthening one another.' Consistent with this view, international law is in force owing to consent and reasonableness, reflected in treaties or common usages, which give rise to customary international law. Positive law is excluded by this formulation because the presence of a coercive authority with the power to sanction—which has never fit well the situation of international law—is not a necessary aspect of law (Pound 1912–13: 126).

The response of the legal positivists has been to hold to their definition of law, and disqualifying international law from claim to the label law 'properly so called' (Austin 1995: 123). Austin (p. 160) referred to it instead as 'positive international morality'. Hart (1961: 226) suggested that international law resembles a 'simple regime of primary or customary law', which he considered to be 'pre-legal'.

Legal Positivist Tradition

John Austin and H. L. A. Hart, respectively, are the most influential early and current theorists of legal positivism. But their forerunner, Thomas Hobbes, merits special mention. Hobbes is an extraordinary figure. As will be analysed further in Chapter 4, he is considered to be both a natural law theorist and a legal positivist, schools of thought that are usually seen as antagonistic. Also of significance, Hobbes is widely credited with placing the problem of social order at the centre of social theory, political theory, and the social sciences generally (Wrong 1994: chap. 2). He also cemented, perhaps irrevocably, the identification of law with order. Hobbes (1996: chaps. 13 and 14) viewed humans in bleak terms, as essentially covetous. Men desire gain, security, and glory (p. 83). Under the Hobbsean vision, as described by Roberto Unger (1975: 65), men 'want not just to have, but to have more than their fellows'; they desire power in addition to material goods, and the 'power of some is the powerlessness of others'. These desires inevitably lead to conflict in the scramble over scarce resources—'a war of every man against every man' (Hobbes 1996: 85). Hobbes (p. 84) concluded, in his immortal phrase, that the life of man in the state of nature is 'solitary, poor, nasty, brutish and short'.

The natural laws he (chap. 14) rationally deduced from human nature involve the right of self-defence and securing a peaceful existence. Thus, Hobbes held, in the interest of obtaining security, people join together to form civil society, handing over virtually unlimited lawmaking power to an omnipotent sovereign. 'The law is a command' of the sovereign (pp. 179, 175); the sovereign is not subject to the law, but above the law (pp. 176, 215). The only basic right the people retain is the right to replace the sovereign if he fails to secure a peaceful social order. Moreover, according to Hobbes, justice is determined relative to the dictates of the positive legal order. 'What the legislator commands, is taken as good: what he forbids, is to be taken as evil. Before his edict, right and wrong do not exist' (quoted in Doolan 1954: 3; see Hobbes 1996: 85). Hobbes eviscerated natural law as a substantive standard for positive law.

Hobbes's view of positive law has similarly negative implications for custom. Huntington Cairns (1949: 261) remarked that Hobbes 'ignores the great mediaeval conception of law as the custom of the community, the idea that law was not primarily the expression of the will of the ruler, but that it was the expression of the habit of the life of the community'. Hobbes (1996: 69) astutely observed the often cynical and instrumental resort to custom and reason: 'they appeal from custom to reason, and from reason to custom, as it serves their turn; receding from custom when their interest requires it, and setting themselves against reason, as oft as reason is against them.' He situated positive law in a position of unquestioned superiority: 'And our lawyers account no customs law, but such as are reasonable, and that evil customs are to be abolished: but the judgment of what is reasonable, and of what is to be abolished, belongeth to him that maketh the law, which is the sovereign assembly, or monarch' (p. 177).

Legal positivists have traditionally evinced an ambivalent or dismissive attitude towards custom. This treatment in part reflects the fact that customs represent a continual challenge to the power and authority of positive law. In the contest between the word (legislation) and actions (customs, usages), the latter has the distinct upper hand. During the Middle Ages, prior to the consolidation of the nation state across Europe, the basic stock of law was customary. To people at the time, 'the law was not primarily something made or created at all, but something which existed as a part of the national or local life. The law was primarily custom, legislative acts were not expressions of will, but records or promulgations of that which was recognized as already binding upon men' (Kelly 1992: 139). Legal positivist views, Pound (1912–13: 128–9, 145) observed, tend to emerge in periods of increased legislation and struggles over the consolidation of state power.

Starting where Hobbes left off, John Austin (influenced by Bentham)[6] defined law as the command of the sovereign. 'Every *law* or *rule* . . . is a *command*' (Austin 1995: 21). 'Every positive law, or every law simply and strictly so called, is set by a sovereign, or a sovereign body of persons, to a member or members of the independent political society wherein that person or body is sovereign or supreme' (p. 165). The 'sovereign' is the determinate and common superior to whom the '*bulk* of the given society are in the *habit* of obedience or submission'; the superior, in turn, 'is *not* in a habit of obedience to a determinate human superior' (p. 166). Any other kinds of rules, like those of morality or custom, are not *law*, 'properly so-called'. Like all legal positivists, Austin saw the fundamental function of law to be the maintenance of social order.

As indicated earlier, Austin insisted on a strict separation between law and morality. 'A law which exists *is a law*, though we happen to dislike it' (Austin 1913: 7). However, he (1995: 141) also recognized the 'frequent coincidence of positive law and morality, and of positive law and of the law of God', and of positive law and customs. Positive law is influenced by the morality and customs of the society. They are, nevertheless, distinct. Morality and customs (which he saw as connected) only exist as rules of positive law when they 'are clothed with legal sanctions by the sovereign' (ibid.; see also 1913: 34–7; 1995: 72–3). Prior to that they are

---

[6] Bentham preceded Austin in formulating the imperative theory of law, and the separation of law and morals, which form the core of legal positivism. Philip Schofield (1991) explained Austin's greater prominence as a legal positivist by a combination of factors, including the fact that Bentham was a sharp critic of the common law while Austin was more conservative.

merely rules set by habit or opinion and sanctioned by social means (Hart 1961: 84–5).

Austin did not construe custom in necessarily negative terms. In an observation that epitomizes the mirror thesis, he (1913: 272) wrote: 'If the people be enlightened and strong, custom, like law, will commonly be consonant to their interests and wishes. If they be ignorant and weak, custom, as well as law, will commonly be against them.' The illustrative example he chose, however, was not flattering to custom. He pointed out that during the Middle Ages people throughout Europe were held in slavish conditions primarily under the rule of custom. 'So that the body of the people in many of the European nations, have been released, by direct legislation, from the servile and abject thraldom in which they had been held by custom, and by law framed upon custom' (p. 273). In this example positive law served as an engine of change, reforming custom.

Austin (1995: Lect. II) affirmed the existence of God's Divine law for humans, which he felt could be revealed to us through utilitarian reasoning. He (p. 158) also suggested that positive law that conflicts with Divine law could be disobeyed (though he was not a strong advocate of this). In addition, Austin believed there is a set of concepts and principles common to all the 'maturer' systems (1913: 147–59); these shared concepts, he suggested, are the product of utility and necessity, 'bottomed upon the nature of man' and the stage of social organization of society (p. 151). 'For we cannot imagine coherently a system of law (or a system of law as evolved in a refined community), without conceiving them as constituent parts of it' (p. 149). It was upon this detailed shared corpus—including, *inter alia*, duty, right, liberty, injury, punishment, redress—that he planned to construct his general jurisprudence.

Austin thus saw law in the terms I have set out as the core view of law in Western legal theory, as an integrated aspect of society which operates to maintain order. His major contribution was to provide a sharp definition of positive law, and to erect a more visible barrier separating the elements on the left side (custom/consent and morality/reason) from the right side (positive law) of the framework. In effect, he contests their claims to also represent a kind of 'law'. Custom/consent and morality/reason, Austin agreed, have a major impact on what ultimately is recognized as positive law, but positive law is still distinct from the other two precisely to the extent that *recognition* by the legal apparatus is a condition of positivity.

H. L. A. Hart's modern classic, *The Concept of Law*, placed legal positivism on a sounder and more readable foundation than that provided by

Austin. His argument will be explored extensively in Chapter 6. In most respects that matter here, his account is not substantially different from Austin's. One relevant aspect is his critique and replacement of Austin's definition of law as the command of the sovereign backed by sanction. Hart felt that Austin's view of law too much resembled a 'gunman writ large'. The sovereign element is unsatisfactory in that it does not fit the situation of modern democracies, where there are no 'uncommanded commanders' habitually obeyed by others (the people rule, and are subject to the rules); and the command element fails because many rules cannot be considered orders backed by threats, but rather are facilitative, or power conferring.[7]

Hart suggested instead that a legal system exists when there is a combination of primary rules of obligation, and secondary rules of recognition, adjudication, and change. Under primary rules, 'human beings are required to do or abstain from certain actions'; secondary rules 'provide that human beings may by doing or saying certain things introduce new rules of the primary type, extinguish or modify old ones, or in various ways determine their incidence or control their operations' (Hart 1961: 78–9). More simply, the primary rules are the rules people in society are to abide by, whereas the secondary rules are the rules legal actors follow in relation to the identification and application of primary rules. For the existence of a legal system, Hart added two conditions on top of the presence of primary and secondary rules: the primary rules must be generally obeyed by the populace, and the legal officials must normatively accept the validity of the secondary rules. Any society that satisfies this description will have a legal system.

Hart's position with regard to the relationship between morality and law shares most aspects of the theories of Hobbes and Austin. His view of human nature was not substantially different from that of Hobbes, and from this he (p. 195) derived a universally applicable 'minimum content of natural law' having to do with the protection of persons, property, and promises which are 'indispensable features of municipal law'. Like Austin, he (p. 199) emphasized that the 'law of every modern state shows at a thousand points the influence of both the accepted social morality and wider moral ideals'. This is, again, the mirror thesis, in Hart's (ibid.) own words: the 'ways in which law *mirrors* morality are myriad.'

With one important exception, Hart also viewed custom in a way similar to Austin. Primitive systems, according to Hart, have only primary

---

[7] Hart's (1961) critique of Austin's account is detailed in chaps. 2, 3, and 4, and summarized on p. 77.

rules, thus lacking legal systems. With the addition of secondary rules they 'step from the pre-legal into the legal world' (Hart 1961: 91). Hart (pp. 44–7) also recognized that customs have become a part of the positive law through recognition. However, Hart differed from Austin in asserting that custom 'has a genuine though modest place in most legal systems' (p. 26). Austin was more generous in crediting the influence of customs on positive law.

This is a telling difference because it suggests a fundamental change after centuries of development of positive law. Hobbes's disregard of custom made it clear that positive law need not necessarily be a reflection of custom. Hart took a further step to indicate that indeed a distance between the two had developed. 'Custom is not in the modern world a very important "source" of law' (Hart 1961: 44; see also Friedmann 1967: 251). Anyone who examines the typical body of laws and regulations produced by legislatures today would confirm Hart's observation.

Custom-Culture Tradition

In the jurisprudential penchant for the classification and discussion of theorists by schools of thought, which I have also indulged in here, there is no category for custom-culture, an absence owing primarily to the historical exigencies of academic traditions and labelling. This category— combined with Maine from the next category—substantially overlaps with what is usually known as the historical tradition. However, my emphasis is not on historicism as such, but on the core views about the relationship between law and society enunciated by its primary theorist, von Savigny. This category counterbalances the categories (natural law and positive law) roughly allotted to the other two elements of the tripartite scheme, and it fits the basic characteristics of an approach that has existed parallel to these others, albeit not generally given separate recognition as such. None of the three categories, I should emphasize, perfectly fits the element with which they most closely correspond. At the broadest level, the present category encompasses the culture of a society, including its customary morality, which has aspects of both custom/ consent and morality/reason. Nevertheless, the emphasis in this category remains with customs and usages as sources of law, so the alignment is appropriate.

When mentioned in legal contexts, Baron de Montesquieu is usually seen either as an early practitioner of comparative law (Zweigert and Kotz 1992: 49), or as one of forerunners of the sociology of law (Ehrlich

1916: 583). Friedrich Karl von Savigny, in contrast, is regarded as the founder of the historical school of jurisprudence, and as one of the pioneers in the development of jurisprudence as the positive science of law (Reimann 1990: 851–8). Yet they shared a view of law as the product of, and intimately related to, the customs and culture of the society. Next to the work of these two scholars, I add Eugen Ehrlich, credited with being the 'inventor' of the sociology of law (Ziegert 1980), who represents the culmination of the custom-culture tradition.

Montesquieu wrote *L'Esprit des Lois* (The Spirit of Laws) during the mid-eighteenth century when the natural law doctrine of Grotius was highly influential. Montesquieu's (1991: 1–5) views of the laws of nature were much closer to those of Hobbes (though with a lesser emphasis on fear), with people primarily concerned to find peace in society. He focused on how positive laws varied greatly in relation to the nation to which they were attached:

> They [positive laws] should be adapted in such a manner to the people for whom they are framed, that it is a great chance if those of one nation suit another. They should be relative to the nature and principle of each government; whether they form it, as may be said of political laws; or whether they support it, as in the case of civil institutions. They should be relative to the climate of each country, to the quality of its soil, to its situation and extent, to the principal occupation of the natives, whether husbandmen, huntsman, or shepherds: they should have a relation to the degree of liberty which the constitution will bear; to the religion of the inhabitants, to their inclinations, riches, numbers, commerce, manners and customs. (Montesquieu 1991: 7)

Montesquieu then went on to establish in detail the connections between positive law and the form of government, climate, soil conditions, morality and customs, commerce, etc., in nations as diverse as classical Rome, France, Germany, America, China, Spain, and various Middle Eastern countries.

The thrust of his view, which was highly influential at the time (Kelly 1992: 273–4), was to challenge the notion of reason-based legal universals. Instead, Montesquieu argued, reason applied to different circumstances would have different results (Stein 1980: 15–16). Thus, positive laws were, and should be, gloriously multifarious, reflecting the local culture and circumstances of each people. He viewed law in a dialectical relation with society: 'law is shaped by society and shapes it at the same time' (Ehrlich 1916: 586). He also observed that the history of legal development helps explain the structure of society (ibid.), a view which anticipates that of the legal evolutionists. In short, Montesquieu presented a classic version of the mirror thesis, though his account went far beyond customs and morality to include the totality of a society and its physical setting.

Almost three-quarters of a century after Montesquieu's classic, von Savigny published his famous tract, *Of the Vocation of Our Age for Legislation and Jurisprudence.* This text, and the Historical School he led, attacked both the philosophical tradition and the legal positivist tradition. 'Fundamentally, the doctrine of the Historical School was a defense both of juristic supremacy against the pretensions of the sovereign and of legal learning and experience—"scientific law"—against abstract "philosophical" approaches to law' (Kelley 1990: 253). Von Savigny's views must be understood in historical context. Germany had recently been freed from Napoleanic occupation, so nationalist sentiments were pervasive (Pound 1923: 19). It was also the time of the Romantic reaction to the Enlightenment emphasis on reason (p. 43), expressed most prominently by Rousseau (1974: 34): 'it is readily apparent that there is no longer any need to ask who has the power to make laws, since they are acts of the general will.' Von Savigny's immediate purpose was to resist the proposed enactment of a Civil Code for Germany based on the French Civil Code, with its abstract principles and claims of grounding in reason. Von Savigny rejected the view that there was a universal law of nature discoverable by reason. Natural law theorists, he (1831: 134) observed, were susceptible to the common self-delusion of 'holding that which is peculiar to ourselves to be common to human nature in general'.

In this exposition I will focus primarily on his polemic on behalf of custom against legal positivist views, just as, in the previous part, I emphasized the legal positivist antipathy toward custom. The imperative theory of positive law—that 'all law, in its concrete form, is founded upon the express enactments of the supreme power' (von Savigny 1831: 23)— failed to appreciate the true source of law, according to von Savigny. From 'the earliest times' the 'law will be found to have already attained a fixed character, peculiar to the people, like their language, manners and constitution' (p. 24); law reflects 'the common conviction of the people, the kindred consciousness of an inward necessity, excluding all notion of an accidental and arbitrary origin' (ibid.). There is an 'organic connection of law with the being and character of the people. . . . Law grows with the growth, and strengthens with the strength of the people, and finally dies away as the nation loses its nationality' (p. 27). All forms of law— customary law, statutes, and juristic law—are the products of the legal consciousness of the people, which is the underlying law-creating force in society (see Ehrlich 1975: 446–8). Hence, the 'first tenet' of the Historical School: 'law is found, not made' (Pound 1923: 16). These views were captured by the notion that the law is a reflection and product of the *Volksgeist*,[8] the spirit of the people. A stronger and more comprehensive statement of the mirror thesis cannot be found.

Since law develops in organic conjunction with society, von Savigny promoted historical study to uncover the root principles of the law, which can then be made systematic. An enduring irony of von Savigny's theory is that the law which he (1831: 59) claimed 'constantly reminded all the Germanic nations of their indissoluble unity' in fact substantially consisted of the *ius commune*, which was derived from the revival of Roman law in the Middle Ages and shared across much of Europe, a fact which von Savigny knew well (pp. 54–5), since he was a great Roman law scholar. Von Savigny solved this apparent contradiction by suggesting that Roman law had been absorbed into German life. In addition, he interjected jurists (professors and learned judges) into a crucial intermediary position. Although the law is originally formed as customary law from ordinary usages, he (p. 30) claimed that with time it is taken over and faithfully developed in technical legal terms by the jurists. Thereafter law would have a twofold existence, with jurists representing the popular consciousness.

Von Savigny's Romanist orientation gave rise to conflicts with 'Germanists', 'who took the idea of law as custom of the people seriously in a traditional, popular sense' (Reimann 1990: 868). Later studies, according to Eugen Ehrlich (1975: 175), showed 'conclusively that with the exception perhaps of legal maxims, legal propositions do not arise in the popular consciousness itself. Legal propositions are created by jurists, preponderantly on the basis of norms for decision found in the judgments of courts.' Critics of von Savigny have suggested that references to customs and consciousness of the people advanced primarily a conservative agenda that included fighting codification and change (Reimann 1990: 877), and enhancing the roles and status of legal scholars (Patterson 1940: 413). Von Savigny's historicism was a formula for preserving the status quo.

It was but a small conceptual step to go from the idea that law can be found in, and emerges from, the customary practices of the people, to the conclusion that, in fact, such practices *are* law. Eugen Ehrlich (1975: 462) made this step, which merely 'carried Savigny and Puchta's very own thoughts to their logical conclusion'. Ehrlich (p. 24) elaborated:

[8] Although this term was adopted by, and is identified with von Savigny, it was actually coined by G. F. Puchta (Reimann 1990: 583).

It is not an essential element of the concept of law that it be created by the state, nor that it constitute the basis for the decisions of the courts or other tribunals, nor that it be the basis of a legal compulsion consequent upon such a decision. A fourth element remains, and that will have to be the point of departure, i.e. the law is an ordering.

According to Ehrlich (pp. 455–71), 'law' consists of the rules of conduct followed in everyday life—the customary practices and usages which give rise to and maintain the inner ordering of associations (the family, village community, corporations, business associations, professions, clubs, a school or factory, etc.). This is the 'living law'. '[L]aw is essentially a form of social life' (Ehrlich 1916: 584). For Ehrlich, this *is* law—not just a source of law, but *law*—regardless of whether it has been recognized by state legal institutions. Ehrlich thus laid a direct challenge to the belief that the state has a monopoly on the creation and administration of 'law', a challenge to positive law as the dominant view of law.

In an important sense, Ehrlich's observations raised a sharp critique of the mirror thesis and the social order function of law. He pointed out that positive law norms often—in certain regions and for certain subjects—had little connection to actually prevailing social norms. Social order is maintained through this 'living law', more so than through the positive law of the state (see Tamanaha 1995a). Ehrlich's work prepared the way for and presaged the later emphasis that legal sociology was to have on demonstrating the frequent 'gap' between law on the books and social conduct.

In another important sense, however, Ehrlich's work is the ultimate extension of the mirror thesis and the social order function of law. In effect, his argument is that if positive law does not mirror social norms, and does not in fact maintain social order, it has lost its superior entitlement to the claim of being *the* law, and the label must be given back, or at least shared with the 'living law', the actually lived social norms that do satisfy these criteria. Legal pluralists, discussed later, have followed this implication of Ehrlich's work.

To conclude this part, I will point out a couple of the parallels this discussion has revealed between the custom-culture tradition and the natural law tradition. Each of these traditions represents the strongest case for the two elements I set out earlier in interaction with positive law, respectively, custom/consent and morality/reason. Montesquieu's and von Savigny's account of custom-culture infusing positive law is parallel to the various claims that positive law is infused with moral rules originating in reason and common human nature. In these cases the reference is often conservative in intention or effect, preserving the status quo, for it suggests that as it stands positive law is the way it should be for legitimate—though different—reasons. Ehrlich's work represents the custom/consent element's counterpart to the natural law tradition's insistence that it has final say over what is valid law; both positions argue, in effect, that they are the *true law*, not (or more so than) positive law. In laying this challenge to positive law, both have a critical potential and bent. Historically, however, for both traditions the legitimating effect on positive law has predominated over the critical.

Law and Social Organization Tradition

This grouping, dealing primarily with the work of Sir Henry Maine, Émile Durkheim, and Max Weber, also consists of theorists who often have been placed under different headings. Maine is considered a seminal figure in historical and evolutionary jurisprudence, and an early (mostly armchair) anthropologist.[9] Durkheim is the leading theorist of Functionalist sociology, and Weber the leading theorist of interpretive sociology. All are alike, however, in that they have formulated highly influential accounts of the way in which the form and content of law is intimately linked to the nature of social organization—the mirror thesis in a different form. Evolutionary jurisprudence is the recognized legal tradition closest to this category. Many of the theories discussed thus far contain an evolutionary component, in the sense that they postulate the emergence of positive law out of custom, usually at some pre-history, pre-writing period. The evolutionary jurisprudence tradition consists of the narrower group of theories that portray the development of law in terms of determinate stages, more-or-less universal, often construed in progressive terms as the movement from a lower or less sophisticated state to a higher state.[10] I have gone outside of this category to emphasize the focus of these theorists on the close links between law and social organization, apart from any evolutionary implications (and Weber is not an evolutionary theorist).

Maine's *Ancient Law*, published in 1861, was extremely influential in its time (Stein 1980: 85). Law developed in stages, according to Maine

---

[9] Some anthropologists might dispute his place in the field. However, one sign of acceptance is that his *Ancient Law* (1986) has recently been republished in the Classics of Anthropology Series of the University of Arizona Press.

[10] An excellent introduction to evolutionary thought in law can be found in Stein (1980); see also Elliot (1985); Hovenkamp (1985).

(1986: 4–29), which moved from pre-customary law (ad hoc decisions of the sovereign), to customary law (maintained by the aristocratic class), to legislation. Although his study examined mostly ancient Roman law and English law, and to a lesser extent, ancient Greek law and Hindu law, Maine drew his conclusions in universalistic terms. His primary focus related to the fundamental differences between primitive and modern society. 'The contrast may be most forcibly expressed by saying that the unit of an ancient society was the Family, for a modern society the Individual' (p. 121). The family is the most elementary group; families aggregate to form clans and tribes; the aggregation of tribes form the commonwealth; the citizens in early commonwealths thus considered themselves to be joined by a common lineage (p. 124). Since the community is the basic unit, an offence committed by, or against, a member of a group is seen as crime of, or against, the group. 'The moral elevation and moral debasement of the individual appear to be confounded with, or postponed to, the merits and offences of the group to which the individual belongs' (p. 122). Relations within the community are governed by *status*, that is, the identity of a person in relation to their group. 'Law is the parent's word' (p. 121); or specifically, the word of the father, to whom the wife and offspring are subordinate.

Thus is the stage set for Maine's (pp. 163–5) most renowned observations:

The movement of the progressive societies has been uniform in one respect. Through all its course it has been distinguished by the gradual dissolution of family dependency and the growth of individual obligation in its place. The individual is steadily substituted for the Family, as the unit of which civil laws take account. The advance has been accomplished at varying rates of celerity. . . . But, whatever its pace, the change has not been subject to reaction or recoil. . . . Nor is it difficult to see what is the tie between man and man which replaces by degrees those forms of reciprocity in rights and duties which have their origin in the Family. It is Contract. Starting, as from one terminus of history, from a condition of society in which all the relations of Persons are summed up on the relations of Family, we seem to have steadily moved towards a phase of social order in which all these relations arise from the free agreement of individuals. . . . [W]e may say that the movement of the progressive societies has hitherto been a movement from Status to Contract.

Maine's work has been subjected to sustained criticism from many directions, including jurisprudence and anthropology, on various counts, from shoddy research to plain confusion, to not being supported by subsequent studies (see Stein 1980: 99–115). Nonetheless, his influence has been immense. He is a key figure for my purposes because he placed law at the very heart of social organization. Social development occurred through, it accompanied and was accompanied by, legal change; legal development *is* social development. Social order is characterized by the order of legal relations. Henceforth society itself could not be understood without attending to its law.

Émile Durkheim, 'an undisputed giant amongst social scientists' (Hunt 1978: 60), went further along this path. He (1983: 34) wrote:

> In fact, social life, wherever it becomes lasting, inevitably tends to assume a definite form and become organized. Law is nothing more than the most stable and precise element in this very organization. Life in general within a society cannot enlarge in scope without legal activity similarly increasing in a corresponding fashion. Thus we may be sure to find in the law all the essential varieties of social solidarity.

Law, for Durkheim, is not just a deeply integrated aspect of society; at a fundamental level it holds together modern society, thereby playing the central role in the maintenance of social order.

Durkheim's account of social–legal development was influenced by Maine's (Lukes 1973: 30), though there are substantial differences. He proposed that the movement from primitive society to modern society was the movement from 'mechanical' to 'organic' solidarity (Durkheim 1972: 123–54). Primitive society was characterized by sameness, by a 'collective consciousness' which covers virtually all aspects of social life; 'social life is made up almost exclusively of common beliefs and of common practices which derive from unanimous adhesion a very particular intensity' (Durkheim 1973: 67). Everything is oriented towards the collective. Strictly speaking, the individual personality was not suppressed; 'at that moment of history, *it did not exist*' (p. 80). What makes the social solidarity 'mechanical' is this sameness. Modern societies, by contrast, reflect a division of labour, with people engaged in specialized activities, forming smaller associations, each with their own sets of beliefs and values. The collective consciousness still exists, but its coverage has dramatically receded, and its orientation has changed to focus on the relations between individuals (pp. 69–85). Social solidarity at this stage is 'organic' because society is bound together through the interdependence of subgroups or segments based upon the nature of their social activity, much like how the organs in a living body each contribute to the survival of the whole (pp. 70, 77–9). Law serves to integrate the various parts of an organic society by replacing what was lost through the diminishment of the collective consciousness.

These two social types each have their own characteristic form of law. 'Since law reproduces the main forms of social solidarity, we have only to classify the different types of law in order to be able to investigate which species of social solidarity corresponds to them' (Durkheim 1983: 37). Durkheim focused on the nature of the legal sanction applied to determine the type of law. Primitive societies are characterized by 'repressive law' (mostly criminal law), modern societies by 'restitutory law' (civil law, procedural, and constitutional law) (pp. 39–58). This difference in orientation is owing to the fact that an offence in primitive society is an affront to the whole, which elicits a strong response; whereas in developed societies the injuries are to the individual, and thus requires an adjustment in the relations between the wrongdoer and the victim.

Durkheim's (p. 34) account of the relationship between law and society presents an extremely tight relationship between law and custom, as well as between law and morality: 'law *mirrors* . . . a part of social life' (emphasis added). His (1993: 82) account of this connection is reminiscent of Montesquieu's: 'Law rests, then, on both objective and subjective causes at once. It is not only relative to the physical environment, to the climate, the number of inhabitants, etc., but even to preferences, to ideas, to the normal culture of a nation.' 'Normally customs are not opposed to law; on the contrary, they form the basis for it' (Durkheim 1983: 35). According to Roger Cotterrell (1999: 91), in Durkheim's view, 'law is to be considered the primary form in which society, as a unity, expresses its moral essence, that is the distinctive moral character that gives it some kind of integrity and cohesion.'

Because he portrays law as representative of the collective consciousness, the possibility for conflict between law and morality is downplayed (Lukes and Scull 1983: 6). As Alan Hunt (1978: 69–70) observed, 'Durkheim posits a *mirror* image relationship between law and social solidarity. This rests upon the unsubstantiated assumption that law embodies the content of all normative systems and necessarily denies the possibility of conflict between legal norms and other normative systems; and such conflict could only be regarded as temporary and abnormal' (emphasis added). Blindness to the possibility of a systematic mismatch between law and morality, or law and customs, is inherent to the mirror thesis.

Durkheim's Functionalist analysis is instructive in another important respect. A number of prominent theorists have characterized law in sociological Functionalist terms, that is, in terms of the necessary function that law satisfies as an integral element within society. For Talcott

Parsons (1980) law fulfilled the crucial function of integrating the subsystems in society (see Cotterrell 1992: 80–92). Niklas Luhmann (1985: 82) saw law as the 'structure of a social system which depends upon the congruent generalization of normative behavioral expectations'. Each asserted that the core service law provided towards the survival of society/social system was the maintenance of order. Thus law must exist in all societies.[11] Luhmann declared: 'Law itself, as a way of constraining behavioral expectations, is found in every society. Without it, social interaction would be impossible' (1982: 124).

This Functionalist-systems approach to law is, in a sense, the purest theoretical representation of the common presupposition that runs through the history of Western legal and social theory: that law is a mirror of society, which functions to maintain social order. Luhmann's suggestion that without law social interaction would collapse epitomizes this idea. For some readers it might seem inapt to characterize Luhmann's account as one in which law is an integrated aspect of society, because his autopoietic theory of law as a closed self-referential system is most often identified with the notion that law is autonomous (see Luhmann 1982: chap. 6; Lempert 1987). This autonomy, however, is the autonomy of a differentiated subsystem *within* society, in which context law continues to play an essential integrative function for society taken as a whole (Luhmann 1985, 1989).[12] In Luhmann's (1982: 128) own words, 'the autonomy of the legal system is significant for the entire social order.'

It is crucial to recognize that sociological Functionalist theories determine the role and nature of law a priori, by theoretical designation, in terms of the function law is deemed to serve in the context of the model of the social system constructed by the theorist. Functionalist analysis therefore cannot account for, cannot even conceive of, the possibility that law would serve almost no social order function, yet operate quite efficiently in other respects, with no sign of consequent breakdown in the social system. This possibility is real, not just hypothetical, as I will later show, rendering Functionalist analysis inadequate for an understanding of law.

---

[11] Parsons might be limited to the assertion that law exists in all differentiated societies.

[12] Cotterrell (1992: 86) argued that with the increasing emphasis on differentiation, Luhmann has moved away from the notion that law serves to integrate the subsystems within society. This interpretation is not consistent with Luhmann's (1982: 128) stated position: 'we can see how the development of a separate legal system not only ensures a degree of rationality and independence in the application of norms, but also provides legal "instruments" necessary for the functional and structural differentiation of society as a whole.' Even when Luhmann (1985: 287) shifted more fully to autopoietic analysis, he continued to discuss law in terms of its 'function'.

Max Weber surpasses Durkheim in stature and influence in the social sciences as well as in legal sociology (Hunt 1978: 93). Trained in law, Weber (1954) produced a detailed sociological study of the relationship between law and society, rich in comparative and historical detail, set in a complex analytical framework. As with all of the previous traditions, I will limit the discussion of his work to those areas that are relevant to this study. Like Maine and Durkheim, Weber believed that there are certain distinct legal types that correspond, more or less, with certain social arrangements. However, he eschewed evolutionary analysis, preferring instead to characterize the categories he described as 'ideal types', heuristic abstractions based upon clusters of characteristics which tend to be found together. His view of the relationship between law and society was also more nuanced, emphasizing multi-causality (see Milovanovic 1989: 30–5). Social influences on the development of law, according to Weber, include religion, political organization, the nature of the economy, and (especially) the interests of the legal profession itself.

Weber (1954: 61–4) set out four basic types of legal thought.[13] The primary distinction was between formal and substantive. A legal system is formal if it has become differentiated to the extent that decisions are based exclusively on considerations internal to the law; a system is substantive if it goes outside of law to base decisions on religion, ethics, policy, or some other ground. Formal and substantive systems are further subdivided into those that are rational or irrational. Rational systems rely upon logical analysis and the application of rules and principles; irrational systems do not. Primitive procedures in which a legal decision is based upon the pronouncement of an oracle are (1) *formally irrational*—formal because it is a closed system that strictly follows certain procedures; irrational because it is not based on any logical analysis (p. 77). (2) *Substantively irrational* systems are those in which the decision is made on an ad hoc basis, focused on the outcome, considering a mix of factors legal and extra-legal. Weber's exemplar for this was Khadi justice—substantive because the decision is based on considerations outside the law; irrational because it is not limited to the logical application of rules pp. 228–9). Priestly-based legal systems are (3) *substantively rational*—substantive because the decision is outcome-oriented based upon fidelity to sacred texts and ethical doctrine; rational because they often are highly casuistic (pp. 205–6). Finally, (4) *formally rational* systems are the modern Western civil law systems—formal and rational because decisions are based exclusively on the logical application

---

[13] My understanding of these categories has been enhanced by the account provided in Kronman (1983: 75–95). Also helpful is Trubek (1972a).

of a comprehensive set of rules and principles to the case at hand (p. 64). Formally rational law, Weber argued, is uniquely suited to the demands of a capitalist economic system, because it provides the highest degree of stability and predictability of decisions which allows for reliable planning (pp. 39–40, 228–9).

Weber's account is especially relevant because he provided a sophisticated analysis of the nature of the relationship in modern society between the three elements we have been tracking. He defined law in legal positivist terms, as the publicly approved institutional enforcement of norms (pp. 5–6). Positive law norms may exist in conformity or conflict with customs/conventions. 'And while it is not at all unusual that legal norms are rationally enacted with the purpose of changing existing "usages" and conventions, the normal development is more usually as follows: a legal order is empirically "valid" owing not so much to the availability of coercive guarantees as to its habituation as "usage" and its "routinization" ' (pp. 34–5). Established custom 'cannot be persistently ignored except under the compelling necessity of certain formal considerations or because of the intervention of authoritarian powers, or where the agencies of legal coercion have no contact with the life of business as is the case where they are imposed by an ethnically or politically alien authority' (p. 72).

This account of the relationship between custom and positive law is familiar enough, but the situation becomes more complicated in the context of formally rational law in modern society. Weber (pp. 307–8) described how formally rational law leads to a gap between legal decisions and the popular expectations and understanding of law:

> Now we have already seen that the expectations of parties will often be disappointed by the results of a strictly professional legal logic. . . . To a large extent such conflicts rather are the inevitable consequence of the incompatibility that exists between the intrinsic necessities of logically consistent formal legal thinking and the fact that the legally relevant agreements and activities of private parties are aimed at economic results and oriented toward economically determined expectations. . . . But a 'lawyers' law' has never been and never will be brought into conformity with lay expectation unless it totally renounces that formal character which is immanent to it.

Internal legal development relating to technical, formal, and logical concerns peculiar to law as a system, thus inevitably pull formal rational law away from common customs and morality. To a certain extent, this distancing is by design, or at least it is entailed by the emphasis on formal rationality. The gain of predictability and stability of outcome comes at the cost of regular failures to match the lay sense of justice. '[F]ormal justice, due to its necessarily abstract character, infringes upon the ideal of substantive justice' (p. 228). Indeed the substantive-oriented systems (rational and irrational), to the extent that they take religious and ethical factors into consideration, are the ones better designed to produce outcomes matching prevailing conventional or moral views. As a consequence of the mismatch in expectations, there is a constant anti-formalist pressure on formal rational systems, reflected in the demands for substantive justice or equity, for purposive adjudication, for 'free law' decisions which focus on the concrete facts of the case more so than on the legal norms, and for the use of juries (pp. 307–21).

A pressing question is raised by this character of modern law. Given the regular mismatch, why do people go along? Weber's answer has to do with legitimation. Weber (pp. 334–7) set out three ways of legitimating a political-legal order in the eyes of the populace: (1) tradition; (2) charismatic or prophetic declarations; and (3) rationality-based legality.[14] Today, according to Weber, the most common form of legitimation in the West is the belief in legality, 'the acquiescence in enactments which are formally correct and which have been made in the accustomed manner' (p. 9). The basis of the claim for legitimacy of legality is that it is a system of rationally made rules. The 'validity of the rules that fix the limits of legitimate authority depends upon their form, their status as formally correct enactments, rather than their specific content' (Kronman 1983: 45). More to the point, 'legal-rational authority employs the principle of positivity as the basis of legitimation' (p. 55). Positive law, in other words, assuming it satisfies certain conditions which render it formal rational in nature, is self-legitimating, is legitimate precisely because it is rational legality.[15] Regardless of this form of legitimation, Weber recognized that a system that satisfies the requirements of legality could nevertheless be nasty—run by a 'violent, or ruthless' minority (p. 9).

Weber's discussion of legitimation has direct implications for the framework regarding the interaction between the three elements. Throughout the history of Western legal theory, positive law has relied upon its consistency with custom/consent and/or morality/reason to

---

[14] In an earlier passage, he (pp. 8–9) adds a fourth method of legitimation, natural law, but it is not further developed.

[15] Weber (p. 64) listed the following characteristics of formal rationality: (1) legal decisions must be based on the application of rules to fact situations (no ad hoc decisions); (2) it must be possible to derive the decision from the rule based upon logic; (3) the complex of rules should be virtually gapless; (4) whatever cannot be construed legally in rational terms is legally irrelevant; and (5) every social action must be seen as either an application or infringement of legal rules.

provide legitimation. With the development of formal rationality, however, positive law began to supply its own legitimation.

Selective Mirror Tradition

Like the preceding two categories, the 'selective mirror' tradition is not
usually found in jurisprudential taxonomies. It encompasses schools of
thought which at first blush may appear mismatched; and all of the schools
in this category might also be placed in the upcoming, final category, the
instrumentalist tradition. However, there is value to understanding them
as examples of a common approach. The schools of thought gathered in
this category all characterize law as a selective mirror: law reflects only certain customs or morals, or values and interests within society. Marxism
presents the best known and most developed version of this thesis. Among
the many variations of Marxism, there is basic agreement on the point that
legal relations '*mirror* and legally define the fundamental economic relationships in society' (Stone 1985: 50, emphasis added), and on the connected point that law's essential function is to maintain order in the interest
of the dominant class (Cotterrell 1992: 106–14).

The notion that law reflects and protects certain interests in society
over others did not originate with Marx. Earlier I recited Plato's and
Aristotle's concerns about this possibility. Thrascymachus declared that
'justice is the interest of the stronger' (Plato 1991: Book I, 344). Adam
Smith actually preceded Marx and Engels in articulating the thesis that
the economic relations of production largely determine the law (Stein
1980: 111). Smith (1978: 208) linked the emergence of law directly to the
accumulation and preservation of wealth:

[When] . . . some have great wealth and others nothing, it is necessary that the
arm of authority should be continually stretched forth, and permanent laws or
regulations made which [secure] the property of the rich from the inroads of the
poor, who would otherwise continually make incroachments upon it, and settle
in what the infringement of this property consists and in what cases they will be
liable to punishment. Laws and government may be considered in this and
indeed in every case as a combination of rich to oppress the poor, and preserve
to themselves the inequality of the goods which would otherwise be soon
destroyed by the attacks of the poor, who if not hindered by the government
would soon reduce others to an equality with themselves by open violence.

Smith's observations are in accord with Engels's (1942: 156–7) description: 'As the state arose from the need to keep class antagonisms in check,
but also arose in the thick of the fight between the classes, it is normally

the state of the most powerful, economically ruling class, which by its means becomes also the politically ruling class, and so acquires new means of holding down and exploiting the oppressed class.'

The 'classic Marxist theorists devoted very little attention to law' (Collins 1982: 107), in large part because law was seen as secondary:

In the social production of their existence, men inevitably enter into definite relations, which are independent of their will, namely relations of production appropriate to a given stage in the development of their material forces of production. The totality of these relations of production constitutes the economic structure of society, the real foundation, on which arises a legal and political superstructure and to which correspond definite forms of social consciousness. The mode of production of material life conditions the general process of social, political and intellectual life. It is not the consciousness of men that determines their existence, but their social existence that determines their consciousness. (Marx 1970: 20)

In this formulation, almost everything not a part of the economic base is a reflection of that base. The ideological superstructure—including law—both maintains and conceals the relations of class domination upon which the economic system is constructed. '[Y]our jurisprudence', Marx (1998: 21) wrote, 'is but the will of your [bourgeoisie] class made into law for all, a will whose essential content is determined by the material conditions of existence of your class.' Thus, legal thought is 'permeated by the dominant ideology' (H. Collins 1982: 71).

Most Marxists would assert, however, as Engels did, that it 'rarely happens that a code of law is the blunt, unmitigated, unadulterated expression of the domination of a class' (reprinted in Campbell and Wiles 1979: 39). Much of the power of law comes from its appearance of neutrality, from the ideology that it is neutral, a general or pluralistic mirror rather than a selective one. '[I]t is advantageous to the ruling class to erect an ideological smokescreen, and to conceal its hegemony beneath the umbrella of the state' (Pashukanis 1989: 140). According to this view, law developed a relative autonomy from the economic base, such that it has its own distinctive features and interests, and logical requirements, which occasionally result in outcomes against the immediate interests of the dominant class.[16] Nonetheless, law still operates within the general confines set by the economic system (Mamut 1993: 3–10), and in the final

---

[16] In this description I have merged the views of two competing Marxist approaches. The 'instrumentalist' approach characterizes law as an instrument of the dominant class; the 'structuralist' approach describes law as a relatively autonomous subsystem in society, which has its own demands, though also, ultimately, in the interest of the dominant class. My account emphasizes the structuralist view, which is conceptually stronger and appears to have more supporters. For an informative recitation of Marxist approaches to law, see Kamenka (1983).

analysis it operates 'to express, regulate and maintain the general nature of the dominant social relations of a social formation' (Sumner 1982: 258; see H. Collins 1982: 47–52).

In terms of the components of the law–society framework, the Marxist account is relatively straightforward. Positive law is viewed as state law, and the role of law in capitalist society is to preserve social order in the face of potential class conflict (H. Collins 1982: 45). Law, morality, customs are all a part of the superstructure, and therefore are basically determined by the same economic factors. The dominant ideology emerges in relation to the prevailing modes of production (Marx and Engels 1947: 39).[17] 'These ideologies will be articulated initially in customary rules and moral standards. Legal regulation inevitably coincides with such norms of behavior as it is merely a more precise and positive articulation of the requirements of the dominant ideology' (H. Collins 1982: 87). 'There is thus a fit between the "intuitive knowledge" or "taken-for-granted morality" and the specific laws and institutions of the particular capitalist social formation' (Kinsey 1978: 219); and positive law rules are often 'first expressed as a custom' (Mamut 1993: 8). This is obviously a strong version of the mirror thesis, in selective terms.

Immediately following a communist revolution and the takeover of the state apparatus by the proletariat, led by the vanguard intellectuals, there will be a gap between the law (now reflecting the interests of this new dominant class), and customs and morality which reflect previous class relations. There may also be a transitional period during which limited aspects of bourgeois law survive. However, in the new proletarian-dominated state the law will be used instrumentally to change customary behaviour and shape moral attitudes to match socialist ideals. Ultimately, in the Marxist ideal, a society will be built 'in which there is no longer any law and where social relations will be ruled by custom alone' (Brierly and David 1978: 254–5).

Critical Legal Studies (CLS) scholars have taken up key aspects of Marxist thought, though they have vigorously attacked 'vulgar' or instrumentalist Marxism (the view that law is *directly* an instrument of the dominant class). Adherents of CLS view law more in terms of an ideology. Law purports to be above it all, neutrally mediating social conflicts, but

---

[17] H. Collins (1982: 50) explains how Marxists view this process: 'The ruling class uses it position to disseminate its own world-views and values throughout a society. If it is successful in the propagation of the dominant ideology then everyone's common-sense ideas about right and wrong, rational and irrational choices, and even aesthetic judgments, will be formed by the assimilation of ideas supplied by agents of the ruling class.'

in actuality legal values are the values of the dominant class, and law operates as a resource of power available especially for the elite segments of society. As Robert Gordon (1990: 419) put it, 'the [legal meaning] systems, of course, have been built by elites who have thought that they had some stake in rationalizing their dominant power positions, so they have tended to define rights in such a way as to reinforce existing hierarchies of wealth and privilege.' Most critical legal scholars adopt the structuralist version of Marxism described above, which grants law a degree of relative autonomy: 'legal autonomy may have some effect in shaping the precise contours of particular disputes or of the narrow problems addressed by lawmakers, but over the long term, the law taken as a whole will take its shape from the interests of socially powerful groups' (Tushnet 1977: 105). This, again, is the selective mirror thesis.

Proponents of Critical Race Theory assert a similar position, except in substituting racial domination for class domination. The 'vulgar' racialist position offers 'theoretical accounts of racial power that explain legal and political decisions which are adverse to people of color as mere *reflections* of underlying white interest' (Crenshaw *et al.* 1995: p. xxxiv, emphasis added). The more nuanced position argues that law also contributes to constructing 'race' itself. 'Laws produced racial power not simply through narrowing the scope, say, of anti-discrimination remedies, nor through racially-based decision-making, but instead, though myriad legal rules, many of them having nothing to do with rules against discrimination, that continued to reproduce the structures and practices of racial domination' (p. xxv). Society is deeply racist, and liberal law allows this racism to be expressed and perpetuated.

Critical Feminist Theory adopts the selective mirror thesis in relation to male domination. 'Feminist legal theorists, despite differences in schools of thought, are united in their basic belief that society is patriarchal—shaped by and dominated by men' (Weisberg 1993: p. xvii). Law reflects and maintains this patriarchy. 'Thus, if critical legal theory is grounded on a belief that the legal system of capitalist society ultimately supports the existing capitalist social order, a feminist critical theory supposes that the legal system of a patriarchal society enforces and maintains a male supremacist social order as well' (Polan 1993: 419). The essential 'maleness' of law is reflected in everything from the 'reasonable *man*' standard, to the adversary system, to the public/private distinction that perpetuates male domination within the family, to predominantly male judges and legislators, to 'masculine jurisprudence' which emphasizes separation over connection and caring (see Bender 1988; West 1988).

'The whole structure of law—its hierarchical organization; its combative, adversarial format; and its undeviating bias in favor of rationality over all other values—defines it as a fundamentally patriarchal institution' (Polan 1993: 425). Patriarchal law thus mirrors patriarchal society, ignoring and suppressing women's interests and values.

The leftist critical branches of legal theory are not alone in formulating a selective mirror account of law in the modern period. In its descriptive mode, the assertion of the economic analysis of law that law reflects efficiency also qualifies: 'many areas of the law, especially but not only the great common law fields of property, torts, crimes, and contracts, bear the stamp of economic reasoning' (Posner 1992: 23). Richard Posner, leader of the law and economics movement, links this pervasive presence of efficiency to a prevailing attitude among certain spectrums in society, historically and in the present. 'It would not be surprising to find that many legal doctrines rest on inarticulate gropings toward efficiency, especially since so many legal doctrines date back to the nineteenth century when a laissez-faire ideology based on classical economics was the dominant ideology of the educated classes' (ibid.). Judges, in particular, were influenced by this ideology (Posner 1990: 359). This account of law is selective because it ignores or downplays the influence of custom on law, and fails to take into account societal moral values generally (although Posner (pp. 374–87) argues that efficiency is in accord with certain notions of justice).

The selective mirror tradition, in its various incarnations, is not directly connected to legal positivism (and Marx disputed the positivist will theory of law (Marx and Engels 1947: 60)), but legal positivism as a doctrine, with its emphasis on will and its strict separation between law and morality, facilitated the perception of law in partial rather than total mirror terms. This category and the next are best seen as straddlers, simultaneously representing the last mirror accounts of law and the first steps away from the mirror thesis.

Instrumentalist Tradition

The schools of thought mentioned in the previous category, as I indicated, might also be considered examples of the instrumentalist tradition, to the extent that law was seen as an instrument of a particular social interest. The instrumentalist approach, however, is broader than the selective mirror notion, and it will be taken up here from this broader perspective. A strong argument can be made that the instrumentalist view of law dominates the late twentieth century in the same way that the past few centuries have been dominated at various times by the philosophical, the analytical, and the historical traditions (see Summers 1982). According to the instrumentalist approach, law is, and should be, an instrument that serves social or individual interests. This is the social engineering view of law. Jeremy Bentham and Rudolph von Ihering are credited with giving rise to the instrumentalist approach, but the Legal Realists are more immediately responsible for its current influence (at least in the United States). All three contributions will be discussed, as will a couple of modern variants of instrumentalist approaches: public choice theory and the process school of legal anthropology.

Bentham was mentioned earlier as an early legal positivist, and is probably most renowned as a major figure in utilitarian theory. Neither of these aspects of his work is necessarily entailed by an instrumentalist view of law, though they tend to overlap. Instrumentalists often adopt the legal positivist will theory of law, as von Ihering and many Realists did, because the notion that law is an instrument to be used for the securing of social or individual needs implies that the law can be made or declared (Pound 1912: 144–5). And while one may hold an instrumentalist view of law without adopting utilitarianism as a moral theory, von Ihering was a social utilitarian, and many Realists adopted versions of utilitarianism (see Summers 1982: 41–59). What they all shared was a scepticism of, and antagonism towards, prevailing views about absolute values represented in the law, whether found in natural law or natural rights principles (which Bentham called 'nonsense upon stilts'), in von Savigny's historical idealism, in Blackstone's view of the common law as the embodiment of reason, or in the conceptualism of formalists. Bentham argued that the two supposed foundations of the common law, that it represents immemorial custom and natural reason, were myths used to conceal subjective preferences and the activities and interests of lawyers (Postema 1986: chap. 8). Roscoe Pound (1908: 609) expressed a view that represents instrumentalists generally: 'We do not base institutions upon deduction from assumed principles of human nature; we require them to exhibit practical utility, and we rest them upon a foundation of policy and established adaptation to human needs.'

By the term 'utility', Bentham (1982: 12) 'meant that property in any object, whereby it tends to produce benefit, advantage, pleasure, good, or happiness . . . or . . . to prevent the happening of mischief, pain, evil, or unhappiness to the party whose interest is considered'. Law should be designed and implemented to maximize the total quantum of happiness over pain in a community, according to Bentham (see James 1973: 6). When calculating the amount of utility of the community, he was a methodological individualist who considered the community to be 'a fictitious body'. 'The interest of the community then is, what?—the sum of the interests of the several members who compose it' (ibid.). Law is 'a social tool, to be used by the legislator to achieve the great end of all social action—the greatest happiness of the greatest number' (P. King 1986: 41). Maximizing the utility of the community thus provides the standard against which both government and law are to be evaluated. He applied this standard to the common law and found it sorely wanting. Bentham scorned the legal profession for the state of the common law and legal procedures, which he considered obscure, too technical, and full of absurd fictions. 'The synonym for technical, he declared, is "fee-gathering". The interests of the legal classes are not the same as those of the rest of society; the lawyers of all classes have the common interest of multiplying suits and complicating procedure and thus harvesting a fruitful crop of fees' (p. 34). His prescription was the replacement of the common law with a rationally designed code based on the fundamental principle of maximizing happiness. 'It was Bentham's great and enduring contribution to legal criticism to insist that the value of a legal rule depends upon its human consequences' (F. S. Cohen 1937: 25).

Just as Blackstone's rationalization of the common law served as the foil for Bentham's polemic on behalf of reform-oriented codification, von Savigny's conservative historical idealism was the target of von Ihering's pro-Code, progressive stance. Against von Savigny's argument that the law developed through the unfolding of the customs and collective conscience of the people, and therefore could only be discovered, not made, von Ihering argued in his text, *Law as a Means to an End*, that the primary driving force behind legal development was human purpose. Law and legal rules are creations that originate in, and exist to serve, human purposes, according to von Ihering, though this is often forgotten with time or through mystification by legal theorists. The primary difference between Bentham and von Ihering is that the latter had a much stronger sense of the social: 'Our whole life . . . [is] a working together for common purposes, in which everyone in acting for others acts also for himself, and in acting for himself acts also for others. . . . Human life and social life are synonymous' (von Ihering 1968: 67). Society, for von Ihering, was more than Bentham's aggregate of individuals. Law reconciled the individual interest with the social interest because the two coincided in so far as the individual lived an elevated human existence through society. Law, as the title to his most influential work suggests, was a means to individual and social ends. The purpose of law was 'securing the conditions of social life' (p. 345). And the only way to discern whether it was serving the ends desired was to observe the actual consequences of legal rules. For von Ihering, 'the first question should be, how will a rule or decision operate in practice?' (Pound 1908: 610).

Oliver Wendell Holmes, grandfather of the Legal Realists, also articulated an instrumental view of law, most prominently in 'The Path of the Law'. Therein he (1897: 465) exposed the fallacy that 'the only force at work in the development of the law is logic'. He criticized both philosophical jurisprudence, for generalizing concepts into unimpeachable dogma, and historical jurisprudence, for sanctifying tradition in a manner that overrode present policy. Holmes (p. 469) urged an 'enlightened scepticism' directed 'toward a deliberate reconsideration of the worth' of existing rules. A 'body of law is more rational and more civilized when every rule it contains is referred articulately and definitely to an end which it subserves, and when the grounds for desiring that end are stated or are ready to be stated in words' (ibid.).

Conceptual formalism, or the 'jurisprudence of conceptions', was the particular target of the Realists. This was the view that abstract legal concepts had an independent existence, with necessary internal structures, elements and implications. This formalist 'transcendental nonsense' was a barrier to legislative attempts at using the law to alleviate social problems (F. S. Cohen 1935). The most infamous examples of runaway conceptualism are the cases that struck legislative attempts to protect employees in the employment relationship on the ground that such regulation violated their liberty of contract.[18] Pound (1908: 616)[19] raised an instrumentalist critique of the analysis in these cases:

> The conception of freedom of contract is made the basis of a logical deduction. The court does not inquire what the effect of such a deduction will be, when applied to the actual situation. It does not observe that the result will be to produce a condition precisely the reverse of that which the conception originally contemplated.

The Realist's instrumentalism, and their critique of abstract concepts, were heavily influenced by the philosophical pragmatism of John Dewey and William James, with its empirical-oriented, consequentialist

---

[18] See e.g. *Lochner* v. *New York*, 198 US 45 (1905).

[19] I have included Pound within the label 'Realist' despite his differences with some in this group. As F. S. Cohen (1937: 8 n. 5) noted, there is a lot of overlap between Pound's sociological jurisprudence and Llewellyn's realistic jurisprudence.

bent (see Summers 1982: 26–34; Tamanaha 1997: 26–57). Dewey (1941) wrote that 'law is through and through a social phenomenon' (p. 76), and that the standard for law 'is found in consequences' (p. 84). 'It can hardly be surprising . . . that when this philosophy became prominent in America, legal theorists came to see law more as an instrument for human use than as an abstract object for disinterested analysis and study' (Summers 1982: 31). So effective were the Realists in advancing the instrumental view of law that few legal theorists today, at least in the United States, would deny that law is an instrument for the achievement of social ends.

Little can be said with regard to the instrumentalist tradition in terms of the framework I have been following in this presentation, in large part because they did not systematically address these elements, nor are they necessarily unified. As a general matter, 'Bentham understood laws as reflective of a state of a people' (Rosenblum 1978: 19). Writing in opposition to von Savigny, von Ihering (1915: 11–19) denied that laws 'come into existence or are formed painlessly, without trouble', out of custom; law emerged in a struggle over power, he thought; so if its source was custom, it would still have involved the selection of one custom over another. The Realists did not pay much attention to custom, but what they did say suggested that custom is more powerful than law and therefore law should be in substantial conformity with custom if it is to be effective (Llewellyn 1962: 401–2). Accordingly, when participating in the drafting of the Uniform Commercial Code, Llewellyn strove to make it consistent with prevailing business practices. Overall, with regard to morality, their positions were consistent with the view that law should reflect prevailing social morality. They were legal reformers who hoped to make law more effective in serving social interests; for the most part these interests were taken as given by society.

Beyond what has already been mentioned, there are two additional similarities among Bentham, von Ihering, and the Realists that bear notice. First, like the theorists in the selective mirror tradition discussed above, the instrumental theorists assumed the position of critics against, and reformers of, the legal status quo. Both categories thereby run counter to the traditional, centuries-old stance of legal theorists serving as rationalizers, legitimizers, and defenders of the existing legal order. Secondly, Bentham, von Ihering, and the Realists thought they were placing law and legal theory on a sounder, more scientific footing. They believed in the scientific model of knowledge and strove to emulate it; and they were empiricist in orientation. They were interested in getting at the actual facts of legal behaviour,[20] in order to make law better. In that sense, although they were critics of existing law, they were not anarchists or social revolutionaries. Their ultimate objective was to improve the law, to make it more rational and effective in the securing of social interests.

The final two versions of instrumentalism I will briefly discuss are public choice theory and the process school of legal anthropology. Public choice theory has recently made a splash in legal theory in the United States. There are different versions of public choice theory, but the basic idea is that legislation is the product of the competition between self-interested groups.[21] Modern society consists of a pluralism of private groups, each seeking legislation favourable to its own position. Legislation goes to the winners in this competition, who directly benefit from the laws enacted. This model stands in stark contrast to the traditional or republican view that legislators enact legislation with a view towards the common good. The cynical interpretation of this interest group model is that the wealthier groups consistently prevail, because economic power is the key to success in the competition (through 'buying' the support of self-interested legislators); the more benign (or naive) interpretation of this model is that legislative outcomes '*mirror* the equilibrium of competing group pressures', which promotes stability and an orderly reflection of the changing political preferences of the community (Farber and Frickey 1991: 17, emphasis added). The implication of public choice theory, which is dominated by the cynical interpretation, is that society as a whole is worse off in instances of this kind of legislation. Therefore, courts would be justified in narrowly interpreting or perhaps even undercutting such legislation, when it is contrary to the public interest (though this raises serious questions about how to identify the public interest).

Public choice theory is interesting because it manifests the culmination of several different trajectories traced through the course of this presentation. It is instrumentalist in the sense that law is portrayed unabashedly as an instrument of particular interests. This theory is also the product of liberal thinking, with its characteristic scepticism of transcendent moral values, and the consequent lack of confidence in the ability to discern *the* public interest from among contesting versions (pp. 58–62). Hence the formerly dominant content-based view of law—that law is substantively

---

[20] Llewellyn (1962: 29) suggested that Bentham and von Ihering were forerunners to Holmes and the Realists in this scientific orientation to legal behaviour.

[21] An excellent introduction to public choice theory can be found in Farber and Frickey (1991).

full, its content determined by social customs or moral norms—has been emptied out. In public choice theory law is an empty vessel, to be filled in by whatever might be victorious following a contest funnelled through the legislative decision procedure.

The process school of legal anthropology stands outside the over-arching framework I have been following in a significant respect.[22] Adherents assume that the function of law is to maintain social order by enforcing shared norms and by resolving disputes, but that assumption views law from the societal perspective, and they are more interested in exploring law from the standpoint of the individuals who resort to law. After all, how many people who invoke the law are concerned about the preservation of social order? And would not the most direct path to peace be to let matters drop? From this perspective, it becomes evident that law often is used by individuals as an instrument—hence its placement in this category—to pursue or generate conflict, to obtain a sense of security, to seek advantage, vindication, or revenge, to appear on a social stage, to gain access to a resource of power, to gain status or wealth, and more. Legal norms, from this perspective, appear less as fixed rules of social order, and more as negotiable, as forms of justification and rational-ization open to interpretation and manipulation in the pursuit of per-sonal ends. The process approach discloses that 'legal systems are the continuing creation of human beings with various, shifting, and contra-dictory motivations and interests, motivations and interests which range from settling disputes to exacerbating them, from using the law as an instrument of social justice to honing it as a weapon of oppression, from making peace with one's enemies to annihilating them with the help of legal institutions' (D. Cohen 1995: 23). An instrumentalist view of law, when pressed to the limit, strips law down to the status of a tool, available for whatever use to which it is put.

---

[22] For examples of this approach, see Roberts (1979); S. F. Moore (1978). An insightful summary and application of process thought can be found in D. Cohen (1995).

3   Loosening the Hold of the Mirror Thesis

Scattered throughout the preceding, mostly historical, presentation, I have made references to modern theorists and theories which represent current versions of the traditions set out, including John Finnis for the natural law tradition, H. L. A. Hart for the legal positivist tradition, legal pluralists for the custom/culture tradition, Niklas Luhmann for the law and social organization tradition, Law and Economics, Critical Legal Studies, Critical Race Theory, and Critical Feminism for the selective mirror tradition, and public choice theory for the instrumentalist tradition. This list is by no means exhaustive. According to liberal theorist Ronald Dworkin (1986), for example, law not just mirrors but inseparably includes aspects of the general principles of political morality within a society. Legal theorist Roberto Unger (1976) provided a neo-Weberian account of the intimate relation between law and social organization, as have legal sociologists Philippe Nonet and Philip Selznick (1978). There are many more examples. Almost every major strain of Western legal and social theory has articulated, or taken for granted, an account of the relationship between law and society as one of close integration and association. It is widely and routinely assumed that law reflects/mirrors society, and operates to maintain social order.

In his insightful discussion of the mirror thesis, William Ewald (1995: 492–6) observed that there are strong versions of the mirror thesis—'Law is nothing but X,' 'Law is wholly explicable in terms of X'—and there are weaker versions—'Law and X are closely related'. And he noted that there are different dimensions of mirroring, whereby 'X' can be filled in with economics, culture, politics, climate, and geography, or some combination thereof. Montesquieu submitted a strong version of the mirror thesis on a combination of dimensions. Marx provided a strong version on the economic dimension. None of the theorists or theories discussed in the preceding chapter could be saddled fairly with the strictest form of the mirror thesis—'law is nothing but . . .'. Indeed, each recognized that law had some role in shaping society, indicating that law occasionally led as well as reflected. Most of the theories discussed also contained prescriptive elements—urging that law should mirror—alongside the descriptive, recognizing that law did not always mirror society, that sometimes it was out of sync. Nonetheless, all of the theories discussed held to at least a weak version, and many to a relatively strong version, of the mirror thesis.

Belief in the mirror thesis among theorists about law is pervasive. Yet I asserted that the selective mirror and instrumental traditions, while they continue to hold onto mirror beliefs, had by implication taken the first steps down a path that ultimately leads away from the mirror thesis, at least as a taken for granted assumption about the nature of law. This chapter, along with the following two, will press harder in this direction. Chapter 5 will discuss concrete empirical reasons to doubt the validity and extent of application of the mirror thesis. To loosen the hold of the mirror thesis, this chapter and the next chapter will consider a series of broader theoretical issues. The first section will articulate and challenge the two legitimating myths about the origins of law that dominate Western theory and consciousness. The second section will raise, in general terms, the implications of the monopolization of legal knowledge by professionals.

Two Legitimation Myths and a Counter Version

The Evolutionary Myth

An evolutionary genesis story about law runs pervasively through Western legal and social theory. A large number of the theories articulated in the preceding chapter, including that of Plato, Aquinas, Maine, Durkheim, Hart, and Luhmann, along with those of most others who have addressed the subject, placed rule by law on a continuum with rule by custom. Although the details differ, generally these theorists posit an initial primordial soup in which habit and custom are dominant in the maintenance of social order, supplemented by an indistinguishable mix of religious or mystical beliefs and morality. According to this account, positive law emerges, in the haze of long forgotten yesteryear, as a distinct mechanism of institutionalized norm enforcement out of the customary order that prevailed in pre-political society. The emergence of positive law reflects and represents an integral stage in the differentiation of society. The separation of public and private realms, ultimately resulting in the formulation of the State, accompanies and gives rise to positive law. Roberto Unger (1976: 58) described this evolutionary process as a 'matter of the changing organization of society'.

Roman law is the most often cited example of this evolutionary process. 'In general the emergence of Roman social thought, paralleling the transition from oral to written culture, was the product of a movement from an agrarian society ruled by unwritten custom (*mos*), sanctified by divine law (*fas*) and faith (*fides*), to an urban community organized by secular and super-familial law (*ius*), written down and extended beyond the old patrician families to the plebs and later to colonies and subject people' (Kelley 1990: 37). At the outset of this process the family is the core unit, and custom rules; at the end it is the State, and law rules. The trajectory involved is characterized as the movement of a society from unthinking repetition and adherence to tradition, towards an order based upon will, upon laws and a social order intentionally forged in our own image for our own ends. The transition is not total, as habit and custom continue to prevail in substantial aspects of social life, and 'customary law' norms are in various contexts recognized by positive law, but there is no doubt that in the end positive law reigns supreme.

Here are excerpts from Aristotle's (1988: 1252b–1253a) version of this evolution:

> The family is the association established by nature for the supply of men's every-day wants. . . . But when several families are united, and the association aims at something more than the supply of daily needs, the first society to be formed is the village. . . . When several families are united in a single complete community, large enough to be quite self-sufficing, the state comes into existence, originating in the bare needs of life, and continuing in existence for the sake of a good life. And therefore, if the earlier forms of society are natural, so is the state, for it is the end of them, and the nature of a thing is its end.
>
> . . .
>
> Hence it is evident that the state is a creation of nature, and that man is by nature a political animal. And he who by nature and not by mere accident is without a state, is either a bad man or above humanity; he is like the
>
> > Tribeless, lawless, hearthless one,
>
> whom Homer denounces . . .

Aristotle's account is typical of evolutionary tales in that he emphasizes the natural inevitability of the process, and in that he ends up with a law-governed state as the standard of rightness and humanity.

Implicit within Aristotle's account, but developed in greater detail by other theorists, are a concomitant series of economic, social, political, and legal developments that occur in sync as core components of the evolutionary process. Economic aspects of this evolution start with the family as a self-sufficient unit of the production and consumption of basic necessities; later moving to the village as a body of collective action in which everyone shares in the production and consumption, with face-to-face transactions and exchanges; and finally ending up with the City or State, in which people engage in functionally differentiated economic activities, with the individual serving as the primary unit of production and consumption, resulting in and necessitating exchanges among strangers, often at a distance in time and space.

Social aspects of this evolution involve a fundamental shift in orientation from the community to the individual. At the outset of this evolution, people are first and always a part of the community of relations into which they are born, with a status and identity tied to that location (as mother, sister, daughter, wife, kin relation, low caste, servant). People live their lives out in continuous face-to-face relations with a limited number of others in a manner that encompasses virtually all aspects of their existence. At the end point of this evolution, people are individuals first who create their statuses and identities through their activities and achievements. People have singularly defined and chosen relations with a multitude of other individuals which amount to strings of encounters that seldom (outside of the family) constitute lifetime face-to-face relations. Society thus shifts from consisting of collections of persons determined by fixed hierarchies and bonds within communities to one of free and equal self-determining individuals relating to others in selected ways.

Political aspects of this evolution begin with the patriarch as the unquestioned authority of the family, which serves as the core political unit. The authority of the father to rule is based simply upon his power and entitlement as father. At the level of the clan or village initially there may be collective leadership, a council made up of each patriarch, perhaps later leading to a tribal leader or Chief. Finally, with the aggregation of villages or provinces there emerges the State with a standing institutional apparatus, representing the separation of the public and private realms, headed by the Sovereign, the repository of power at the highest level of political development. The basis of authority of the Sovereign to rule changes over time in a progressive order that initially begins with charisma or Divine endowment, and ends in the consent of the governed.

According to most accounts, the development of law is a key aspect of this process. Talcott Parsons (1966: 26) identified the emergence of an institutionalized legal system as *the* 'critical development' or 'watershed' in the 'transition from intermediate to modern society'. Law serves the essential functions of coordinating behavioural expectations, responding to disruptions of order, and resolving disputes. Laws protecting property encourage and allow for productive activity by preserving its fruits; laws enforcing contracts provide a degree of reliability in transactions among people outside the family; criminal laws preserve order; the judge is a neutral third party whose decision disputants can abide by. At the simplest stage of social development many of these activities are satisfied by customary mechanisms oriented towards the achievement of a consensus; but beyond the rudimentary stages of social development custom proves inadequate to these tasks (see Unger 1976: 48–86). Social theorists from Durkheim to Habermas (1996: 66–81) have concurred that in differentiated societies, with their attendant value pluralism and increases in interactions between strangers, law serves the core function of integrating society.

Depending upon the nature of the account, this integration operates in one or both of two ways: in coordinating behaviour among individuals, and by serving as the background infrastructure which holds together the various subsystems (moral, political, economic, lifeworld, etc.) comprising society. In the following passages Habermas describes how law functions simultaneously at both levels:

Unlike postconventional morality, law does not just represent a type of cultural knowledge but constitutes at the same time an important core of institutional orders. Law is two things at once: a system of knowledge and a system of action. . . . (p. 79)

From the vantage point of the theory of communicative action, we can say that the subsystem 'law,' as a legitimate order that has become reflexive, belongs to the societal component of the lifeworld. Just as this reproduces itself only together with culture and personality structures through the flow of communicative actions, so legal actions, too, constitute the medium through which institutions of law simultaneously reproduce themselves along with intersubjectively shared legal traditions and individual competences for interpreting and observing legal rules. As a part of the societal component, these legal rules constitute a higher level of legitimate orders; at the same time, however, they are also represented in the other two lifeworld components, as legal symbolism and as competences acquired via legal socialization. All three components [culture, society, and personality] share co-originally in the production of legal actions. Law includes all communication oriented by law, such that legal rules refer reflexively to the function of social integration directly fulfilled in the process of institutionalization. But the legal code not only keeps one foot in the medium of ordinary language, through which everyday communication achieves social integration in the lifeworld; it also accepts messages that originate there and puts these into a form that is comprehensible to the special codes of the power-steered administration and the money-steered economy. To this extent the language of law, unlike the moral communication restricted to the lifeworld, can function as a transformer in the society-wide communication circulating between system and lifeworld. (pp. 80–1)

Thus is law touted as the essential glue that bonds individuals and society (as a system) in the disenchanted, post-traditional, post-custom dominated era.

This evolutionary tale serves to legitimate law in several different ways. First, the postulated emergence of the legal order out of the customary order confirms the continuity of the former with the latter. As Luhmann (1985: 83) described it, 'The development of law is not to be understood as the step from a pre-legal to legal forms of societies, but as a gradual differentiation and functional independence of law.' ' "Custom," in Ulpian's formula, "is the tacit consent of the people confirmed by long-established practice"; it was the residue or recollection, of the ways of the father. . . . Habit, sanctioned by family patterns, communal pressures, and cultural inertia, fixed social usages and created a sort of proto-legitimacy finally expressed in "customary law" ' (Kelley 1990: 90). Under the evolutionary tale, the connotations of consent that attach to the customary order carry over to the newly emergent legal order. It portrays a bottom-up process of natural development, law and legal institutions growing out of society and the consensual actions of the people. The norms of positive law, by this account, *are* one and the same norms of custom, merely enforced by a different, institutionalized mechanism, a view made popular among legal anthropologists by Paul Bohannan's (1967: 47) definition of law as custom that has been reinstitutionalized for the purposes of enforcement by legal institutions. This characterization was also dominant during the medieval period, when 'enacted laws were still justified, for the most part, as restatements of existing custom' (Berman 1983: 145). Custom, according to this evolutionary account, undergoes a process of 'gradual crystallization' to reach the stage of positive law (Kelley 1990: 91). It is this connection with custom that licenses the legitimating claim that 'Law originates in fact' (pp. 92, 100).

Secondly, the evolutionary account legitimates law in a sense much stronger than that law is good or useful. The emergence of law is itself a crucial stage in social development. Law is necessary to the continued functioning and survival of society. Without law, society would fall apart and descend into chaos. '[T]he constitution of the legal form became necessary to offset deficits arising with the collapse of traditional ethical life,' Habermas (1996: 113) asserted, following Durkheim. Law is thus portrayed as essential, foundational, irreplaceable, heroic.

Finally, as with all evolutionary accounts, this story about the emergence of law is legitimating in so far as it explicitly or implicitly describes law in progressive terms, as the result of eons of gradual improvement. The evolutionary development of law represents an advance over previous mechanisms of social order, not just in terms of greater efficiency and flexibility as an instrument of social policy, but as a manifestation of our will, wresting our freedom from the binds of the unthinking demands of tradition. When social life was dominated by custom and by religion, we were dictated to by the past or by Divine Will; but with positive law, for the first time in the history of humankind we control the circumstances of our existence. Furthermore, in this progressive account, the law we have developed in modernity accords a greater degree of freedom and equality for the individual. We thus stand flattered at the pinnacle of the entire trajectory of history, with law as one of our proudest achievements. 'Law is that expression of civilization which most closely approaches perfection' (Ullmann 1969: p. vii).

The Social Contract Myth

The second great story about the origin and legitimacy of law is the social contract tale of classical liberal theory, articulated most prominently by Hobbes, Locke, and Rousseau (see Morris 1999), and more recently Rawls. Like the evolutionary account, versions of the social contract tale trace back to early Western legal thought. 'Some Greeks appear to have floated the hypothesis that the state and its laws (as opposed to earlier forms of natural human associations, or natural societies) came into being as a contract between individuals for the mutual self-preservation of the contractees, so that the political realm of the city-state was nothing more than a product of convention' (Janet Coleman 2000a: 36). In contrast to the gradualist, unintentional cast of the evolutionary tale, however, this story postulates a conscious moment of decision, whether in a 'state of nature' or in an 'original position', when individuals agree to create and subject themselves to a governing legal authority.

Also unlike the evolutionary tale, from the very outset in the social contract approach individuals are free and equal and serve as the primary focus of orientation.[1] Individuals are autonomous and rational beings who exercise their will. It is precisely owing to their rough equality— under conditions of scarcity, general covetousness, and limited altruism—that people join together and voluntarily forgo their natural liberty, choosing instead to live under law in the furtherance of creating an ordered society to better enable them to pursue their interests. Although some social contract theorists (like Locke) postulate a kinder state of nature than others (like Hobbes), they virtually all conclude that rational beings would prefer to live under a system of law. The law is necessary to

[1] A different but complementary articulation, and comparison, of these two approaches is provided by Norberto Bobbio (1993: 1–25).

protect the populace from disorder and avoid the war of all against all, or at least to avoid the general insecurity and regular eruptions of violence that would ensue in its absence. The law is thus constituted by, and legitimated by, the consent of the individuals who live under it. From the standpoint of those entering the contract, the State born of this contractual moment is *their* State, the law *their* law, reflecting their desires and interests, possessing power because and in so far as the people have granted it.

Marcel Gauchet (1997: 173) articulates the image conveyed by social contract theory in his description of the understanding of the modern state:

The sovereign tended ideally to replace the systematic plurality of communities and bodies with the reflexive unity of a collective being constituted from its individual members' social desire. The order governing human communal life was no longer an external given but had to be willed into existence. . . . This was the new face of power in the modern State: the specialized instance through which the community achieved subjectivity, the unifying operation of the sovereign making the community correspond with itself in all details and coincide with its own instituting principle—its founding pact.

It must be emphasized that this is the *image* perpetuated by social contract theory—an image of identity. Gauchet (p. 58) also observed, but failed to critically elaborate, that 'modern individualist theories of the social contract appeared as soon as so-called absolute power was installed'.

A Critique of the Two Myths

These two tales, which have dominated the Western consciousness and understanding of law, are not necessarily competitors. A number of theorists, like Rousseau, articulated both evolutionary elements and social contract elements in the emergence of law. Furthermore, one may adopt the evolutionary theory as a general historical account, while also applying social contract theory as an actual constitutional moment in certain societies, or as a hypothetical exercise for the purposes of analysing the legitimacy of political and legal arrangements. It is not accidental that the endpoint (individualism) of the evolutionary tale is the starting point of the social contract tale. Both tales obtained special prominence during the Enlightenment, which celebrated individualism. And both were articulated by Western theorists who took their own situation to represent the epitome of political, legal and social development. While political philosophers often portray them as alternative models (see Bobbio 1993), many people have internalized both. So reassuring are these stories that the wish to believe is compelling.

I have referred to these accounts as 'myths' or 'tales' to emphasize that neither is factual, regardless of pretensions to that effect. By necessity, evolutionary theorists have engaged in projection laid upon conjecture, since the starting point of these theories is a pre-historical, pre-writing period. Locke (1980: s. 101) acknowledged this, prefatory to embarking upon his own speculation: 'Government is every where antecedent to records, and letters seldom come in amongst a people till a long continuation of civil society has, by other more necessary arts, provided for their safety, ease, and plenty: and then they begin to look after the history of their founders, and search into their original, when they have outlived the memory of it: for it is with *common-wealths* as with particular persons, they are commonly *ignorant of their own births and infancies*.' Views of social and legal affairs during this period are thus based invariably upon non-existent or extremely limited evidence. Many accounts consist of extrapolations from knowledge of the development of Roman law or from exposure to exotic peoples. Drawing from examples like this, however, presupposes the very point to be proven—that evolution has in fact occurred in a manner such that they provide reliable representatives of past stages of development.

Recapitulations of the evolutionary tale seldom suggest a persuasive social mechanism that would lead time and again to the emergence of public-oriented legal institutions.[2] One popular explanation—for both evolutionary accounts and social contract accounts—points to the need for a neutral third party to enforce norms and resolve disputes within a community, without which normative violations would lead to acts of private retribution. Disputes would fester unresolved, under this scenario, threatening the cohesion and existence of the group. This third party becomes institutionalized in the form of law, over time in the evolutionary account, or following agreement in the social contract account. The problem with this explanation is that, as legal anthropologists have demonstrated, small-scale communities enforced norms and resolved disputes in a variety of ways—ranging from self-help to political solutions—many of which did not involve the development of public legal institutions.

Another explanation offered as the social mechanism leading to the emergence of public legal institutions is the interaction between different

---

[2] A recent evolutionary account can be found in Jenkins (1980: chap. 8). The following discussion responds to the explanations for the emergence of law put forth by Jenkins, as well as upon the accounts of others.

communities with contrasting norms and interests, giving rise to trade disputes or conflicts over land or resources, which necessitates the intervention or creation of a neutral third party to resolve disputes. This account is belied by the history of interaction between communities, which has seldom resulted in the voluntary creation of, endowment of power upon, and permanent submission to, a third party public authority. The perennially weak state of international law demonstrates the implausibility of this account. The few occasions on which it has occurred, like the creation of the World Trade Organization, merely confirm how difficult and unlikely it is.

Finally, a popular explanation focuses on the larger scale community and points to the division of labour, or the differentiation of society, as leading to the emergence of positive law. 'Today legal norms are what is left from a crumbled cement of society; if all other mechanisms of social integration are exhausted, law yet provides some means for keeping together complex and centrifugal societies that otherwise would fall into pieces' (Habermas 1999: 937). Law saves society from collapse by filling the integrative function formerly satisfied by shared values. But this account is circular. The emergence of positive law is thought to be a fundamental aspect of the differentiation of society. Parsons (1966: 25) stated that the 'development of autonomous legal systems is perhaps the most important indicator of differentiation'. As a key aspect of societal differentiation, it can hardly be a consequence of such differentiation, leaving unanswered the question of precisely why or how law emerges under these circumstances. This explanation contains a magical quality shared by all functionalist accounts, whereby a system-based need to hold society together arises, and, *ipso facto*, it is filled by law. But functionalist theory recognizes the existence of functional equivalents in social life, and thus nothing in this scenario requires that *law*, as opposed to some other mechanism, emerges to satisfy the functional needs generated by differentiation. The only way functionalism can avoid this problem is by a priori designating as 'law' *whatever* holds society together, an approach that many functionalists adopt. A consequence of this approach, however, is that it includes all sorts of phenomena under the label 'law', and gives rise to insurmountable problems of distinguishing law from other sources of social order, as will be discussed in greater detail in Chapter 7. More to the point, the functionalist 'explanation' for the emergence of law is implausible on its merits. If society were headed towards a state of collapse owning to a loss of shared values (to anomie), the law and legal system would be swept in its wake.

A functioning legal system cannot exist in the absence of a substantially cohesive society.

Speculation aside, the evidence is lacking or contrary to evolutionary theory.[3] With regard to general social evolution, supportive 'evidence is radically incomplete—indeed it is almost non-existent!' (Maniacs 1987: 71–2). Evidence regarding legal evolution is worse. 'The main result of anthropological research is that any scheme of universal legal evolution must be rejected. Such is the variety found in different societies at the same stage of social and economic development that we must hold with Hoebel that "there has been no straight line of development in the growth of law." There is no automatic connection between a particular level of cultural development and particular legal techniques or legal ideas' (Stein 1980: 104).

An unstated but necessary—and patently implausible—assumption underlying evolutionary accounts is that societies develop in relative isola-tion, with limited intervention or influence from outside. Once the reality of outside influence is acknowledged, it is evident that the classical evolu-tionary tale, even if true, could not have been played out in more than a few situations, because outside influence necessarily alters the trajectory of actual development away from whatever path that might have occurred without such influence. The history of the world is testament to this point.

If the evolutionary account has initial plausibility, it is the result of the fact that it plays to, and is built upon, stereotypes of what primitive life was like, and upon the common notion that primitive (or non-Western) society stands in relation to modern (or Western) society as a child does to an adult. It feeds and reinforces the sense of the West that it represents the high point towards which history has aimed. During the mid-to-late nineteenth century, when evolutionary theories were especially popular (Manicas 1987: 52–72), coinciding with the work of Maine and Darwin, educated persons naturally 'saw their whole mode of life, including their conceptions of rationality and of science, as part of a history of inevitable progress, judged by a standard of progress which had itself emerged from that history' (MacIntyre 1990: 24). Many people still see things this way today.

---

[3] A comprehensive discussion of the criticisms of Durkheim's evolutionary account of law can be found in Cotterrell (1999: chap. 6). Cotterrell defends Durkheim's account against most of these criticisms on the grounds that he did not mean it to be an actual his-torical account, and on the grounds that his concepts were sociological not legal, and thus cannot easily be tested in terms of legal categories. Cotterrell is perhaps correct with regard to Durkheim's position, but that does not detract from the validity of the criticisms of evo-lutionary accounts.

Puncturing the evolutionary myth, it must be emphasized, does not deny that law's relationship with society can change, or that there have been fundamental differences in manifestations of law in relation to differences in society. Rather the points are that there is no universal pattern, that there is no inherently progressive aspect to changes, that there are substantial reasons to doubt the functionalist account of law and its relationship with society, that positive law in many instances is not in fact derived by descent from prevailing customs, and, most important, that the evolutionary story is simply false as a historical account of the emergence and development of the overwhelming bulk of legal systems in existence around the world today.

Like the evolutionary tale, the 'state of nature' of social contract theory has never been observed, nor has any evidence of it survived, nor is it clear that this state has ever existed. As David Hume (1966: 22) long ago observed, 'Whether such a condition of human nature could ever exist, or if it did . . . may justly be doubted.' We are born into a family, into pre-existing communities, Hume pointed out, and we rarely ever thereafter exist as autonomous individuals. Immanuel Kant (1991: 79) observed that the idea of people coming together to form a social contract of this kind should not be understood in factual terms 'for it cannot possibly be so'.

The strongest critique of social contract theories comes from naturalist or communitarian approaches that deny its individualist starting point. Living in society is our natural condition. This natural social condition is one of order, not a war of all against all. What binds us to one another and to the larger community and State is not consent but the language, culture, and complexes of social obligations, practices, and institutions within which we exist, and apart from which we cannot long survive. The State and law do not exist outside of or set against society, and are not created whole in one moment. The entire scenario of individuals joining together out of necessity to form a society and State is alien to our nature as social beings. Marx put it thusly: 'it is natural necessity, the essential human properties however estranged they may seem to be, and interest that hold the members of civil society together . . . only political superstition still imagines today that civil life must be held together by the state, where as in reality, on the contrary, the state is held together by civil life' (quoted in Pashukanis 1989: 91–2).

Another familiar critique is that the very possibility of entering into a binding contract presupposes the presence of social and legal norms, which means the state of nature cannot be one devoid of law or social order (MacIntyre 1998: 136–40). An analogous critique can be lodged against the hypothetical social contract theory espoused by John Rawls. The choosers in the original position must be informed by thick notions of social mores if they are to make any choices at all, and the thicker these notions are the more one determines the outcome of the decisions supposedly to be made.

Yet another common critique is that the consent involved is not true consent, even aside from the non-existence of the state of nature, because people never really have or make a choice. Prominent examples of what appear to be actual social contracts, such as the drafting and enactment of the US Constitution, upon closer inspection are revealed to invariably involve the consent of selected members of the population. Moreover, these are rare, one-time events, which means that successive generations have not in fact consented. Consent, at least according to Locke, must be actual for each individual. Given this demand, and the rarity of occasions for express consent, Locke (see 1980: s. 119) was forced to fall back on the notion of tacit consent, and pointed to indicia of such consent as owning possessions, travelling on the highway, and remaining on the territory. To be told that one consents by not leaving, however, by partaking of the benefits provided by the society and legal system, presumes that one has the financial resources to leave, and places a heavy burden on those who wish to indicate that they do not consent by requiring that they forgo possessions and leave behind friends and family. Tacit consent understood in these terms has three unpalatable implications for social contract theory: either the consent required is unintentional and thin (since few people travelling the highway understand themselves to be thereby expressing acceptance for the system of government), giving rise to a commensurately thin obligation; or it is a consent given under duress (motivated by the high cost of non-consent), which vitiates the consent; or the term 'consent' is used but not really meant by social contract theorists (see Simmons 1993: chap. 7).

Defenders of hypothetical social contract theory will respond that critiques to the effect that the state of nature has never existed, that the positing of autonomous individuals is unrealistic, and that people do not really consent, are beside the point. The state of nature and the social contract are metaphors or ideas meant to help us evaluate the legitimacy of our political arrangement (see Kant 1991: 79). As Rawls (1971: 13) put it:

No society can, of course, be a scheme of cooperation which men enter voluntarily in a literal sense. . . . Yet a society satisfying [hypothetical social contract demands] comes as close as a society can to being a voluntary scheme, for it meets the principles that free and equal persons would assent to under circumstances that are fair. In this sense its members are autonomous and the obligations they recognize self-imposed.

Locke repeatedly refers to actual (including tacit), not hypothetical, consent, and would therefore not likely accept this defence. Moreover, this defence is not effective against the argument that the scenario does not reflect our nature, and therefore the outcome of the hypothetical would differ from the outcomes postulated by social contract theorists.

Above all else, however, once it is admitted that this scenario is articulated in terms of hypothetical consent, a thought experiment conducted from the luxury of the library, the very characterization of it as entailing 'consent' or involving a 'contract' is false, insidiously drawing upon the language of choice, agreement, and will without the semblance of any being present. What exists is the veneer of consent polished to a shine by the theorist's seductively crafted hypothetical. John Stuart Mill (1985: 141) made the point bluntly: 'society is not founded on a contract, and . . . no good purpose is answered by inventing a contract in order to deduce social obligations from it.' The only obligation to abide by the law that may arise from a hypothetical contract is a hypothetical obligation. If a real obligation is to exist, it must be based upon the merits of the situation, which has nothing to do with the hypothetical contract.

Habermas's discourse theory of law is the most sophisticated recent variation of social contract theory—drawing upon hypothetical consent to legitimate the law—and it (inadvertently) highlights its dangers. According to Habermas (1996: 104), 'the legitimacy of law ultimately depends on a communicative arrangement: as participants in rational discourses, consociates under law must be able to examine whether a contested norm meets with, or could meet with, the *agreement of all those possibly affected*.' Owing to the unanimity requirement, this system is a truly free one in which 'the addressees of law are simultaneously the authors of their rights' (p. 104). Put in more concrete terms, this means that the law is legitimate if (*ab initio*) the homeless man rousted from the park bench would agree to vagrancy laws, or the prisoner awaiting execution would agree to the imposition of the death penalty for heinous murders. These examples are intended to suggest that, despite repeated and rather forceful assertions regarding the necessity for acceptance 'by all citizens' (p. 135), Habermas does not *really* mean *unanimous* consent, or even *actual* consent. His discourse principle is meant to serve as a regulative ideal. Not surprisingly, the net effect of his theory, common to the social contract tradition, is to legitimate the status quo of law in liberal democracies under the banner of consent, cleansed of any odour of coercion (Tamanaha 1999).

There are other critiques of social contract theories (see Morris 1999), but the relevant criticisms for the purposes here have been conveyed. In so far as evolutionary theory characterizes the emergence of law in continuity with a customary order, and in so far as social contract theory characterizes the existence of and submission to law as a matter of consent, both myths lend strong support to the mirror thesis. Under both accounts, the law is *our* law, *our* creation, an integrated aspect of society. Likewise, in both accounts, law serves the essential function of maintaining social order. Under the evolutionary account society would collapse without law; under the social contract account, the threat of social disorder is what prompts us to enter into the contract to constitute law, or at least to endorse it as a hypothetical matter.

It is telling—nay, extraordinary—that the two most influential, enduring, and still salient accounts in Western legal and social theory for the emergence and legitimation of law are myths. It is also telling that both tales acquired prominence during the Enlightenment, one of the key themes of which was the debunking of myths. What in fact occurred was the construction of legitimating accounts of law by updating and reconfiguring old myths into the language of science (evolutionary) and rationally exercised free will (social contract).

A Counter Genesis Story

Consider another account. Say through ruthlessness, greed, savvy, the accumulation of wealth, or a greater number of offspring or relatives or population from which to draft, or through superior armaments or better tactical abilities or access to militarily advantageous animals like horses, a strongman or warlord, or a gang, or an entire clan, or an alliance, or an outside power, was able to set up and enforce an order of rules—by maintaining a staff prepared to exert coercion—which were then effectively enforced upon anyone within reach. The primary object of the rules was to maintain the wealth and power of the leader or core group, and to exploit the populace and local resources. Among other matters, this body of rules encompassed social relations among the subject populace—the simplest form of which would simply allow existing customs to remain in effect so long as they did not conflict with the interests of, and rules imposed by, the governing power. Within this jurisdiction that would be *the law*. People would avoid the reach of this law whenever possible, but otherwise would abide by the rules out of fear, coercion, a lack of alternatives, inertia, and that fact that they could conduct much of their daily activities in the shadow of the law anyway, and perhaps out of a sense that the law was entitled to a claim of right owing to the ability of the strong man or group to effectively exert its will. The power to rule, in this view, supplies the authority to rule. In earlier periods, von Ihering (1968: 191) observed, people 'did not look upon force with our own eyes; they saw nothing improper in such a condition; nought detestable and damnable, but only what was natural and self-evident. Force as such made an impression on them and was the only kind of greatness they could appreciate.' Under this alternative scenario there is no presumed continuity with or descent from an existing customary order. There is no moment of consent. If anything, the rules imposed by the institutionalized enforcement apparatus may well exist in a state of conflict and competition with the customary order, though the holders of power would be quite happy to downplay the conflict and claim that the law they impose is in the interest of all.

Many theorists would reject this as not qualified for the label 'law'. Rather, it is the 'gunman writ large' H. L. A. Hart so vehemently protested. But it is difficult to disqualify this scenario from constituting positive law. The standard protest that this does not consist of an *approved 'public' authority*, and therefore is not law, is unpersuasive. It presupposes whose consent is necessary (certainly the strong man or group enforcing its will consents), and it assumes that the subject populace in this scenario would not accord this form of positive law a measure of approval, underestimating the belief that the power to rule entitles one to rule. Significantly, it also assumes that measurably more public approval is in fact accorded in the paradigm case of positive law they have in mind. Even Hart (1961: 113) allowed that the primary rules of obligation need not be approved by the public for a legal system to exist, as long as the primary rules are generally obeyed by the populace and the legal officials approve the secondary rules, which exactly matches this scenario.

Furthermore, this protest fails to recognize the extent to which the category 'public' authority is contestable. This label has the effect of symbolically clothing an actor or group of actors in garb that entitles them to a claim of being above the struggle among 'private' actors, or representing the general good rather than any particular interest (Pashukanis 1989: 134–50). Any institutionalized resource of power would be pleased to make this claim. The evolutionary and social contract tales build upon the public/private distinction assuming that it represents a fundamental, identifiable social divide. The alternative genesis story, in contrast, views the distinction from the standpoint of its rhetorical import. It recognizes the possibility that a self-interested group dons the 'public' mantle for the legitimation benefits that flow therefrom. They simply claim to be 'the law', and thereby benefit from the connotations of public authority that attach to this label. In a study of medieval European legal systems, Robert Bartlett concluded that 'The distinction between public and private violence was a rhetorical weapon of the monarchy as it entered, one contestant among many, an arena of conflicting powers and authorities' (quoted in Cohen 1995: 17). According to Pashukanis (1989: 1936), feudal authorities did not make the public/private distinction until it was advantageous to do so. Throughout history the State has been a constant player in the private arena, and private companies have exercised public functions and activities. In the Babylonian period, about 2000 BC, for example, 'State and private roles were interwoven' (Jay 2000: 24). Conversely, in the seventeenth century the Dutch East Indies Company had 'the power to build forts, maintain armies and negotiate treaties' (p. 139). During the Middle Ages in Europe, local bishops combined political, legal, religious and economic activities, as did kings, emperors, lords, and local rulers (Berman 1983: chaps. 1 and 2). These examples can be vastly multiplied, up to and including present variations. Hence, the very notion of the separation of public and private realms, repeated by so many legal and social theorists, is completely suspect, yet it forms an essential pillar of both the evolutionary and social contract tales.

Unpleasant as it may be, this alternative scenario for the origins of legal systems is certainly plausible. Adam Smith suggested it, at least partially. In Book I of Plato's *Republic*, Thrasymachus argued at length that 'as a matter of historical fact, rulers and ruling classes invented the concept and the standards of justice for their own purposes' (MacIntyre 1998: 34). Aristotle (1988: 1324b) recognized that 'in some states the entire aim both of the laws and of the constitution is to give men despotic power over their neighbor'. Marxists have claimed that law is organized force that safeguards the interests of the dominant class (Pashukanis 1989: 134–50). Von Ihering (1968: 185) went the furthest in elaborating it. 'Whoever will trace the legal fabric of a people to its ultimate origins will reach innumerable cases where the force of the stronger has laid down the law for the weaker.' Law and force, according to von Ihering, are intimately connected, indeed inseverable, with force maintaining priority of position. 'Force produces law immediately out of itself, and as a measure of itself, *law evolving as the politics of force*. It does not therefore abdicate to give the place to law, but whilst retaining its place it adds to itself law as an accessory element belonging to it, and becomes *legal force*' (p. 187). Von Ihering also suggested a plausible account of how law as a weapon of the powerful might transform into law as a limitation of the powerful (or as a weapon within limits): the dominant power realizes that its own interest is served if law undergoes this transition. Another possible explanation for this transition, *if and when it occurs*, one not offered by von Ihering, is the transformative power of ideas. Over time the claim that law represents the 'public' may begin to have a moderating influence on the conduct of those who control the legal apparatus, either owing to the necessity to occasionally live up to this claim to lend it credibility, or by those in power coming to believe genuinely in its truth and thereafter acting accordingly.

In contrast to the scanty evidence and weak analytical underpinnings of the evolutionary tale and the social contract tale, this alternative scenario has direct and ample evidence to point to in support. It captures the spread of state law around the world through colonization, as will be elaborated on in Chapter 5, and it bears a strong resemblance to many historical and current systems of state law dominated by authoritarian, totalitarian, or military regimes. John Morrall (1960: 13–14) described the early medieval period in terms reminiscent of this alternative:

To the German successor-kingdoms of the Western Roman Empire, the monarch was not primarily the head of a territorial State but a personal tribal leader; it might not be too wide of the mark to think of him as a gangster chief, surrounded by his henchmen and living with them off the country they had conquered. The Romanized subjects of his conquered territory would be taken under his protection and preserved, for concessions in money or in kind, from attacks by other gangster leaders.

The principle of protection in return for service is one of the keys to the complex of personal legal relations so characteristic of medieval society.

When the State is relatively weak, as it often is in its inception and as it currently is in a number of formerly colonized countries, it is not difficult to seize control over the State and its legal apparatus, and apply them to the benefit of those in power.

The mechanism that underlies this alternative scenario is human covetousness—the Hobbsean desire for glory, material goods, and power in situations of scarcity. Rather than the Hobbsean solution, however, which involves the voluntary submission of the populace to law in the interest of maintaining order, this scenario involves the imposition of rules on a group by organized, self-interested agents who seize the mantle of Sovereign or don the cover of 'public' actor. Instead of the gradual evolutionary differentiation of society leading to the emergence of law, this scenario involves conquest by internal or external powers who thereafter impose a system of laws as a way of consolidating their rule, although they may well claim to operate in the interest of the subject people as well as representing the highest achievement of human development.

The argument pressed here is not the extreme one that law has never evolved out of an order of custom, or that law has never been the conscious creation of a newly formed political community. Only that these scenarios have as a matter of historical fact occurred far less often than the alternative genesis story presented here. The majority of state legal systems in existence today originated through imposition from outside or were created by imitation by local authorities to meet the threat posed by conquest from outside powers. It bears noting that perhaps the most often cited example of the evolutionary tale, the development of Roman law, can also be cited as a prime example of the alternative account of law as an instrument of power which was applied in the wake of Roman conquest.

Despite the plausibility of this alternative account, it is not discussed in a manner even close to approaching the frequency or prominence given to the two myths. When it has been articulated, usually it is offered as an exception or deviation from the norm. The centuries old pattern of perpetuating idealizations when describing the origins of law is strong evidence that theorists have been concerned primarily with rationalizing the law, with giving support to the status quo. An uncharitable explanation for this tendency is that theorists are routinely members of the elite groups that benefit from the legal order. A more charitable explanation is that they were genuinely concerned about an impending breakdown of society, a prospect that is explicitly prominent in both myths. Presumably everyone, including the poor and disadvantaged, would prefer order to chaos, and law appeared to theorists to be the final bulwark against the impending disorder pressing against the window. These theorists' anxiety was heightened by the Enlightenment generated disenchantment of the world—the loss of belief in God. Locke expressed his almost palpable angst: 'Promises, covenants, and oaths, which are the bonds of human society, can have no hold upon an atheist. The taking away of God, though but even in thought, dissolves all' (quoted in Gauthier 1999: 73).

If God does not exist, why be good? Historian Carl Becker (1932) identified this as *the* compelling question that confronted eighteenth-century
philosophers. Without the opiate of religion and its promise of rewards
and eternal paradise hereafter, why would the poor put up with their
perennially and hopelessly abysmal state, with the grossly unequal distribution of wealth and privilege in society, inevitably bolstered by and
enforced by the law? Absent divine punishment and rewards, it appeared
to many theorists that people would abide by the law only if they fear it,
or if they believe it to be right. Instilling fear was the business of the legal
apparatus. Theorists created stories about law that made it appear right.

The collapse of the hegemony of the Christian world-view that dominated Europe for more than a thousand years, and its replacement with
a focus on humanity—liberty, equality, fraternity, the rights of man—
prepared the way for these myths to take hold. As God was shunted to
the sidelines, self-determining Man took centre stage, ushering in 'the
new religion of humanity' (Becker 1932: 139). Absent divine religion, 'A
religion which made the fatherland and the laws the object of adoration
for all citizens would be in the eyes of a wise man an excellent religion'
(quoting de Bonneville, Becker 1932: 156).

Alastair MacIntyre (1998: 17), a prominent moral philosopher,
describes, in the context of moral discussions, the core motivating factor
shared by both myths—concern about the darkness in the heart of man:

> Morality is then explicable as a necessary compromise between the desire of nat-
> ural men to aggress upon others and the fear of natural men that others will
> aggress upon them with fatal consequences. Mutual self-interest leads men to
> combine in setting up constraining rules to forbid aggression and lust, and pow-
> erful agencies to inflict sanctions on those who break the rules. Some of these
> rules constitute morality; others law. A good deal of variation is possible in the
> way that this intellectual fairy tale is told, but its central themes, like those of all
> good fairy tales, are remarkably constant. And above all, at the heart of the
> account there remains the idea that social life is perhaps chronologically and cer-
> tainly logically secondary to a form of unconstrained non-social human life in
> which what men do is a matter of their individual natural psychology.

As the pervasiveness of the two myths demonstrates, the fear of human
aggression and disorder runs deep, at least among theorists about law. An
alternative account of the sources of social order offered in Chapter 8
will, it is hoped, help lessen this primal fear sufficiently to wean theorists
from these myths.

This more realistic alternative story about law as power can be aligned
with legal positivism. No legal positivist has described law in the bare

terms set out here. It is more accurate to say that this scenario is made more imaginable by legal positivism's will theory of law. If positive law is whatever legal actors say is law, pursuant to the rules they follow in the creation and identification of law, as strict legal positivism holds, then it is evident that state law need not have any particular relationship with the society to which it is attached. Positive law need not necessarily mirror the society's customs or moral values; it need not even be derived from that society. The legal positivist notion of the separation between law and morality contains precisely this implication, though legal positivists have shied away from recognizing it, often assiduously noting the frequent coincidence of law with morality. Legal positivism contains the seeds of subversion of the mirror thesis within it precisely because it holds that, at root, positive law is indeed a system of power.

The Implications of Legal Professionals and Legal Knowledge

The preceding section focused on piercing two familiar and powerful myths about the origins of law, myths that have the effect of perpetuating the assumption that law is a reflection of society. This section will address a more mundane subject—the implications of the development of legal specialists who monopolize knowledge about law and control the operations of the legal system. Legal specialists are the medium through which societal input must pass in order to be manifested in the law. All mediums have an impact, and so too with legal specialists.

As indicated in Chapter 2, theorists have increasingly begun to take note of the emergence of jurists or legal specialists—lawyers, judges, legal scholars, all those who utilize legal knowledge and participate in legal discourse. Maine mentioned the aristocratic order which monopolized knowledge about law in the customary period. Von Savigny recognized the role of jurists in developing the technicalities of law. More than any other social theorist, Weber emphasized the professional interests of lawyers and the nature of legal rationality in shaping law, as did, in their various ways, Bentham, Engels, Luhmann, Unger, and Posner. The monopolization of legal knowledge by a discrete group in society is a real social phenomenon, one that has advanced to the point of perhaps irreversible entrenchment.

Concerns about lawyers have abounded as long as the profession has been in existence. Donald R. Kelley (1990: 130–1) recounts complaints that existed at least as early as Roman times, and carried through the medieval period during which the legal profession became firmly established:

Jurists were still, in Ulpian's phrase, 'priests of the law.' Yet priesthoods are always suspect, especially when they are also a social and economic elite; and hardly less than usurers and soldiers, the lawyers were the targets of the bitterest satire and denunciation, the source of a powerful counter-mythology. Not only could lawyers be 'mean and mercenary,' as Cicero had lamented, but they were by instinct as well as method and motives, duplicitous and out for hire to the devil himself. Long before Luther's famous complaint it was proverbial that 'a lawyer's a bad Christian.'

In fact the legal profession reflected, morally and perhaps socially as well, the heights and depths of the human condition in late medieval Europe. It was an international force, in effect taking over the guidance of secular institutions as canonists had done for the church. . . . In 1300 there were perhaps twenty European universities with some significant instruction in law; by 1500 the number was closer to eighty. Despite ideological differences within communities of students and masters, their common language and methods gave them the coherence virtually of an international intelligensia rivaling the clergy, but possessing a secular and in some circumstances even an anticlerical character. What guaranteed the success of the profession of law was the general 'triumph of the professionals' noted by John P. Dawson, which took over the distribution of justice on every level from the popular to the political, and which established a vast complex of court systems forming their own relationships and rivalries.

Resentment of the priesthood of lawyers reached a fevered pitch during the French Revolution. The rallying cry for a Civil Code based upon reason and general principles, understandable to all, was promoted on the grounds that it would free the populace from the clutches of lawyers (pp. 226–7; Merryman 1985: 28). Bentham pressed the same argument in England. He criticized the common law as a 'partnership' 'having for its object the extracting, on joint account, and for joint benefit, out of the pockets of the people, in the largest quantity possible, the produce of the industry of the people' (quoted in Postema 1986: 273). Shakespeare immortalized anti-lawyer sentiment when one of his characters declared, 'The first thing we do, let's kill all the lawyers.'[4] Today, the proliferation of mean-spirited lawyer jokes is ample (and perhaps unnecessary) evidence that distrust of lawyers has not appreciably lessened.

The monopolization of legal knowledge and discourse by a discrete and insular group provides an independent ground to question the mirror thesis, for three reasons in particular. Once legal professionals control

---

[4] William Shakespeare, *Henry VI, Part 2*, IV. 2.

the administration of the legal apparatus, they have the capacity to wield it to their own advantage because outsiders have a limited capacity to exercise oversight of their activities. Unnecessary procedures, complicated pleading requirements, obscure legal language, rules requiring that certain matters be handled by lawyers, strict limitations on entry to the profession, restrictions on competitive practices like advertisement, self-regulation, and self-enforcement of ethical, legal, and professional violations, and a multitude of other techniques, inure to the benefit of individual lawyers as well as the profession as a group, both financially and in terms of power. Echoing Bentham, Weber (1954: 202–3) elaborated on this tendency in common law systems: 'Wherever legal education has been in the hands of practitioners, especially attorneys, who have made admission to practice a guild monopoly, an economic factor, namely their pecuniary interest, brings to bear a strong influence upon the process not only of stabilizing the official law and of adapting it to changing needs in an exclusively empirical way but also of preventing its rationalization through legislation or legal science.' It is not just that many transactions have been structured in a manner that requires the participation of lawyers, for which they—always involving at least two—must be paid; in many situations lawyers must be consulted, a position which grants them power. These advantages are the strongest precisely when the law is not an obvious mirror of society, or at least not a clear one, for those are the instances in which the assistance of lawyers is indispensable.

A second consideration with implications for the mirror thesis follows from the specialization of a body of knowledge, as has occurred with law. Especially with regard to formal-rational rule of law systems, legal knowledge has its own internal logic and demands that constantly push it to develop in directions that differ from commonsense notions. The impact of legal knowledge is unavoidable because all input is filtered through a legal lens, as Weber (p. 307) recognized in terms that presage autopoiesis:

> Now we have already seen that the expectations of parties will often be disappointed by the results of a strictly professional legal logic. Such disappointments are inevitable indeed where the facts of life are juridically 'construed' in order to make them fit the abstract propositions of law and in accordance with the maxim that nothing can exist in the realm of law unless it can be 'conceived' by the jurist in conformity with those 'principles' which are revealed to him by juristic science.

The various techniques applied to the interpretation of statutes (plain language, legislative intent, express mention/implied exclusion, internal consistency, adherence to precedent), for example, can lead to outcomes counterintuitive for lay people (including sometimes the legislators themselves), many of whom would think the obvious approach is simply to make the most sense of the statute under current circumstances. Another example is the existence of legal fictions, which are the product of the requirements of pleading and legal reasoning. The more law becomes a specialized body of knowledge, the greater its potential to diverge in form and outcome from the understandings of the society to which it is attached. Again Weber (p. 278) saw this better than any other theorist: 'The consequences of purely logical construction often bear very irrational or even unforeseen relations to the expectations of the commercial interests. It is this very fact which has given rise to the frequently made charge that the purely logical law is "remote from life." This logical systematization of the law has been the consequence of the intrinsic intellectual needs of the legal theorists and their disciples . . . of a typical aristocracy of legal literati.'

A third consideration is the possibility that law will be developed, not in connection with the society below, but rather through contacts among jurists as a transnational group. Lawyers, in other words, might have more in common with, and be more influenced by, lawyers and legal knowledge from other societies than by their own society. The implications of this phenomenon, which must not be underestimated, will be developed in greater detail in Chapter 5, though a few preliminary observations are in order here. The *ius commune*, the common law of Europe that held sway in the later Middle Ages, which was implicitly referred to in the passage by Kelley quoted earlier in this section, is a prominent example of the extraordinary influence this factor may exert. After falling into relative disuse for centuries, Roman law was revived in the late eleventh century by academics, initially at Bologna, who proceeded to spread this body of law throughout Europe (Berman 1983: 123–7). So effective were they that substantial vestiges of Roman law can still be found in European legal codes today (Zimmermann 1994). A similar phenomenon is again now occurring in relation to the *lex mercatoria*, as I will later relate.

All three possibilities, which pull law in different directions, increase the likelihood that positive law will reflect the interests and concerns of legal specialists, of legal knowledge itself, and of the legal culture, at least to some extent, rendering it less of a mirror of the particular society to which it is attached. There are restraints on this process. Active intervention through legislation helps bring the law in line with society (or at least in line with policy initiatives which prevail in the legislative process), though as Weber (1954: 203) noted this is not always successful owing to resistance at the stage of interpretation and application by members of the legal profession. Furthermore, since the legal actors themselves are members of that society, presumably to some degree their decisions and actions will reflect (at least selected) prevailing social values. Again, the point is not the extreme one that social values are never reflected in the law; rather, it is the more modest reminder that legal indoctrination and the internal dictates of legal knowledge have a real influence that suggests that the mirror thesis should not be taken for granted.

Lawyers and legal theorists may well be sceptical of these claimed consequences of the professional monopolization of legal knowledge. Law, like politics, seems quintessentially local, and it deals with everyday social events. It is important to recognize, however, that the specialization of bodies of knowledge and its various consequences are not limited to law. In his analysis of modernity, social theorist Anthony Giddens (1990) provided an account of the general phenomenon of the emergence and 'disembedding' of systems of expert knowledge that is characteristic of modern society. 'Disembedding' 'means the "lifting out" of social relations from local contexts of interaction and their restructuring across indefinite spans of time-space' (p. 21). Law, according to Giddens (pp. 27–9), is one of the expert systems that have become disembedded. These systems involve bodies of knowledge that lay people have a limited ability to check. People are forced into a position of trusting, or at least relying upon, both the system of knowledge and the capacity of the individual experts (lawyer or judge, or legal theorist) who represent that system to them in a given context of interaction (pp. 79–92). The only alternatives are avoidance or opting out, which often are not viable or attractive options.

Alasdair MacIntyre (2000: 91–2) recently expressed concerns about legal professionals in terms that tie together many of the above points:

Ours is a culture dominated by experts, experts who profess to assist the rest of us, but who often instead make us their victims. Among those experts by whom we are often victimized the most notable are perhaps lawyers. If you as a plain person take yourself to be wronged and you wish to achieve redress, or if you are falsely accused and you wish to avoid unjust punishment, or if you need to negotiate some agreement with others in order to launch some enterprise, you will characteristically find yourself compelled to put yourself into the hands of lawyers—lawyers who will proceed to represent you by words that are often not in fact yours, who will utter in your name documents that it would never have occurred to you to utter, and who will behave ostensibly on your behalf in ways that may well be repugnant to you, so guiding you through processes whose complexity seems to have as a central function to make it impossible for plain persons to do without lawyers.

If still not persuaded (and perhaps only lawyer readers remain so), consider medical science, which is now the collective product of worldwide development. Advances in medical knowledge and technology have their own internal impetus, and have led to developments with serious social, economic, moral, and political consequences—like the capacity to maintain life support for terminal patients indefinitely, advances in the viability of foetuses, and genetic testing and cloning. Consider the common suspicion that certain techniques or treatments are conducted mostly for the financial interests of the individual practitioner or the medical profession as a whole. Consider the inability of the uninitiated to check what medical practitioners and researchers are up to. Consider their insistence on self-regulation, and the zealousness with which medical professionals police the borders of what they consider to be legitimate medicine. Consider that when called upon to justify their actions the routine response is to cite the public interest. If those considerations sound like plausible grounds for concern in relation to medical knowledge and practices, and concern about whether their actions indeed reflect prevailing social values, the very same conclusion is appropriate for law.

4 Fundamental Shifts in the Law–Society Relationship

Fundamental changes have occurred in the way in which theorists talk about and understand the relationship between law and society, changes that have taken centuries to develop and are the result of a cluster of philosophical, political, economic, social, and cultural factors. This chapter will elaborate on several key changes. The instrumental tradition discussed in Chapter 2 is a product of and has contributed to these changes, as have some of the issues and developments mentioned in the previous chapter, especially those related to the Enlightenment. The overall thrust of the theoretical challenge to the mirror thesis set out in this and the previous chapter can be envisioned through the law–society framework set out in Chapter 1, now in altered form:

(A) CUSTOM   →   → CONSENT

(C) POSITIVE LAW

(B) MORALITY →   → REASON

The alterations in the representation of the framework are meant to convey two basic points. The first point has to do with the internal relations within each of the two elements on the left side—the elements representing societal input—in their relationship with positive law. Within element A, there has been a distinct shift in emphasis away from custom towards consent; within element B, a shift away from substantive morality towards reason, seen in formal or procedural terms. The second point is that there is now a greater distance between the left and right sides, between societal input and positive law, with the interjection of a non-transparent medium—legal professionals—between the two, and with a greater degree of independence of positive law from its former reliance upon the other two elements for legitimation. Observing these shifts and considering their implications should help open up a critical distance from the mirror thesis.

Key Background Ideas of the Enlightenment

Science and the Enlightenment

The Enlightenment can best be understood as a cluster of ideas and attitudes, dominant among which was belief in the power of science and reason to inform us of the true circumstances of our existence, to dispel superstition and magic, to free us from the chains of traditions, to seize control over and shape our present and future, and to lead us to a more civilized existence (see Tarnas 1991: chaps. 5 and 6). Following the triumph of Newtonian physics, science achieved unparalleled prestige based upon its ability to offer access to an understanding of nature. Advances in technology connected to industrial development confirmed the power of science as a source of knowledge. The scientific model began to colonize and dominate other fields, including morality and philosophy. Science and reason brought 'timeless, universal, and objective truths' (MacIntyre 1990: 65). Knowledge and progress constituted the self-image of the age.

Although identifying the Enlightenment with an emphasis on reason is commonplace, in his seminal study of this period Ernst Cassirer (1951: 5–6) cautioned that what they meant by reason is very different from modern understandings of the term:

'Reason' becomes the unifying and central point of this century, expressing all that it longs for and strives for, and all that it achieves. . . . The eighteenth century is imbued with a belief in the unity and immutability of reason. Reason is the same for all thinking subjects, all nations, all epochs, and all cultures. From the changeability of religious creeds, or moral maxims and convictions, of theoretical opinions and judgments, a firm and lasting element can be extracted which is permanent in itself, and which in this identity and permanence expresses the real essence of reason. For us the word 'reason' has long since lost its unequivocal simplicity.

Cassirer explained that the eighteenth-century understanding of reason also differed from that of the seventeenth century. The latter, following the Cartesian model, focused on the construction of systems of ideas. 'Truly philosophical knowledge had seemed attainable only when thought, starting from a highest being and from a highest, intuitively grasped certainty, succeeded in spreading the light of this certainty over all derived being and all derived knowledge' (Cassirer 1951: 6). In contrast, for the eighteenth century, reason in the context of science rejected abstract systems in favour of discovering 'the regularity in the phenomena themselves' (p. 9). Reason in this sense was less the logic of mathematics than an analysis of phenomena and propositions about phenomena, identifying connections in a manner which transforms a mass of empirical material into a few basic principles.

Cassirer (p. 13) pointed out another key difference between those two centuries: between reason in the context of a pervasive religious world-view, versus reason in the context of a scientific world-view:

In the great metaphysical systems of that [seventeenth] century—those of Descartes and Malebranche, of Spinoza and Leibniz—reason is the realm of the 'eternal verities,' of those truths held in common by the human and the divine mind. What we know through reason, we therefore behold 'in God.' Every act of reason means participation in the divine nature; it gives access to the intelligible world. The eighteenth century takes reason in a different and more modest sense. It is no longer the sum total of 'innate ideas' given prior to all experience, which reveal the absolute essence of things. . . . It is not the treasury of the mind in which the truth like a minted coin lies stored; it is rather the original intellectual force which guides the discovery and determination of truth.

There is no need to further elaborate on these ideas. Despite the work of Thomas Kuhn and Paul Feyerabend and others who challenge the progressive view of science, despite the findings of quantum mechanics and relativity theory which have buried the mechanistic view of the natural world, despite talk of postmodernism, despite the Romantic and New Age backlash to the dominance of science and reason, despite a loss of faith that science holds all the answers, Enlightenment ideas continue to shape the world-views of Western societies. Science has become tarnished of late, and it no longer holds the lofty position it once did in the early modern period, but every other knowledge system, including religion, philosophy, and morality, has suffered at least as much as science. Therefore, its prestige remains high on a relative basis. Science works, and produces concrete results, which is more than can be said about many other fields of knowledge.

As Cassirer points out, however, reason is not understood in the same terms as the Enlightenment. The diminution in the standing of reason has had significant consequences for law and morality, as will now be discussed. The focus of the discussion will be on Hobbes, who wrote in the mid-seventeenth century, and on Hume, who wrote in the mid-eighteenth century. They took positions with regard to morality and reason that went against the spirits of their respective ages, contributing to a legacy that continues today.

Hobbes's Rejection of the Ultimate Good

Thomas Hobbes has always been an ambivalent figure. At the time he wrote his work generated a backlash from both sides of the political spectrum, from liberals because he justified absolute power in the Sovereign, and from (fellow) conservatives because he suggested that the Sovereign obtained its power through consent of the governed, and because he gave people the ultimate right of self-defence (see Hampton 1999: 41–57). Viewed from the modern standpoint, he is a monumental figure for initiating the social contract tradition, which forms the basis for liberal democratic societies, but the authoritarian conclusions he drew are an embarrassment. Another peculiarity of Hobbes's legacy is that he is at once a natural law theorist and the grandfather of legal positivism, which, as indicated earlier, have historically been starkly opposed schools of thought. It is this latter straddling which matters most here. For the purposes of this analysis, Hobbes's significance is not so much owing to his actual influence; rather, his way of thinking about a key set of issues is representative of views that later came to dominate.

Hobbes's (1996: 86) account of natural law begins in a manner consistent with the traditional approach that natural law could be identified through reason: 'a law of nature (lex naturalis), is a precept, or general rule, found out by reason.' But he immediately diverges from this tradition in a fundamental respect. From antiquity through its absorbtion by Christianity, up to the time of Hobbes, thought about natural law and morality always had a substantive orientation. That is, one of its 'deepest assumptions' is that 'the question of how we are to live must be answered in terms that show us how to attain the highest good that the individual can hope for' (Schneewind 1998: 57). Hobbes (1996: 65) rejects this approach, stating that 'there is no such Finis ultimis (utmost aim) nor *Summum bonum*, (greatest good,) as is spoken of in the Books of old Moral Philosophers.' The absence of an ultimate aim or greatest good 'ariseth partly from the diversity of passions, in divers men; and partly from the difference of knowledge, or opinion each one has of the causes, which produce the effect desired' (p. 66). Hobbes held to a 'radical subjectivism' according to which standards for right and wrong, good and evil, are determined relative to civil society and its laws (Postema 1986: 48–51).

Norberto Bobbio (1993: 118–19) articulates the unique aspect of Hobbes's approach to the role of reason in relation to natural law:

What distinguishes Hobbes's definition from the definitions offered by other natural law theorists is the different meaning which *reason* has for him. . . . Reason has only a formal, not a substantive value. It does not reveal essences to us, but it enables us to draw certain consequences from certain principles. . . . Reasoning does not consist of learning evident principles, but is rather a method for thinking. Hobbes's concept of reasoning is not metaphysical, but instrumental. . . . For other natural law theorists, naturalis ratio [natural reason] or recta ratio [right reason] prescribes what is good or evil in itself. For Hobbes, on the contrary, reason indicates what is good or bad in relation to a given end. . . . From Hobbes's utilitarian point of view, the supreme end of human beings is peace. For other natural law theorists, the supreme end is the (moral) good.

Self-preservation is fundamental for Hobbes, from which all else follows. Applying reason to this fundamental principle, Hobbes uses a natural law argument to give rise to a system of positive law, as a means of preserving peace in the interest of self-preservation. Unlike traditional natural law approaches, however, he does not allow natural law to serve as a standard against which to determine the validity of the positive law system (in part because that would reintroduce instability), thus 'repudiating a major point in classical natural law theory' (Schneewind 1998: 93). '[N]o law can be unjust,' according to Hobbes (1996: 230), for what is just is determined by positive law. Natural law in effect falls away once the positive law system has been established, thereafter serving primarily as a guide in conscience, although he does assert that the Sovereign is bound by natural law. This is how Hobbes at once belongs to two opposing traditions, though it might also be said that his embrace of natural law is a death clinch.

Although responsibility cannot be attributed to Hobbes alone, from this period forward there was an inexorable shift away from discussing morality in terms of the ultimate good. This shift culminated in liberalism. Like Hobbes, Locke—the theorist most responsible for articulating the basic elements of liberal democracies in existence today—thinks 'that there is as little point in discussing the highest good as there is in disputing "whether the best Relish were to be found in Apples, Plumbs, or Nuts." The greatest happiness consists, then, in having what pleases and avoiding what pains; but since "these, to different Men, are very different things" ' the ancient question of the *summum bonum* cannot be answered in a way that is both valid for everyone and useful in guiding action' (Schneewind 1998: 143). It follows from this that the best political and legal system is the one that consists of a neutral framework that allows people to pursue their own vision of the good, consonant with the right of others do the same. Substantive natural law was thereby transformed into content-empty natural rights to liberty and (formal) equality. The best law is the one that maintains order, and for the rest simply leaves people alone and gets out of the way. John Stuart Mills's essay *On Liberty* (1985: 68) is the most succinctly powerful statement of the furthest extension of this view, insisting that law has no business interfering in private morality—'the only purpose for which power can be rightfully exercised over any member of a civilized community, against his will, is to prevent harm to others.'

Hume's View of Reason and the Fact/Value Distinction

Hume is relevant owing to his extraordinary influence in solidifying the instrumental view of reason and in establishing the fact/value distinction. With regard to the former, he famously observed that 'Reason is, and ought only to be the slave of the passions, and can never pretend to any other office than to serve and obey them' (Hume 1978: 415). Reason does not provide motives to act, nor does it inform or supply the will or desires. It operates on premises, or serves in making probablistic calculations. 'Reason, in short, is relevant to the means not the end; it determines not what you want but how to get it. Now the means, by definition, is subordinate to the end and therefore reason is subordinate to passion. For it is passion which determines the end and reason only the means' (Mounce 1999: 69). Reason is an instrument. Hobbes had also espoused an instrumental view of reason, but Hume made it stick in philosophical terms, and Hume's view significantly diminished the standing of reason in a way that Hobbes' did not. '[A]ll authority which pure reason had wielded had been unjust and unnatural, in short, had been usurped authority. Reason not only loses its position of dominance; even in its own field, in the domain of knowledge, it has to surrender its leadership to the imagination' (Cassirer 1951: 305).

This view of reason has direct implications for the ability—or, more accurately, inability—of reason to produce substantive moral principles:

Take any action allow'd to be vicious: willful murder, for instance. Examine it in all lights, and see if you can find that matter of fact, or real existence, which you call *vice*. In which-ever way you take it, you find only certain passions, motives, volitions and thoughts. There is no other matter of fact in the case. The vice entirely escapes you, as long as you consider the object. You can never find it, till you turn your reflexion into your own breast and find a sentiment of disapprobation, which arises in you, towards this action. Here is a matter of fact; but 'tis the object of feeling, not of reason. It lies in yourself, not in the object. So that when you pronounce any action or character to be vicious, you mean nothing, but that from the constitution of your nature you have a feeling or sentiment of blame from the contemplation of it. (Hume 1978: 468)

Morality, like passion, is a matter of feeling, not reason. '[T]he distinction of vice and virtue is not founded merely on the relations of objects, nor is perceived by reason' (p. 470).

Hume's fact/value (or 'is'/'ought') distinction also had a monumental impact. His basic point can be simply stated: statements about matters of fact are of a different quality or category than statements about normative obligation, and one cannot deduce the latter from the former. There is a logical barrier between the two. Factual assertions are descriptive, while value assertions are prescriptive. The fact that something is or has occurred does not, of itself, license the assertion that it should or ought to occur. A justification must be interjected to go from a factual observation to a normative assertion.

Hume's arguments gradually came to affect profoundly philosophical and cultural understandings of reason, morality, and the relationship between the two. He dramatically restricted the range of reason and reduced it the status of an instrument with far less stature than its former claim as the diviner of moral truths. The long-term impact suffered by morality owing to Hume's restriction of reason and his fact/value distinction, however, was far worse than the harm suffered by reason.

Morality was left mired in a quandary from which it has yet to emerge (though Hume alone cannot be blamed). The question at issue is not the concern of Locke expressed earlier wrought by the exit of God—Why be good? It is the equally primary question—What is the good? If Divine revelation is no longer a source of knowledge about morality or the good, then reason applied to the study of human nature and conduct—which appealed to the scientific strain of the Enlightenment—was the most obvious alternative. That strategy, however, generated its own problems. Here is the dilemma that stumped Enlightenment philosophers: 'if nature is good, then there is no evil in the world; if there is evil in the world, then nature is so far not good' (Becker 1932: 69). It cannot be asserted that there is no evil in the world, at least not without emptying the term of all recognizable meaning.

Since the Enlightenment, the question that has never been answered satisfactorily is how to locate a standard by which to distinguish good from evil. God is out of the picture. Nature, again, cannot provide the standard. By natural inclination, people regularly do what many would

consider evil (witness human history of ever-present violence and domination, from war to spousal abuse), to a degree which cannot be dismissed as errant or exceptional. Many Enlightenment philosophers felt
that culture was progressive and therefore the furthest developed cultures
carried moral standards within them (Cassirer 1951: 268), but this self-
congratulatory posture could not withstand recognition that this kind of
morality is merely conventional, combined with growing awareness of
the variety of cultures in the world and the lack of a culture-independent
standard to determine which is the furthest developed. Furthermore, any
attempt to derive a standard from what people typically do (whether by
nature or convention) potentially runs afoul of the fact/value distinction
(see Finnis 1980: 33–42), and eliminates the possibility of having unreal-
ized moral ideals toward which to strive as a guide to improve the human
condition. It would turn the status quo into the ideal. One evident alternative is to construct a standard based upon those norms apparently necessary for the survival of the human species (assuming such survival is a
moral good), but this would lead to a minimalist conception of morality,
with a small number of basic rules and no aspiring content, hardly worthy of the label morality, and it would be compatible with many forms of
evil (see e.g. Hart 1961: 189–95). This bare minimum could be uplifted
by changing the standard from human survival to human flourishing;
however, disputes over what 'flourishing' entails would follow immediately, requiring a standard for the standard. Another alternative, the one
taken by many after the failure of these others, known as utilitarianism,
is simply to equate the good with what people desire, or with happiness,
and to construct a moral system oriented towards the maximization of
the total quantity of happiness. There are many difficulties with utilitarian theory—including its hedonistic bent, the lack of a non-controversial
way to quantify and weigh desires or happiness, and the fact that there
are alternative ways to construct utilitarianism (act or rule)—but the most
serious problem is that it licenses the treatment of others as a means to
one's own end (constrained in some versions by the do no harm principle), which carries a stain of repugnancy. A final alternative is the natural
law approach—shorn of its religious garb—which insists that we all (or at
least the wise) know the moral good, that what is moral conduct is self-
evident. 'But no fact seems to be plainer in the modern world than the
extent and depth of moral disagreement, often enough disagreement on
basic issues' (MacIntyre 2000: 93). Moreover, if we all know the moral
good, if it is in some way a part of our natural inclination, why is there so
much evil in the world?

Thus have we returned full circle to the dilemma bestowed by the Enlightenment philosophers and Hume. The former took out religion and the latter took out reason. In hindsight, once the first step was taken, each additional step on the path toward the current dilemma seems almost inexorable. Before the Enlightenment, reason provided knowledge of substantive principles of the good by gaining direct access to the Divine order set by God. With the Enlightenment, reason (as a form of analysis that helps intuit patterns and connections) was applied to human nature or culture, but this could produce little beyond a narrow set of minimalist rules, with no insight into the substantive moral good. Belief in a morally infused Divinely inspired nature gave way to nature understood in purely empirical morally indifferent terms (Cassirer 1951: 246). After the Enlightenment, God was gone (at least philosophically), nature was seen as amoral, and reason was at best an instrument. The possibility of gaining access to the source and content of morality and moral norms beyond what cultural conventions provide seemed closed, or it was a mystery with no obvious solutions.

Revealingly, many of the critiques levelled above against the various possible approaches to morality—that it does not account for evil, that it lacks aspirations, that it has repugnant implications—are *morally* based. The state of moral discourse today is that it continues apace despite the lack of apparent grounding and shared standards. The core of this situation lies in the idea of the subjectivity of values (see Unger 1975: 76–81). Values are subjective in the sense that whether or not an individual accepts a set of moral values—granting that they are socially generated and shared—depends upon a feeling or personal faith, often the product of socialization, and sometimes choice. Whether characterized in cultural or individual terms, the content of moral norms can no longer be seen as objective, rationally derived, or of universal application.

The exploration and colonization of the world that accompanied the Enlightenment had the effect of solidifying this cluster of ideas:

The global explorers had . . . expanded Europeans' geographical knowledge, and with it their exposure to other cultures and other histories. With the continuous growth of information in these areas, it gradually became evident that human history extended back in time far longer than had been assumed, that there existed many other significant cultures past and present, that these possessed views of the world widely divergent from the European, and that there was nothing absolute, immemorial, or secure about modern Western man's present status or values. (Tarnas 1991: 330)

A pluralism of moral values among and within communities; a pluralism of desires and visions of the good among and within individuals; a loss of tradition and faith in God; an eviscerated reason, stripped down to the status of a tool, unable to generate moral norms or to arbitrate among existing candidates; these are the conditions for modern law in society.

A departing note on Hume relates to how he dealt with the implications of his position for the common law of his time, which claimed origins in the natural reason he had so effectively debunked. Hume supported the common law by pointing to its other primary justification, that of being rooted in the custom and tradition of the realm. Indeed, Hume apparently held to a relatively strong version of the mirror thesis, believing that 'law is a development from and is always intimately tied up with the basic structuring conventions and customs of a community' (Postema 1986: 84). The function of law, according to Hume, is to secure the stable conditions of social life, in particular facilitating coordination, which is why laws reflecting prevailing customs are especially useful. Hume is a conventionalist like Hobbes in insisting that justice has meaning relative to the legal rules and to achieving the function of the legal system (ibid., chap. 3). To a significant extent, his understanding is contingent upon the correctness of the mirror thesis.

Three Changes in Relative Proportions Making Up Positive Law

Before elaborating on the relevance of the foregoing ideas, three unrelated factors will be mentioned briefly, all of which have led to general changes in the make up of positive law systems and have contributed to the diminished connection with custom and moral principle.

The first factor has to do with a substantial increase in the proportion of positive laws dedicated to economic matters. That there are links between law and the economic system is obvious and has long been recognized. A society that has exchange through direct bartering will require a different complex of rules from one using currency-based market transactions at a distance. A society that allocates production and distribution activities through central planning will have different rules from one based upon free market principles. Despite the evidently close relation, until relatively recently Western legal theory has not paid much attention. Montesquieu was one relatively early theorist who emphasized the close link between the economic activities of a nation and its laws.

Marx and Engels argued, at a high level of generality, that the law is determined by the economic base, and they demonstrated how specific bodies of law, like labour law, inured to the benefit of the capital owners (see Cain and Hunt 1979: 62–107). Pashukanis (1989: 40–1) extended the argument to show how the form as well as the content of the law matches and is a product of the market system, resulting in a profound transformation 'making human relations into legal relations'. Weber showed that capitalist market systems require regimes of property, to encourage productive activities, and of contract, to allow for planning and provide security for transactions at a distance (in both time and location) (see Trubek 1972a). In particular, Weber argued that market systems have a strong preference for predictability, which he believed formally rational law was uniquely suited to provide.

When simple transactions are the core economic activity, as it was for millennia of human existence, economic-related rules can be and often are an aspect of the general body of customs and morality. At more complex levels, however, a great deal of economic-related legislation has no counterpart in social customs. Laws addressing the constitution of corporations, for example, have no parallel in social custom—indeed corporations are creatures created by law—nor do laws prohibiting monopolistic behaviour, nor do laws relating to the regulation of securities, and so forth. In the modern period, market systems, economic entities (like corporations), and commercial transactions have increasingly become detached and driven by their own imperatives. Weber (1954: 96) recognized the impetus that economic activities provide for legal development: 'This growing demand for experience and specialized knowledge and the consequent stimulus for increasing rationalization of the law have almost always come from increasing significance of commerce and those participating in it.' His point is even truer today. This body of economic-related law has moral implications and consequences, but in large part it no longer is an aspect of general social customs and morality as such, and it has been successfully kept insulated from them, except to the extent that business customs are embodied in the law. A significant bulk of the laws in many Western states today fall in this category.

The second factor is the growth of administrative law in modern social welfare systems. Administrative law generally encompasses either regulatory activities—e.g. protection of the environment, consumer protection, insuring drug and food quality, regulating communications, transportation, and immigration—or social programmes—e.g. welfare benefits and

emergency management. What is involved is the effectuation of government policy, with little or no relation to prevailing social customs and
indirect connections with moral norms. Much of the decision-making is
technocratic in nature, oriented towards finding and implementing the
strategy best able to achieve the stated policy, or political in nature, oriented towards appeasing the contesting interests at hand. For many of
today's social welfare states, administrative laws and regulations comprise a substantial portion of the law.

The third factor is the formidable proportion of legal development of
late that has come in relation to the governmental apparatus itself. 'Law
by no means exhausts itself in behavioral norms but increasingly serves
to organize and regulate state power' (Habermas 1996: 144). The modern *Rechtsstaat*—a government run by and through laws—devotes substantial lawmaking and law application energies to its own structure and
activities. In many states, virtually every branch and department of the
government is constituted by a background framework of enabling,
directive, and restrictive legal rules, which create it, empower it, and
guide and govern its activities. In ever-increasing detail and volume, law
and regulations spell out what and how government officials do things.
Governments today are legal creatures (like corporations, only more so),
at least in the West. Usually these self-oriented legal rules have little to do
with prevailing social customs or with morality.

As a consequence of the three factors mentioned above, although the
growth of positive law in the last few generations in the West has been
extraordinary, large chunks of these new legal rules have scarce connection to social customs, and much of it is only indirectly related to moral
norms. Earlier manifestations of positive law may have allocated a substantial degree of attention to social customs and morality, when it was
concerned with the affairs of everyday life in the village (along with
enriching the rulers), but the kinds of things done with and through law
have substantially changed in the last two hundred or so years.
Administrative law and law related to the government itself, in particular, are relatively recent developments, at least in terms of their hefty
bulk. Likewise, the scope and detail of economic-related law has
exploded, matching the exponential growth in the pace and sophistication of economic activities. Accordingly, on a relative basis the amount of
lawmaking today directly connected to custom or substantive moral rules
has markedly diminished.

Reduction in Custom as a Source of Positive Law, and the Shift to Procedural Consent

As recounted in Chapter 2, twentieth-century legal theorists have noted the diminishing connection between social customs and positive law in the West. Hart commented that custom is a marginal source of law in modern society. Ehrlich, responding to von Savigny, suggested that positive law did not in fact arise from, nor necessarily match, the collective conscience and prevailing social customs, but rather was almost exclusively the product of the jurists. The very point of Ehrlich's 'living law', and his distinction between rules of conduct (based upon customs and usages people actually followed) and rules for decision (the rules applied by courts), was to emphasize that positive law rules and lived social customs regularly diverge.

Many factors have contributed to this trend, including the emergence of legal specialists and changes in the make-up of state law mentioned earlier. Two principal explanations for the diminishing influence of custom on positive law will be articulated here, one focusing on concrete factors and the second operative in the realm of ideas. After elaborating on these factors, their implications will be played out in a review of the history of theoretical discussions related to the common law. The overall thrust of this discussion will be to establish the existence of a general shift away from substantive custom towards procedural consent in relation to positive law.

The concrete factors relate to various kinds of tensions that exist between custom and positive law. The struggle to incorporate custom or customary law into positive law in Europe during the later medieval period may serve as exemplary, with the lessons revealed having broader application. A primary aspect of the establishment of state power during this period entailed legal unification—an imposed uniformity of positive law, at least on paper, at a national or provincial level. 'The consolidation of societies into great states or principalities favoured not only the revival of legislation but also the extension of a unifying jurisprudence over vast territories' (Bloch 1967: 43). This strategy has been followed many times in the course of history, repeated on a grand scale during the period of Western colonization. The process of implementing legal regimes with broad territorial scopes inevitably results in a disparity with prevailing customs, which often are diverse within a territory. When positive law enacts customs, one available set must be selected over others. Given the detail, multiplicity, and local nature of customs, and the fact that many cannot be embodied easily in rule form, it is exceedingly difficult for customs to be reflected faithfully in positive law (as demonstrated anew by the general failure of efforts, despite best intentions, to codify native customary law following decolonization in the 1950s through 1970s). Moreover, in medieval Europe, once customary law was 'taught and set down in writing and was in part fixed by legislation, it inevitably lost much of its variety and flexibility' (p. 44). When customs are placed in written form they are frozen and their development thereafter influenced by the legal context within which they exist—in contrast to the fluid situation of social life in which customs change according to various influences—which results over time in a divergence between the two (Ehrlich 1975: 121–36). Furthermore, the enactment of Codes in the style of the French Civil Code, written in the form of general principles, are not amenable to the restatement of customs.

Finally, as mentioned earlier, custom poses a constant challenge to the power of positive law because it has populist connotations and because it is difficult to alter lived patterns of behaviour. It is thus in the interest of positive legal systems to maintain their supremacy over custom ('generously' incorporating or allowing the customs it cannot defeat), to delegitimize custom (as the product of ignorance), and to lessen its connection with custom as a source of law (in favour of the 'dictates of reason'). Hence the author of an early treatise on English law 'emphasized the contrast between the discouraging multiplicity of local usages and the much more methodical practice of the royal court' (Bloch 1967: 43). Accordingly, it is not unusual for positive law (especially in its nascent period) to claim allegiance to custom when advantageous and to reject custom when perceived as a threat, or when it is no longer needed. As a positive law system becomes more securely established, its stance often shifts from the former to the latter. It is important to understand that positive law has *always* had an opportunistic relationship with custom and so-called 'customary law', as Donald Kelley (1990: 106) implicitly suggests:

> With the advent of written forms . . . even with the provisio of popular 'approval' and 'tacit consent,' custom lost its primary ties with its social base and came under the control of legal and political authorities. . . . [The] true significance of the transition from 'custom' to 'customary law' . . . is that once again the legal experts have begun to take over. This is indeed the import of the twelfth-century revival of 'legal science,' in which custom joins civil and canon law in the arsenal of the 'language of power' which jurists come in large part to monopolize.

Contrary to what the label might suggest, it is usually legal officials who determine what qualifies as 'customary law'. To state the point more directly: even when positive law *claims* to enact or recognize custom or customary law, it may well nevertheless reflect neither.

The broader ideas that contributed to a change in the relationship between custom and positive law can be traced back to the Enlightenment. The eighteenth century was called the 'age of criticism' (Cassirer 1951: 275). The philosophy of the Enlightenment 'opposes the power of convention, tradition, and authority in all fields of knowledge' (p. 234). 'Enlightenment thought originally contrasted belief crystallized in tradition, dependent on the overriding of reason by authority and collective pressure, with belief consistent with reason and able to sustain its credibility directly in the face of the rational scrutiny of a questioning individual' (Barnes 1995: 119). Under this view, custom represents the worst kind of unthinking behaviour. Custom and tradition were seen 'as likely to be or more likely to be obfuscating than illuminating and which, even when they do happen to transmit truths, do so in a way which still requires the scrutiny of tradition-independent rationality for what is transmitted to be justifiably accorded the status of truth' (MacIntyre 1990: 65). Custom, which once had a status that rivalled that of written law, was thereafter regarded with suspicion, as an embarrassing vestige of the past out of place in the modern legal system.

With the new individualist, humanist orientation becoming dominant in social thought, law increasingly came to be seen as an instrument applied by our will to achieve our social purposes—custom and convention became its antithesis. This represents a major shift in the view of custom in relation to positive law. Numerous scattered references have been made in the preceding text to views that custom is a source of positive law, is equal in power to positive law, is necessary to positive law, is the ancestor out of which positive law emerged, and is supported by and reflects the direct consent of the people. 'In the words of Bartolus and Baldus, "Custom represents the will [or reflects the mentality] of the people" ' (Kelley 1990: 147). Custom was attributed with possessing the 'triple force' as 'founder, interpreter, and abrogator of law' (p. 133). Custom was seen as 'grounded in common sense or, in Gaius's famous phrase, "natural reason" ' (p. 91). Indeed, in Grotius's account, which is still operative today in international law, natural law rules are identified by the common customs of civilized people, which is taken as evidence of their consistency with the natural reason implanted in humankind (Stein 1999: 99). Following the Enlightenment, however, custom was transformed from representing the epitome of reason and general consent to being the blind fetters of the dead past.

No transition is total, however, and residual views that identify custom with consent can still be found, as in international law, and as reflected in the following relatively recent passage from sociologist Levy Bruhl (1964): 'Statutory law is not essentially different from custom: both are the expressions of the will of the group' (translated and quoted in L. L. Fuller 1975: 95). Legal anthropologists, in particular, have regularly expressed romanticized views of custom in consensual terms. But in general positive law, with an assist from democracy, took on the connotations of consent, at the expense of custom's former claim to represent the same, and it was law's superiority over custom in this respect which licensed its power to prevail over custom in instances of direct conflict.

A number of these changes, and the general shift from custom to pro-cedural consent in relation to positive law, can be illustrated concretely by tracing the progression of how the common law of England (and the United States) was characterized by theorists. Common law theory has a special relevance to the argument of this book because it has character-ized law in strong mirror thesis terms. In the following passages Gerald Postema (1986) sets out the classical theoretical description of the relation between the common law and society:

[C]ommon law is common and immemorial custom, an 'ancient collection of unwritten maxims and customs' (1 *Comm.* 17), recorded in the memory of the people. (quoting Blackstone, p. 4)

The conviction of the authority of the law is the sense that the rules and practices of the Common Law at present are continuous with the life and the history of the people whose law it is. . . . [C]ommon law is seen to be the *expression* or manifesta-tion of commonly shared values and conceptions of reasonableness and the com-mon good. (pp. 6–7)

And that order [of the common law] is not created, or imposed from outside the common life of the people, rather it is the *expression of* that life. . . . In this extended sense the Common law can be said to rest on the *consent* of the people. This con-sent is deeper than agreeing to have other persons represent one in a legislative assembly. It comes from a recognition that the rules that govern one's life are *one's own*, they define that life, give it structure and meaning, are already practised and so deeply engrained that they appear to one as purely natural. (pp. 16–17)

If it is possible, then, to capture in a single phrase what law *is*, according to classi-cal Common Law theory, one might say that it is a form of social order manifested in the practice and common life of the nation. (p. 38)

A closer inspection uncovers revealing changes in this understanding. Initially *social customs* were identified as the primary source of the common law, despite the reality of the substantial residue of imposed Norman law. And although significant aspects of the common law had demonstrably more recent origins (p. 19), by 'the sixteenth century the myth of "immemorial custom" had become a cornerstone of the legal profession' (Kelley 1990: 22). 'Maitland noted a three-stage progression from customs originating in the "common wisdom and experience of society," through the stage of becoming "established customs," to the point at which they receive "judicial sanction in courts of last resort" ' (Hogue 1966: 190). But a subtle yet significant shift occurred after which the claim that the 'customs' reflected by the common law became, not so much those of society itself, but those of the judicial tradition; the common law was characterized as the *customs of legal practice itself*.[1] The break represented by the shift from social customs to judicial customs was softened by claims that judges merely acted as Oracles who discovered and spoke the law on behalf of the society; and the transition was facilitated by ambiguous references to 'custom' without further specification, at least in general declarations. Roscoe Pound (1911: 604) noted in the early part of the twentieth century, however, that among theorists of the common law, 'it has been recognized repeatedly that law represents commonly not customary modes of popular action, but customary modes of judicial decision or juristic thinking, rooted in either case in a purely juristic tradition.'[2]

Accompanying and supporting this shift were assertions that the common law represented the progressive judicial working out of reason and principle. Following the Enlightenment it would have been harder to claim that a body of social customs conformed to reason, but the claim could be made more easily in relation to the practices of judges. 'This conception gives reflective reason a much wider scope in the law and portrays the Common Law as a *rational science* based on first principles, or at least potentially transformable into such a science' (Postema 1986: 33).[3]

---

[1] Peter Stein (1999: 63) offers an account which suggests that this is not a shift so much as a reference to two different courts. He indicates that the local courts did indeed apply local customs, while the common law courts elaborated their own customs. This may in fact be an accurate historical account, but the distinction was not made in theoretical references.

[2] See also A. W. B. Simpson (1994: 133) ('the common law system is properly located as a customary system of law in this sense, that it consists of a body of practices observed and ideas received by a caste of lawyers, these ideas being used by them as providing guidance in what is conceived to be the rational determination of disputes litigated before them').

[3] Postema (1986: 30–8) points out that two different references to reason were applied to the common law: particularistic legal reasoning (especially analogical) and reasoning towards principles, although the distinction was often not recognized. Here I refer to the second usage of reason.

These principles were immanent in the body of cases, Christopher Columbus Langdell and others asserted, and legal rules and principles could be discovered inductively as a science. 'In [nineteenth-century] England the prevailing view was still that enshrined in Blackstone's Commentaries on the Laws of England of 1765: the law was essentially common law, which was ancient custom, refined over the centuries by the practical reason which resided in the capacious bosoms of the king's justices' (Stein 1980: 69).[4] Legitimation for the common law was thus dual: custom and reason, with reason carrying more of the weight following increasing acknowledgement that the customs involved are judicial, not social.

Owing to this characterization of the common law in terms of (consensual) custom and judicial reason, legal professionals were long able to resist inroads from legislation. Legislation never had a comfortable place in common law theory because it is the product of will and political expediency and hence could not be expected to fit within the (claimed) overarching rational structure of the common law. But this reassuring representation was difficult to maintain in the face of Bentham's excoriation of the English legal profession and the common law, and the later critique pressed by the American Legal Realists. Over time pressing social problems, and the expansion of the state bureaucracy and the scope of activities it engaged in, in combination with the growing view that law was an instrument with which to achieve social purposes, helped shift the lawmaking momentum away from the conservative common law onto legislation. The weakness of the rationale supporting the common law was ultimately revealed in the demise of the long-standing rule of construction that statutes in derogation of the common law were to be narrowly construed.

The capitulation of this rule can be understood as a manifestation and symbol of the shift from custom to procedural consent that is the subject of this section. Here is a quick summary: Prior to the Enlightenment consent for legal rules was found in (claimed) consistency with custom. Then, Edmund Burke aside, custom came to represent the unthinking chains of the past more so than consent. The common law was only dubiously connected to social customs anyway; and Hume's critique of reason rendered suspicious talk of the discovery of substantive principles and rules through judicial reason. Bentham's and the Realist's critique further deflated these claims. Law was increasingly seen as an instrument of our

---

[4] An informative essay on this subject is Whitman (1991).

will, in contrast to custom. Consent to positive law thus shifted onto the democratic election of representatives authorized to make law through legislation. This left common law systems with an uneasy combination, as described by Roberto Unger (1996: 115):

The key point is that a common law after democracy and with democracy must mean something different, and develop in a different way, from a common law outside and before democracy. To be tolerable within democracy a common law cannot represent the cumulative discovery of a natural and stable world of custom by a group of legal wise men. Nor can it be the basic system of private-law categories defining the necessary legal forms of free economies and societies. . . . From the perspective of democratic beliefs and practices, we can no longer interpret the body of statutory law in light of statutory analogies, nor acquiesce in the strict construction of statutes in derogation of common law.

Despite this problem, the common law carries on, albeit more circumscribed relative to legislation, even as it has been deprived of its former sources of legitimation with no clear replacement. Given current understandings, if the common law did not already exist, it could not likely be created today. In this sense it is a thriving vestige of the past. Although this example is taken from the common law, many analogous developments occurred in civil law systems (except that the emphasis was on the Code rather than the judges), which shifted grounds of legitimation over time from claimed consistency with custom, to reason-generated principles, to democracy. In many civil law countries, the prestige of jurists and the Codes they drafted remain relatively high, but even then much of the lawmaking impetus of late has shifted onto legislatures, rendering problematic former claims that the Codes were comprehensive and gapless statements of the law.

A final important aspect of this shift must be recognized, something that distinguishes custom from democracy as sources of law. In both cases consent for law is claimed, but of a qualitatively different kind. The consent of custom was direct and substantive, in the sense that the *content* of positive law norms were (supposedly) taken directly from prevailing customs. The consent of democracy, in contrast, is indirect and procedural or formal, in the sense that (except for instances of lawmaking referenda) the populace does not vote directly for the content of laws, but rather elect through a formal (vote counting) procedure the people authorized to make the laws, who then use a formal (vote counting) procedure to enact the laws. The formal procedures at these two levels allow for the expression of, concealment of, and combination of, an extraordinary mix of motives and underlying reasons that go into generating a positive or

negative vote, only one of which—and not necessarily the most important one—is support for or opposition to the content of any particular law.
Despite the efforts of theorists like Habermas to construe democratic procedures as a form of consent for the content of laws, it is more descrip-
tively true to this process to recognize elections and voting as a form of
political accountability. There are too many layers between the election
(or eviction) of legislators and the creation of law to lend plausibility to the
claim that there is direct consent for the substantive content of law. The
shift to indirect and procedural is significant because, in contrast to
the direct and substantive (claimed) identity between custom and positive
law, law can no longer be assumed to be a mirror of lived social relations.

Supporters of the mirror thesis may still point to two factors that keep
the law directly in line with the customs and morality of society: lay participants like juries, and open-ended legal standards like fairness or reasonableness. But again there is a significant difference from past practices.
Formerly, when custom was claimed as a law, often people from the community were called in to attest to the custom directly (Stein 1999: 83). In
contrast, juries today, to the extent that they still exist, are generally limited to finding the facts, not determining the law. Furthermore, as Weber
(1954: 321) observed: 'The use of jurors and similar lay judges will not
suffice to stop the continuous growth of the technical elements in the law
and hence of its character as a specialists' domain.' Standards like fairness and reasonableness invite the input of prevailing customs and social
views, but often they come encrusted with legal meanings and constraints. The existence of these kinds of mechanisms, even where they are
effective, do not detract from the general points that the connection
between custom and positive law has altered in the modern period, and
that there has been a distinct shift away from custom towards procedural
consent.

Away from Substantive Morality towards Procedural
Rationality—The Rule of Law

The final shift to be addressed consists of an interconnected twofold
change: the relationship between morality and reason was fundamentally
altered; and the direct connection between positive law and substantive
morality was severed (or at least substantially lessened) and replaced with
a connection between positive law and procedural rationality, resulting
in an increased distancing of positive law. These shifts will be taken up in
order.

As discussed in the first section of this chapter, in the Western tradition morality and natural law have throughout history been associated with reason. Moral philosophy is replete with assertions that substantive moral principle can be discerned through the application of reason (see Schneewind 1998). Under the pervasive Christian world-view, the connection between reason and morality was straightforward: God implanted reason in humankind as a means to identify morality. Voltaire analogized it to the cooperative instinct God gave to bees: 'He endowed each man with certain inalienably feelings; and these are the eternal bonds and first laws of human society' (quoted in Cassirer 1951: 245). Even after this religious connection was lost, and the search for grounding transferred to human nature, it was still routinely asserted that moral principles could be identified through the application of reason. ' "Nature" and "Reason" are the substantive criteria of what is legitimate from the standpoint of natural law' (Weber 1954: 290).

Then came Hume's critique of reason and all that followed in its wake, articulated earlier, after which reason was no longer seen as capable of identifying substantive moral norms or natural law principles whether from human nature or any other source. In combination with the successful march of science, the result was a bifurcation after which science and (instrumental) reason were placed together on one side representing the sources of verifiable knowledge, with morality and religion on the other side representing belief and faith.[5] After being identified together for so long, a gap between the two was opened, situating morality and reason on either shore with no bridge between them. Thereafter rationality was understood in instrumental terms and morality was relegated to the status of subjective preference or a cultural product. Indeed, by this logic, morality was characterized as conventional and subjected to the same treatment as custom. As Habermas (1996: 95) put it, 'cultural traditions and processes of socialization came under the pressure of reflection, so that actors themselves gradually made them into topics of discussion. To the extent that this occurred, received practices and interpretations of ethical life were reduced to mere conventions and differentiated from conscientious decisions that passed through the filter of reflection and independent judgment.'

One consequence of the complex of factors surrounding this change in the relationship between morality and reason was a fundamental shift away from substantive morality towards procedural rationality relative to

---

[5] Richard Tarnas (1991: 375–8) identifies a similar though not identical bifurcation.

positive law. Until this shift, the connection between positive law and morality was always seen in substantive terms, in the sense that the key was law's consistency with the *content* of moral norms. Legal positivists, according to Hart, confirmed that 'the content of many legal rules mirrored moral rules or principles' (1958: 596). The emphasis of natural law thought, in particular, was 'on the law's content and on substantive standards for evaluating that content' (Summers 1984: 65). In a gradual process following from, and as an aspect of, the earlier described developments, however, law became separated from substantive morality: 'it was eventually taken for granted that law as a product of reason, is capable of functioning as an instrument of secular power, disconnected from ultimate values and purpose' (Berman 1983: 198). Just as reason came to be seen in substantively empty instrumental terms, so too with positive law.

The culmination of this shift from substantive morality to procedural rationality in relation to law is that positive law came to point to its own nature—to legality—for legitimation. The existence and nature of this shift will be established through a discussion of the notion of the rule of law, and of the theories of Lon Fuller, Max Weber, and Jürgen Habermas, each of which represents an aspect of this shift.

Judging from the frequency with which it is referred to—by legal theorists, social scientists, politicians, and members of the public—the idea of the rule of law is the dominant legitimating slogan of law at the close of the twentieth century. Although there are competing versions of what this notion entails, its core characteristics can be stated without much controversy. In the narrowest terms, it means that the government rules through law, and that the government is itself under the law. 'The ideal of the rule of law in this sense is often expressed by the phrase "government by law and not by men" ' (Raz 1979: 212). One way to understand the rule of law is by way of contrast to what it is not: being subject to the arbitrary whims or subjective views of the individuals (including judges) who act in the name of the government. If the government takes actions against individuals, it must do so in accordance with duly enacted laws. These laws should have, at least, the qualities of generality, prospective application, open public notice, and reasonable clarity (pp. 214–18).[6]

For the purposes here, the crucial point is that the rule of law, as formulated, is substantively empty. 'It is evident that this conception of the rule of law is a formal one. It says nothing about how the law is to be made: by tyrants, democratic majorities, or any other way. It says

---

[6] Raz lists additional characteristics, but here I provide the bare minimum.

nothing about fundamental rights, about equality, or justice' (p. 214). Thus, the rule of law is compatible with, and may be instituted by, a system that contains the most immoral of laws. 'A non-democratic legal system, based on the denial of human rights, on extensive poverty, on racial segregation, sexual inequalities, and religious persecution may, in principle, conform to the requirements of the rule of law' (p. 211). The rule of law, at least under this dominant theoretical view, contains no substantive moral standards as an aspect of its definition. Those who doubt this minimalist conception should recall that by all accounts the United States has long complied with the requirements of the rule of law, including during the periods of legalized slaveholding and segregation. From the standpoint of the rule of law, the law is an instrument with exclusively procedural characteristics. 'Like other instruments, the law has a specific virtue which is morally neutral in being neutral as to the end to which the instrument is put' (p. 226).

Prior to elaborating further on the modern instrumental view of law, to appreciate the remarkable change entailed in the shift to this view it must be compared with the pre-Enlightenment theoretical view, which is a lineal ancestor of current views. The medieval idea of law as espoused by theorists, Walter Ullmann (1946: 3) observed, was steeped in Christian moral philosophy and Aristotelianism:

The central theme of this conception was the relation of mankind to God. Created and ruled by God—philosophically conceived as the first cause of all Being—mankind was deemed subject to the eternal laws of the Universe. The divine Will and Reason were clearly perceived to be the ever-active powers in the government of the world. Essential to this thought was the idea that the cosmos is one well-ordered, harmonious, and articulated whole, whose parts are at the same time both parts and wholes, and that God is the supreme Ruler of the Universe, its sole source and aim. Human conduct was thought of as purposive and destined to a definitive end. . . . Furthermore, since the relationship of man to his Creator was of an internal character, and therefore of a moral nature, the transplantation of ethical ideas into the sphere of law was an argument which suggested itself as being fundamental to this conceptual framework. . . . The consultation of Aristotle's *Ethics* and of the Christian teaching was merely an articulate expression of this reasoning, which finally led to an infiltration of ethical content into fundamental legal principles. The self-sufficiency of law was herewith denied.

The contrast between this description and the modern rule of law ideal could not be greater—the most striking difference being the latter's lack of ethical content. It is also immediately evident why the religion-steeped understanding of law could no longer hold today. Notably, this idealized view of the order of the Universe and moral law stood in stark opposition to the social reality of the time.

Lon Fuller's influential account of the rule of law, what he calls the principles of legality, is likewise substantively empty. According to Fuller (1969: 33–94), by its nature law must have the following qualities: (1) be general; (2) be publicized; (3) not be retroactive; (4) be understandable; (5) not be contradictory; (6) be such that the legal requirements can be complied with; (7) be relatively stable; and (8) have a congruence between the rules announced and the rules applied. Fuller recognized that his account of the nature of law was neutral with regard to, and could accommodate, a range of substantive aims. Nevertheless, he claimed that these eight conditions amounted to the 'internal morality of law' (pp. 220–4). Fuller's account of what this morality consisted of was less than clear. He asserted at various points that an aspect of this morality is that the principles of legality help to achieve human aims or other moral goals (p. 205), that it assists individuals in making plans (p. 210), and that it facilitates social interaction (p. 223). The basic idea appears to be that the principles of legality afford people a 'fair opportunity to obey the law' (Summers 1984: 37). Another aspect of this morality is that legality imposes certain minimal restraints on a tyrant, at least by way of contrast to a totally arbitrary application of power. The main point is, as Fuller recognized, 'the concept of the internal morality of law is essentially procedural' (quoted p. 71); though he also believed that the legality described has a kind of affinity with substantive moral good or justice (L. L. Fuller 1969: 157–9, 1958: 636). Despite his content-empty view of the morality of law, Fuller identified himself with natural law schools of thought (Summers 1984: 62). He 'once referred to his theory as "a procedural, as distinguished from a substantive natural law"' (quoted in Bix 1999a: 76). His 'affirmation of the role of reason in legal ordering' placed him solidly within the natural law camp (Summers 1984: 63).

Weber's account of formal legal rationality, which he saw as characteristic of Western civil law systems, was described briefly in the an earlier chapter. In essence, it exists when 'the legally relevant characteristics of the facts are disclosed through the logical analysis of meaning and where, accordingly, definitely fixed legal concepts in the form of highly abstract rules are formulated and applied' (Weber 1954: 63). This kind of law is 'formal' in that legal decisions are based on legal criteria only. Like the rule of law and Fuller's account of legality, Weber's formally rational law is substantively empty in the sense that it is open to, and can function with, any set of substantive norms. Indeed, he contrasts formal legal rationality with substantively rational systems that are designed to achieve substantive justice (pp. 61–4). A 'formal legal system is one that eschews all ethical ideals based either upon a conception of the good or considerations of distributive justice' (Kronman 1983: 95). Formal law is an instrument to serve our ends. The formal and rational aspects of the law—its rationalization and systematization—render its outcomes more predictable, allowing people to plan better, which enhances their free-dom and ability to engage in transactions (Weber 1954: chap. 11; Hayek 1973). Formally rational systems derive legitimation from the character-istics of formal legality itself—'only legal-rational authority employs the principle of positivity as the basis of legitimation' (Kronman 1983: 55). Habermas (1996: 73) characterized Weber's theory in these terms: 'legit-imation is premised solely on aspects of the legal medium through which political power is exercised, namely, the abstract rule-structure of legal statutes, the autonomy of the judiciary, as well as the fact that adminis-tration is bound by law and has a "rational" construction.'

Habermas's approach to the legitimation of law also begins with ratio-nality or, more specifically, with his notion of communicative rationality. As with all of these substantively empty approaches, his use of reason 'no longer provides a direct blueprint for a normative theory of law and moral-ity' (Habermas 1996: 5). The problem that leads to this normatively empty approach to law is familiar: the disenchantment of the world, combined with the pluralism of modern society, through which 'comprehensive worldviews and collectively binding ethics have disintegrated' (p. 448). If there is no agreement on the substantive moral good, there must at least be a procedure by which the contesting views can come to a decision. This is what Habermas's discourse theory provides. Pursuant to discourse theory—described earlier in the social contract theory discussion—the law is legitimate because the authors of the law are also its addressees, and there is no coercion owing to the unanimous agreement of all those affected (at least in theory). The relevance of Habermas's theory here is that it once again demonstrates a shift away from substantive morality towards reason and procedure. Habermas described his own approach in such terms: 'the legitimacy of positive law is conceived as procedural rationality' (p. 453). Similar to Fuller, Habermas appears to believe that decisions made under the conditions of discourse theory would produce morally right outcomes,[7] and thus his approach also has an affinity with the good.

---

[7] Habermas writes that it would lead to 'rational outcomes', but he appears to mean by this morally correct, and made this statement to the author in a personal conversation.

Although the above theorists approach from completely different directions, they are in agreement on fundamental points. All of them view law in instrumental terms, and identify (in different ways) law with reason. Their approaches to law are substantively empty. All of them focus on the procedural and formal aspects of law. Indeed, their descriptions of law—instrumental, formal, substantively empty—echo Humean-inspired conceptions of reason. All of them, in their own way, shift away from the traditional test for the legitimacy of law in its consistency with the content of moral principles or with prevailing customs, towards focusing on the 'legitimacy of legality' itself (see Dyzenhaus 1996).[8] They point to the nature of the rule of law itself as the grounds for its own legitimation, separate from and regardless of the content the law enacts. Locating legitimacy in legality itself is the companion and legacy of the moral pluralism of the modern age.

It can be argued in response that legality, or the rule of law, is still consistent with the mirror thesis in so far as positive laws that are democratically enacted will reflect prevailing morality. Law is still a mirror, but now it obtains this quality through an indirect mechanism. Habermas's discourse principle, in effect, works this way. David Dyzenhaus observed of Bentham's position, but also capturing a more broadly applicable view, that 'what is important about the institutions of radical democracy is that they permit the positive law to *reflect* the desires or preferences of at least the majority of individuals' (p. 161, emphasis added). Both democracy and law are instrumental, under this view. 'Democracy is the best available means for revealing preferences and positive law is the best available mechanisms for implementing them' (ibid.). As custom and morality have been relocated to greater distances from positive law, democracy—this discussion and the discussion of the preceding section have established—has been handed an increasingly heavy burden for consent and the mirror thesis.

The difficulties with this allocation of weight upon democracy were alluded to earlier and can be stated briefly here. A threshold point of doubt is that representative democracy, which is the ubiquitous form of democracy today, by way of contrast to almost forgotten direct democracy, is suspect. 'Since the late eighteenth century, the idea that "the people" should themselves make the rules which "govern" their lives has been a key feature of the *ideology* of the modern state, ideology exactly because, as the writers of the eighteenth century acknowledged, "representative government"

---

[8]   David Dyzenhaus (1996) used this phrase, and discussed the themes surrounding it, in a superb analysis of Habermas's view of law.

is *not* "democracy" ' (Manicas 1987: 34). Indeed representative democracy was thought to be superior by many political theorists precisely because it would allow elected elites to restrain the excesses of the (ignorant) masses (ibid.). Moreover, as public choice theory suggests, it cannot be assumed that votes are cast by representatives based upon whether the proposed law reflects their constituents' views rather than upon the best chance of obtaining a significant campaign contribution. Self-interest and vote trading are notorious constants of the political process. Nor can it be assumed that the majority view prevails. The alarmingly low levels of participation in the elections of many Western countries—not infrequently less than half the eligible voters—raises additional concerns about reliance upon this process. Furthermore, in a pluralistic society, there will be at least one group, and perhaps others, whose views will not be reflected in the law, groups which when combined may outnumber the view that does prevail. Finally, a great deal of lawmaking is in fact the product of legal professionals—judges, legal academics, code commissions—and is either not democratic at all, or at most is formally endorsed by a superficial democratic stamp. Once again, reasons to doubt the mirror thesis remain.

A second argument in response, a powerful one, might be that the mirror thesis continues to hold, though in a qualitatively different way. Instead of reflecting the substantive content of moral beliefs, the liberal (empty) rule of law reflects a liberal culture, both embodying the value of toleration for different views in an age of irreducible moral pluralism. That begs the question of whether the cultures with the rule of law are indeed liberal in this sense—whether toleration is truly a prevailing cultural value. It might instead be the case that the cultures are simply morally pluralistic; and given this situation there is no alternative other than the use of formal procedures in relation to the production and application of law, making no promises about what the substantive outcomes of these procedures might be.

Even theorists who acknowledge and try to accommodate the existence of moral pluralism in their theory of law, however, hang on to the substantive mirror claim. An example of this can be found in Jeremy Waldron's (1996: 1566) recent characterization of Kant as a legal positivist for the modern age:

Kant insists that we must now appreciate that there are others in the world besides ourselves, and that we are to see the others not just as objects of moral concern or respect, but also as agents of moral thought that is coordinate and competitive with our own. When one thinks about justice, one must recognize that others are thinking about justice and that one's confidence in the objective

quality of one's own conclusions is matched by others' confidence in the objective quality of theirs. . . .

If, nevertheless, there are reasons for thinking that society needs just one view
on some particular matter to which all its members are to defer, then there has
got to be a *way of identifying a community view* and grounds for one's allegiance to it
that are not predicated on any judgment one would have to make concerning the
view's moral rectitude (emphasis added).

This passage asserts reasonably that there are certain matters in which
the law must pick one view over others. It becomes questionable when it
makes the separate assertion that the *community view* prevails, which is, of
course, the mirror thesis (unless the argument is that whichever view prevails is, therefore, the community view). Two unstated assumptions contained within the italicized language of this passage help make it
persuasive: first, that there is a view sufficiently widespread to constitute
a 'community view'; and secondly, that democratic procedures are an
effective way of identifying it.

These are no small points because Waldron builds upon the argument
to derive an obligation to abide by the positive law apart from and without regard to whether it might be considered unjust by an external standard. Concern about this argument is heightened when one recognizes
that Kant (1991: 81–7, 143–7) himself issued an 'absolute' prohibition
against resistance to a law by a citizen, recommending 'severe treatment'
of those who do resist, even with regard to a law he or she sincerely determines to be unjust, because such resistance would defeat the legal order,
and there would be no one to judge the dispute. If instead Waldron's
assertion was more frank—that a selection had to be made, it was made
according to formal procedures, and the ultimate winner might not be
just and might not in fact represent the community view—the conclusion
that an obligation to abide by the law that results would not follow as easily and would more quickly give way in the face of justice claims. The
undeniable, if often ignored, implication of the rule of law as substantively empty, and of procedural consent for rules based upon democratic
elections of representatives and formal voting for the laws they enact, is
that non-mirroring is always a real possibility. My argument, to repeat, is
not that law is never a mirror of society; it is rather that we should not so
readily take for granted that it is.

Hence the image portrayed of law by theory in the modern age is legality as an empty vessel, drawing upon democracy for consent-based legitimacy in the making of laws (serving as the mechanism for allowing the
mirror effect), and staking its own claim to legitimacy based upon its ability

to maintain order and to apply the law according to procedures consistent with formal requirements. There continue to be views of law in substantively rich terms, of course, the most prominent representative of which is Ronald Dworkin's law as integrity, but the formal procedural view of law is clearly dominant among theorists. Studies have also shown that among lay people evaluations of procedural justice are an important consideration in determining whether legal proceedings will be seen as legitimate (Lind 1998). If these studies are correct, either theorists have succeeded in purveying this view of the law more broadly, or procedural views of fairness have seeped into the public consciousness independently, perhaps also as a consequence of the spread of Enlightenment ideas and recognition of the inevitability of moral disagreement owing to the subjectivity of values.

This formal view of law dominates at the same period in which certain legal developments appear to point in anti-formal directions. Roberto Unger, Philippe Nonet and Philip Selznick, Patrick Atiyah, and Harold Berman, among others, have remarked upon a recent shift in Western legal systems away from strict rule application toward greater explicit consideration of substantive justice (see Tamanaha 1997: 236–40). The growth in administrative law has also brought an increase in the balancing of interests, goal-oriented reasoning, and use of discretionary standards, away from strict rule application.

An even more striking trend potentially along these lines is an apparent 'global expansion of judicial power', in which 'the phenomenon of judges making public policies that previously had been made . . . by legislative and executive officials appears to be on the increase' (Tate and Vallinder 1995: 2). A leading factor in this development is the spread of judicial review of legislation by Constitutional Courts, or by supranational courts such as the European Court of Justice and the European Court for Human Rights (see Sweet 2000). Constitutional judicial review does not necessarily represent a breakdown of the procedural view of law, because the review is justified typically as the interpretation and application of the Constitution, which is itself a positive law. However, judicial decisions giving direct effect to human rights norms, even though they might also be considered positive law when embodied in Declarations or Bills of Rights, come much closer to re-injecting substantive moral standards into the law along the lines previously suggested by natural law, although in more restricted terms.

Predictably, following quickly on the heels of observations about courts taking on a greater role, statements can be found that 'in contemporary government it is the judge's mind that most closely *mirrors* that of the demos' (Shapiro 1995: 61, emphasis added); and that 'most men and women who come to the bench bring with them views that *reflect* the general consensus of those holding high political offices' (Jacob 1996: 390, emphasis added). The mirror thesis is always close at hand.

It is too early to tell whether these developments will bring about a change in the instrumental, procedural view of positive law that is currently dominant among theorists. It may be that this view is now at its apex, poised to begin a downward descent, with theorists lagging behind in recognizing changes that will lead to its demise or reformulation. Hold the dirges, however. It will not be buried easily. In an era of pluralism, the complex of ideas surrounding morality, reason, and law appear to preclude a return to the only evident alternative, a substantially rich ethical view of law. What remains to be seen is whether an empty, formal view of law can suffice for long.

5   Against the Mirror Thesis

Powerful as the mirror thesis is, a few voices have expressed caution or out-right opposition. This chapter will elaborate on concrete social-historical reasons to question the assumption that law mirrors society's customs and morality, and to question assumptions about the social order function of law. The discussion will be divided into three sections, the first dealing with legal transplants, the second with the globalization of law, and the third with the 'gap problem'. This chapter is a mostly empirical complement to the mostly theoretical analysis of the preceding two chapters. Together, they constitute a response to the views set out in Chapter 2.

Legal Transplantation

Legal transplantation, whether by voluntary borrowing or by imposition, poses an obvious problem for the mirror thesis: how can positive law reflect society if it is derived from elsewhere? Transplantation also raises a question about law's social order function, since the assumption is that law is effective in this respect primarily because it reflects prevailing social customs and values. Two distinct streams of thought that focus on legal transplantation will be discussed in separate parts in this section: the work of Alan Watson and other legal comparativists; and the work of scholars who have traced the impact of the spread of law through colonization, especially legal anthropologists. Their different backgrounds have led to different approaches and emphases, though there are points of convergence.

Watson and Legal Comparativists

Watson is a prolific legal historian and comparativist who, in a series of books and articles, has presented a powerful case against the mirror thesis: 'the dynamic causal relationship between law and society which is often thought to keep the former in close harmony with the latter simply does not exist' (1983: 1136).[1] He (pp. 1131–42) insists that 'much of law

---

[1] An informative account of Watson's views is presented in Ewald (1995). Ewald makes a distinction between a weak and strong form of Watson's argument. The weak form merely seeks to challenge the strong mirror thesis; the strong form is the argument that law is autonomous or insulated from society. Ewald encourages the weaker reading of Watson's argument, though he recognizes that Watson has made many explicit statements asserting that the law is insulated.

is out of step with the needs and desires of society "to an extent which renders implausible the existing theories of legal development and of the relationship between law and society" '. Law, Watson (1985: 119) argues, 'is largely autonomous and not shaped by societal needs'. He relies on two basic propositions in support of this view: (1) that legal development throughout history, in the West and elsewhere, has primarily been the product of transplantation from one legal system to another; and (2) that, more than any other factor, the legal culture itself determines and controls legal development, mediating the influence of surrounding social, economic, and political factors. These two propositions are connected. 'To a considerable degree, the lawmakers of one society share the same legal culture with the lawmakers of other societies' (Watson 1983: 1157). A central aspect of this shared legal culture is the need for prestige: '[lawyers] are creatures of habit; they tend to view legal rules as ends in themselves; in altering the law they seek either to play down the extent of the change, or to borrow a rule from some foreign legal system with great prestige and authority' (Ewald 1995: 499). Another aspect is the tendency to see law as a specialized realm, or as Watson (1985: 119) put it, 'Law is treated [by the legal elite] as existing in its own right; hence it is being in conformity with lawness that makes law law.' These attitudes, shared among legal professionals regardless of national boundaries, generate a predisposition towards borrowing, which explains 'the transnational character of legal change' (Watson 1983: 1157).

Watson (1987) argues that legislation, one direct method by which prevailing social values can become a part of the law, has in the past had a relatively small role in legal development. He (1985: 58) also contends that 'to a great extent customary law does not derive from what the people of a locality habitually do'. His argument is that small communities did not typically resolve disputes through the application of legal rules but instead though determinations of what is fair. In those situations where customary law is cited in the course of adjudication, often there are many different possibilities from which to chose, or the customs are unclear or had not previously been declared, so the decision itself actually creates the customary law. Furthermore, he (pp. 43–65) argues, what is called customary law is often in fact borrowed from elsewhere. Thus, even positive law that cites customary law as its source, one of the stronger forms of the mirror thesis, does not escape Watson's sceptical challenge.

Following detailed studies of legal development, substantially though not exclusively focused on Roman law, Watson concludes:

to a large extent law possesses a life and vitality of its own; that is, no extremely close, natural or inevitable relationship exists between law, legal structures, institutions and rules on the one hand and the needs and desires and political economy of the ruling elite or of the members of the particular society on the other hand. If there was such a close relationship, legal rules, institutions and structures would transplant only with great difficulty, and their power would be severely limited. (1978: 314–15)

Law . . . is above all and primarily the culture of the lawyers and especially of the lawmakers—that is, of those lawyers who, whether as legislators, jurists, or judges, have control of the accepted mechanisms of legal change. Legal development is determined by their culture; and social, economic, and political factors impinge upon legal development only through their consciousness. (1985: 118)

These passages reveal that Watson rejects not just the mirror thesis, but also to a significant extent the selective mirror thesis as well.

Weber's description of the emergence of the legal profession as a group of legal specialists with its own interests, and of legal knowledge presenting its own internal demands, is a precursor to Watson's account. And Luhmann's and Teubner's autopoiesis bears similarities to it, especially in the view that the external environment influences law only as it is filtered through legal discourse. But Weber, Luhmann, and Teuber, I have argued, all still see law as a deeply integrated aspect of society. Watson, in contrast, allows for the possibility that there can be a fundamental disconnect between law and society. He (1983: 1137) gleefully acknowledges that his view 'contradicts virtually all scholarly research on law and society'. The problem, according to Watson, is that this research has been conducted by scholars beguiled by a functionalist perspective into misperceiving reality. '[T]raditional sociologists of law and legal anthropologists cannot admit that important legal rules may be largely dysfunctional; that would be to deny the possibility of any theory of legal development based on sociological or anthropological observations' (ibid.).

Watson does not deny that society influences law. The consciousness of lawmakers, he (1985: 118) allows, is influenced by social values. And he (1983: 1135) concedes that the 'cause' of legal rules 'is commonly, but not always, rooted in social, economic, or political factors important to the life of society or its leaders'. Watson (1993: 116) also recognizes that 'transplanting frequently, perhaps always, involves legal transformation'; the surrounding social circumstances influence how the rules are interpreted or function. Nonetheless, he (1985: 17) maintains that 'the input of the society often bears little relation to the output of the legal elite'.

Although few theorists agree entirely with Watson's position, comparativists are paying increasing attention to the fact that the phenomenon of legal transplantation through voluntary borrowing is presently accelerating, given momentum by the collapse of the socialist legal systems and the rise worldwide of political and economic liberalism (see Ajani 1995; Wiegand 1991). 'Yet again law is crossing geographic, cultural and linguistic boundaries. It is traveling from system to system' (Jagtenberg, Orucu, and de Roos 1995: 1). Comparativists who focus on this phenomenon have drawn the conclusion that all systems of law are mixed, with combinations of foreign and homegrown ('autochthonous') elements (see Orucu 1996; Kocourek 1936: 229). According to these theorists,[2] following a sufficient passage of time, and when the socio-cultural circumstances of the receiving system match (relatively) those of the generating system, the blend may become seamless, which for all practical purposes will amount to a unique combination that does fit with the surrounding society.[3] In contrast, when less time has passed, and when there are substantial differences in the socio-cultural circumstances of the generating and receiving systems, the positive law system will consist of an uneasy mix of elements and the likelihood of divergence from societal customs and norms is great. Most comparativists studying the mixed nature of legal systems (still a small group), it should be noted, are more reticent than Watson when drawing conclusions about the relationship between society and law. Their emphasis to date has been mostly on the legal systems themselves, and less so on the relations between law and society.

A study by Marc Galanter (1972) of law and society in India following over a hundred and fifty years of the reception of English law, first under British colonial administration then under Indian control, paints a complex portrait that will set up the transition to the next part. Typical of such situations, there were loud and long-standing complaints that the law was alien to Indian culture and values, especially vociferous during the struggle for independence. Yet following independence the system remained virtually intact. The legal system was supported by 'a wealthy and influential class of lawyers' (p. 61) who resisted change. Indeed, to the Indian legal profession the law felt fully Indian, as expressed by an Indian Attorney General:

[2] In particular, Esin Orucu (1996) has provided a sophisticated analysis of mixed systems. See also D. Goldberg and E. Attwooll (1996).

[3] Thus Neil MacCormick (1993: 355) can make the assertion that Scottish law—which contains elements of civil law, common law, and indigenous customs—is 'curiously well adapted to "metaphysical Scotland," perhaps because it itself is one of the moments that shaped the national spirit captures in that phrase.'

For over a hundred years distinguished jurists and judges in India have, basing themselves upon the theories of English common law and statutes, evolved doctrines of their own suited to the peculiar need and environment of India. So has been built up on the basis of the principles of English law the fabric of modern Indian law which notwithstanding its foreign roots and origin is unmistakably Indian in outlook and operation. (quoted in Galanter 1972: 63)

Despite this rosy assessment, the move to revive a traditional legal system for dispute resolution had enough support to be allowed a limited presence alongside the state legal system. This newly restored traditional system, however, absorbed aspects of the official legal system and thus was not 'traditional' in the historical sense (p. 64). Moreover, the villagers became adept at using the co-existence of the two systems to their personal advantage. Thus, the society adapted to the law and the law adapted to the society, but in various and complicated ways not captured by the metaphor of a mirror.

Galanter (p. 66) concludes his study with a series of observations that go to the heart of this book:

The Indian experience provides an occasion for questioning the familiar notions . . . of what is 'normal' in legal systems; that law is historically rooted in a society, that it is congruent with its social and cultural setting, and that it has an integrated purposive character. These notions express expectations of continuity and correspondence, of present with past, of law with social values, or practice with precept; expectations which are in part projections of the working myths of modern legal systems.

The Indian experience suggests a set of counter-propositions. It suggests that neither an abrupt historical break nor the lack of historical roots prevents a borrowed system from becoming so securely established that its replacement by a revived indigenous system is very unlikely. It suggests that a legal system of the modern type may be sufficiently independent of other social and cultural systems that it may flourish for long periods while maintaining a high degree of dissonance with central cultural values. It suggests that a legal system may be disparate internally, embodying inconsistent norms and practices in different levels and agencies.

These counter-propositions point to the need for some refinement of familiar notions of what legal systems are normally like.

Legal theorists have almost entirely ignored this reality. A general jurisprudence of law and society must be able to recognize and encompass situations like this, for they are far more prevalent than is typically recognized.

Colonization and the Findings of Legal Anthropologists

The second stream of thought that focuses on transplantation looks at the role of law in colonization. Legal anthropologists have been the major contributors to this approach, which has shaped the perspectives and interests they bring to bear. Their work is oriented primarily towards the study of law in non-Western countries, especially non-state or indigenous law. They accept the mirror thesis with regard to the West (law reflects Western cultural values), and build upon this to show the mismatch between transplanted law and the customs and values of the colonized society. In particular, they have emphasized the relationship between indigenous systems of law and state law. Finally, the key conceptual notion legal anthropologists have developed to study and explain these situations is legal pluralism.

European colonization of the non-Western world began in earnest in the late fifteenth century, peaked in the late nineteenth century, and for the most part ended by the 1970s, though a number of colonies remain in existence today. There were differences among the various coloniz-ers,[4] but, speaking generally, for the first two centuries colonization efforts concentrated on economic exploitation of resources and Christian proselytizing of indigenous populations. Actual conquest or colonial con-trol was often limited to coastal areas or other easily accessible trade routes. Law brought to the colonies was dominated by economic considerations. In a classic mix of public/private functions, for example, at the beginning of the seventeenth century the English and Dutch East India companies were given royal charters that authorized them to make and enforce laws in the interest of insuring the success of their economic activities (Leue 1992).

Initially, transplanted law from home governed predominantly the settler communities, which consisted of expatriates. 'On the whole there was a striking reluctance to accept jurisdiction over subject people. Up to the late eighteenth century there was no serious European endeavor to develop jurisdiction over an indigenous population according to their own law. Nor were there attempts on a large scale to extend European law to the subject population' (Fisch 1992: 23). In most cases it was not necessary, nor practicable, nor economically efficient to extend legal rule over indigenous populations, especially when the actual presence outside

---

[4] Excellent historical descriptions of the relationship between law and colonization, which I have relied upon in this account, can be found in W. J. Mommsen and de Moor (1992), esp. Fisch (1992).

of the main colonial centres consisted of little more than a few officials, merchants, and missionaries, along with a small militia. 'Accordingly indigenous legal institutions were mostly left alone, unless they directly affected the state of the European traders, missionaries, settlers, or officials' (Mommsen 1992: 4). Jurisdiction was determined by the 'personal principle', pursuant to which the colonizer's law applied to any cases involving expatriates (including cases between expatriates and natives).

By the mid- to late eighteenth century the situation began to change. Colonial rule was extended further inland and more indigenous people came to work in the growing trading centres, increasing the degree of interaction. Most colonizers instituted systems of indirect rule, especially in the rural areas. Indirect rule involved relying upon (and enhancing) the authority of local chiefs, and respecting customary law, subject to 'repugnancy clauses' under which local customs were disregarded when contrary to general—that is, colonizer—notions of justice (Fisch 1992: 27–33; Mommsen 1992: 6–10). This policy led to the creation of an officially endorsed dual system of law. It was argued for on moral terms, and was seen at the time by many as enlightened, but there were clear advantages to the colonizers in this policy, which enhanced stability by ruling through indigenous elites while maintaining the superiority of Western law when the colonizer's vital interests were at stake (Mommsen 1992: 10–11). Labour laws that permitted imprisonment for breach of employment contracts, general taxation that forced people to work for the colonizer's economic enterprises in order to earn money, and land reform designed to allow the purchase and use of land for expatriate owned and run mining and agricultural enterprises, all played an important role in solidifying colonial exploitation though law (Chanock 1992). In summary, colonial law was designed 'to structure and to legitimate the relations of political domination and economic exploitation of the natural and human resources in the colonies' (von Benda-Beckmann 1992: 318). The colonial state was an economic predator, and positive law provided its claws. The law was by no means a reflection of society.

It might be said in response that positive law still matched prevailing social customs and norms to the extent that it recognized the validity of customary law. But the situation is more complicated than that.[5] Three basic strategies were applied to bring customary law within the ambit of the state legal systems: the codification of customary law; use by state

---

[5] Informative studies on the situation that has resulted from the colonial imposition of law can be found in B. Morse and G. Woodman (1987), A. Allott and G. Woodman (1985), and S. B. Burman and B. E. Harrell-Bond (1979).

courts of customary law as a source of law in a fashion analogous to common law; and the creation of informal 'native' or 'village' courts that applied customary law (Tamanaha 1989: 102–6). All of these strategies suffered from various defects, which can be pared down to the basic problem that customary norms and processes could not be removed from their original medium without losing their integrity. '[I]ndigenous rules are not seen *a priori* as "laws" that have the capacity to determine the outcome of disputes in a straightforward fashion. It is recognized, rather, that the rules may themselves be the object of negotiation and may sometimes be a resource to be managed advantageously' (Comaroff and Roberts 1981: 13–14). A review of the literature reveals the following problems:

Assuming that customary norms can be identified and labeled as such, they have been found to be in a state of flux with different versions; there are conflicting or contradictory norms; norms are described in a 'vague or elusive' manner; norms have multiple contingencies or exceptions; stated norms often do not match actual behavior; it is not always clear how to move from the abstract norm to application in a give case; and sometimes a number of normative orders coexist. (Tamanaha 1989: 103–4)

All of these problems reflect the flexible nature of the traditional normative systems, many of which were not as rule-oriented as Western law (though it should be noted that the Legal Realists pressed similar critiques of US common law). Customary systems of rules characteristically were highly contextualized. In the selection, formulation, and application of norms in a given situation, many customary systems took into consideration the history and relationships between the individuals and groups involved. Frequently, the vindication of stated norms was of secondary importance to achieving a consensus. As a consequence of these and other factors, customary norms which were incorporated into the legal system (by codification or judicial decision) did not mean the same thing or function in the same way, and informal or village courts (which frequently tended to take on the forms or style of colonial law) did not operate like pre-existing indigenous institutions. 'The essence of the customary systems may be said to have lain in their processes, but these were displaced, and the flexible principles which had guided them were now fed into a rule-honing and -using machine operating in new political circumstances' (Chanock 1985: 62).

Customary law recognized and incorporated by the state legal system, therefore, was not the same as customary law and norms as they may have existed in society. Further complicating matters, a growing chorus of legal anthropologists have argued that much of what passed for customary law was not customary or traditional at all; rather, it was selectively created to meet current interests, including colonial or indigenous elite domination (Chanock 1992, 1985; Snyder 1981). Customary law, in this view, was an artificial construction, a product of and reaction to the colonial legal systems, a label used to convey a sense of consistency with indigenous norms for the purposes of legitimation, while concealing the underlying fact of recent invention.

Regardless of the messy reality, the revival of customary law was one of the leading slogans of the worldwide decolonization movement of the 1950s and 1960s. In practice, however, following decolonization in many places the transplanted legal regimes were left virtually intact through 'transitional' clauses that continued existing colonial law in effect until repealed. Such repeal, if it occurred at all, was often substantially delayed, resulting in anomalies like the Dutch Civil Code surviving in Indonesia for decades following decolonization, and written in the Dutch language despite the fact that a small proportion of the Indonesian population spoke the language. Quite commonly, the law has remained in the colonizer's language long after their departure, and often only the indigenous elite are conversant in this language. After decolonization, in many locations, the borrowing of Western law actually increased in the 1960s and thereafter, under the influence and prompting of international aid agencies, of transnational banks and other corporations that required familiar legal regimes as conditions of investment, and through the advice and actions of participants in the Law and Development Movement, guided by the belief—partially inspired by Weber's argument that formally rational law best suits the needs of capitalism (Trubek 1972b)[6]—that Western law was a necessary aspect of modernization (see Tamanaha 1995b).

Legal anthropologists studying law and society in the wake of colonization formulated the doctrine of legal pluralism, which has been touted as 'the key concept in a postmodern view of law' (Merry 1992: 358), and crowned as the dominant new paradigm in the sociology and anthropology of law (Griffiths 1995: 201). There are two distinct versions of legal pluralism (Griffiths 1986; Merry 1988). The first, older version applies to the earlier described attempts by colonial legal regimes—often continued by their indigenous successors—to incorporate customary law

---

[6] For a contrary view, see C. A. Jones (1994).

norms into the state legal system. Law in these situations is plural in the sense that different kinds of legal norms and institutions are encompassed within a single state legal system (see Hooker 1975).

The second, newer form of legal pluralism makes the point that there are many 'legal' orders operative in society, of which state law is just one, and often not the most powerful one. This version has been developed primarily by legal anthropologists who studied non-state systems of social order that continued to thrive in the shadow of state law in colonial and post-colonial societies. It was openly apparent to these social scientists that the reach and influence of state law was limited, that the state legal norms were alien to and often inconsistent with the norms people actually followed, and that state law had a relatively minor role in maintaining social order. Under a functional view of law as the maintenance of social order within groups, it made sense to conclude therefrom that there were other 'legal' systems operative in the same social arena. Eugene Ehrlich's theory of 'living law' as the rules of conduct adhered to by people in their routine social behaviour provided a precursor to and source for this view of law. It was but a small and logical step for legal pluralists to also conclude that legal pluralism is a condition of all societies, Western and non-Western (Galanter 1981). According to new legal pluralism, non-state legal orders range from the interstices within, or areas beyond the reach of, state legal systems where custom-based norms and institutions continue to exert social control, to the rule-making and enforcing power of institutions like corporations and universities, to the normative order that exists within small social groups, from unions, to sports leagues, community associations, business associations, clubs, and even the family.

Both versions of legal pluralism are relevant for the purposes of this analysis. The older version is relevant because it describes an ongoing condition prevalent in formerly (and presently) colonized countries around the world, wherein the bulk of the positive law remains law transplanted from elsewhere, often still in the long-departed colonizer's language, unknown and inaccessible to vast portions of the population, available mostly to lawyers and indigenous elites.[7] Positive law in this context cannot be said to mirror social customs or values. The incorporation of customary law, to the extent that it is effective, hardly ameliorates this mismatch because often it operates only on the margins of the law, usually limited to a few subject-matters (like family law). Moreover,

---

[7] For a detailed case study of this kind of situation, see Tamanaha (1993b).

as indicated earlier, serious questions have been raised about whether the results of such attempts at incorporation truly reflect lived customs and values, either because incorporation into the legal system results in distortions, or because what goes by the name of 'customary law' is sometimes comprised of inventions. Too often after decolonization the exploitative colonial legal apparatus was simply taken over by the indigenous elite—including lawyers—for their own benefit.

It might be argued that legal pluralism is consistent with the mirror thesis in so far as it is a reflection of the pluralism of non-Western societies, with their sharp divisions between urban and rural, educated and uneducated, elite and poor, new economy and old economy, modern and traditional, and often with different languages and groups coexisting. According to this view, situations of legal pluralism can be described as a variation of the selective mirror tradition wherein the law operates to the advantage of some within society at the expense of others, though the favoured group in many of these cases is an extremely small and narrow one, sometimes limited to only the legal actors themselves (which would reduce the mirror thesis to the absurd assertion that law is a mirror of itself). Even if the mirror thesis is understood in this way relative to situations of old legal pluralism, new legal pluralism still differs in a significant respect. In the selective mirror tradition state law is an important force in the maintenance of general social order. But in new legal pluralism, at least in the context of non-Western countries, state law is often considered to have a weak role in the maintenance of social order, and to not be an integrated aspect of society. Not only is positive law not a mirror of general social customs and values, under this view, it is a peripheral player in the social context.

New legal pluralism is thus especially relevant because it highlights the point that state law is often powerless—ignored or ineffectual—with regard to the governance of lived social relations in non-Western countries, and perhaps even in certain contexts in Western countries. This weakness is obvious in the rural areas of many non-Western countries, where the legal apparatus is nowhere to be seen. But it is also evident in Western countries, in the sweatshops in the heart of New York City, where labour and safety regulations are ignored, or in South Central Los Angeles, where the state legal presence is weak, or in Chinatowns all over the West, where inhabitants often live by their own set of rules, and fear or avoid state law. State law, in many of these contexts, often does not maintain social order to any substantial degree, and, within these communities, does not reflect lived customs or prevailing social values.

The Implications of Legal Transplantation

To conclude this discussion of legal transplantation, a table of the connection between law and society will be constructed to help illustrate the consequences of transplantation. This table will consist of a set of ideal types based upon the work of the theorists recited earlier, including Maine, Durkheim, Weber, and Unger, among others.

		Traditional society	**Modern society**
SOCIAL ASPECTS		Basic Unit: Family	Basic Unit: Individual
		Collective Orientation	Individual Orientation
		Ascriptive-Based Status	Achievement-Based Status
		Multiplex Relations	Simplex Relations
		Diffuse Roles	Specific Roles
		Shared Values	Anomie or Diverse Values
		No Public–Private Distinction	Public–Private Distinction
LEGAL ASPECTS		Custom Governed	Law Governed
		Status-Based Relations	Contract Based Relations
		Duty Emphasis	Rights Emphasis
		Punitive Oriented	Restitution Oriented
		Irrational (i.e. Ordeals)	Rational
		Substantive Justice	Legal Justice
		Objective is Consensus	Winner/Loser Determined by Rules
		Private Sanction	Public Sanction
		Not Institutionalized	Institutionalized

The first row of the first column represents the social organization of traditional societies; the second row of the first column consists of the legal aspects that accompany and match this form of social organization; the second column provides the same with regard to modern societies. Although the labels 'Traditional' and 'Modern' have been used to mark the contrast, consistent with their characterization in the literature, the terms 'Communitarian' and 'Individualist', or non-Western and Western, or *Gemeinschaft* and *Gesellschaft*, respectively, could also be applied. This table, it should be evident, is a representation of the strong mirror thesis— the characteristics in the bottom row are thought to be directly connected to, and reflect, those in the top, for a given type of society.

A myriad of specific and general objections can be raised against the above categories and their connections. It can be correctly pointed out, for example, that many traditional societies had restitutive law and modern societies have strong punitive dimensions to law; that certain traditional societies were oriented to the application of rules, and had winners and losers, whereas modern legal systems also consider substantive justice and are concerned about achieving a consensus; that traditional societies did consider achievement, while modern societies continue to attach significance to ascriptive status; and that traditional societies had elements of individualism while modern societies have pockets where a communitarian orientation prevails. The most vehement objections raised to contrasts of this sort rail against its apparently evolutionary and ethnocentric implications, which sets up the modern as superior to or at a higher stage than the traditional. I shall not attempt to defend against these and other objections, many with which I agree. And I explicitly disavow any connotation that the right column is superior to the left. No evaluative implications should be attached to either column.

There is another concern with this table which suggests that it should be read with caution. Any representation based upon the work of legal and social theorists assumes that their representations of the law–society relationship are correct at some fundamental level. But the survey of theories in Chapter 2, and the critiques pressed in Chapters 3 and 4, support a suspicion that many are idealized accounts. Many early modern accounts of traditional society were based upon pure speculation, or upon reading travelogues or diaries of adventurers or missionaries, not on actual field investigation. The fact that many theorists have presented roughly overlapping accounts does not of itself establish the truth of these accounts. Many of these theorists were influenced by the work of others, and by shared themes and attitudes permeating the intellectual milieu within which they wrote, especially during the nineteenth-century heyday of evolutionary theorizing.

Cognizant of these concerns, my objective in formulating the table is to draw the contrast in the sharpest possible terms to illustrate the implications of transplantation, given widely held theoretical understandings of the law–society relationship. Consider them ideal types drawn from the accounts of theorists, designed to illuminate what would occur in the purest (and hence non-existent) case. Suffice it to say that the above contrast is a fair representation of the work of legal and social theorists on the subject, and it still dominates theoretical understandings today, as reflected in this recent observation by prominent legal historian and sociologist Lawrence Friedman (1994: 125): 'Modern law presupposes a society of free-standing, autonomous individuals. Many past legal systems were strongly communal; the unit of legal analysis was the family, the clan, the group.' Analysts continue to observe that, at least in modern Asian societies, the 'rule of relationships' predominates over legal regulation, even in the transnational commercial context (C. A. Jones 1994).

To put the point in basic terms, when legal transplantation occurs across two similarly organized societies there is no change in terms of the basic relations specified by the table. But when legal transplantation occurs from a modern (or Western) society to a traditional (or non-Western) one, the legal box on the bottom right-hand corner is superimposed on the social box in the top left-hand corner. The clash that results is evident. Obviously, neither the society nor the law would remain the same. As studies of such situations have shown, society would change because the transplanted laws and legal institutions provide a new resource of power in society for individuals to resort to as a means to escape from, or with which to contest, the traditional order and social understandings (see Tamanaha 1989: 94–6), though people would often also attempt to avoid this alien source of power. The law changes because it operates in a totally different social context. Law in Japan, for example, mainly the product of the transplanted German Civil Code, with certain post-war American influences, completely overlaid by Japanese cultural attitudes and orientation, has a quite different relation to society than law in Germany or the United States (see Chiba 1989; Sanders 1996). The training and nature of the legal profession plays a key role, in some ways helping make the law better fit society but in many ways not. Meanwhile, people and institutions within society react and alter their conduct and attitudes in response to the presence of the transplanted law. Extensive as the consequent changes to society and to law might be, the result of these changes is not necessarily that law and society move entirely in sync; often mismatch, rather than mirror, remains.

The Implications of Globalization

Globalization Generally

No new subject has captured the fancy of current legal and social theorists more than globalization. Globalization means, in essence, that the world is being linked together in a variety of different ways. Advancements in transportation make it possible to go just about anywhere in a day or two, thereby shrinking space; innovations in communication, from the fax machine to the Internet, allow instantaneous communication around the world, thereby shrinking time. American dominated popular and consumer culture, from Hollywood, to Madonna, Coke, and Nike, spans the globe. Multinational corporations and international conglomerates distribute their production facilities around the world, and sell to markets around the world, such that it is difficult to identify a single national home (see Walker and Fox 1996; Thurow 1995). Major financial markets are involved in worldwide equity trading and foreign exchange transfers at huge volumes that dwarf the capacities of nations to control, interconnected in a way such that a crash in one market will immediately affect others (Held 1995: 127–34). Transnational business transactions have become routine. A 'world economy' has come 'into existence which actually has no specifiable territorial base or limits, and which determines, or rather sets limits to, what even the economies of very large and powerful states can do' (Hobsbawn 1994: 277). Ecological events in one nation—like deforestation, the burning of fossil fuel, release of chlorocarbons, use of pesticides, nuclear waste or disasters, pollution of rivers and oceans, over-fishing—unavoidably influence other nations, and sometimes the entire world (Seita 1997). Under globalization, the local has a global influence and the global has a local influence (Giddens 1990: 64). Boaventura de Sousa Santos (1995: 263) distinguished between these, respectively, as 'globalized localisms', wherein a local phenomenon—like the English language or Coca-Cola—becomes global, and 'localized globalisms', wherein local conditions—like the environment—are affected by transnational influences.

Globalization has thus been observed in a variety of different realms—especially economic—and it covers a range of dimensions, from the development of globe-spanning linkages, to worldwide destructive consequences, to intentional harmonizations, to unplanned convergences. In a multitude of different respects, it entails a unification, a coming together, a mutuality of influence, a connectedness or sameness of some kind (including shared suffering), all on a global level.

Social theorist Anthony Giddens (1990: 70–8) identified four institutional dimensions to globalization. First, there is a global political order, dominated by nation states separated along territorial lines (though competing with various non-state political entities above and below the nation state), each with an internal monopoly over the means of violence.

Secondly, there is a capitalist world economy, including commodity and money markets, dominated by the activities of transnational corporations and banks. Thirdly, there is a world military order, involving the world-wide flow of weaponry, the spread of military knowledge (techniques and training), and the development of alliances. Fourthly, there is global spread of industrial development, including the transfer of technology, a shift in the distribution of production, and the development of an international division of labour. A fundamental aspect lying behind each of these dimensions, according to Giddens, is cultural globalization, based upon developments in communication, especially those related to mass media.

One may quibble with Giddens's categories, all of which are interpenetrating and could have been divided differently, but the framework he constructs is helpful in highlighting the different aspects involved. A notable omission from his scheme, however, is any mention of law. Like culture, law in some form or another, from treaties to private contracts to the regulation of markets, to the spread of legal institutions, constitutions, and the rule of law, also lies behind each of these developments. If it can be said that culture has provided the ideational infrastructure for the different dimensions of globalization, then law has provided a part of the formal infrastructure. Law travels with politics and economics, especially in transactions between relative strangers or actors (political or economic) at a social distance.

A growing body of literature,[8] including the inevitable inauguration of the *Journal of Global Legal Studies*, has begun to analyse the various aspects of law in relation to globalization. Among the scholars who specialize in this field, the 'globalization of law' refers to 'the degree to which the whole world lives under a single set of rules' (Shapiro 1993: 37). Judged against this high standard, law is certainly not global and will not be global any time soon. However, there have been tangible developments that point in this direction. One example can be found in assertions that certain universal human rights norms govern over state laws (see Bianchi 1997; Weiner 1992), as occurred with the Nuremberg trials and the Bosnian and Rwandan war crimes trials, recently given a more permanent institutional presence in the creation (or attempted creation) of the International Criminal Court. Other examples are the World Trade Organization and the General Agreement on Tariffs and Trade, which promulgate a basic set of rules and procedures governing trade on a global level. The creation of entities with overarching supra-state structures, like the United Nations

---

[8] The most recent contribution to this literature is William Twining's fascinating and ambitious book, *Globalisation & Legal Theory* (2000).

or the European Union, are another example of unification; as are the enactment of internationally binding treaties like the Law of the Sea Convention, and the drafting of internationally applicable guidelines, albeit not legally binding, like a Code of Conduct for Transnational Corporations.

At the same time, however, there have been countervailing occurrences of nation states breaking up or becoming divided along ethnic or nationalist lines (see Weiner 1992), from the internal destruction of Rwanda and disintegration of former Yugoslavia, to the Quebec separatist movement, to the calls for greater Scottish independence, to the increasing polarization of racial tensions in the United States. According to some analysts, when 'viewed from the ground up, "globalization" does not mean homogenization, but quite the opposite. It means an *intensification* of differences conceived in racial, ethnic, and class terms' (Greenhouse 1994: 23). As Santos (1995: 262) remarked: 'Far from being linear or unambiguous, the process of globalization is highly contradictory and uneven. It takes place through an apparently dialectical process, whereby new forms of globalization occur together with new or renewed forms of localization.' Observers of the situation have thus theorized about a coming together and falling apart at the same time (Barber 1993: 121–7).

The effect of these developments has been to chip away at the sovereignty and the autonomy—two distinct concepts—of the nation state. Sovereignty is a political concept with an internal and an external aspect. The internal aspect holds that the state has 'final and absolute authority' within its territory; the external aspect holds that there is no 'final and absolute' authority above the state (Held 1995: 100). The notion of the direct effect of human rights, for example, cuts back on the internal aspect; while subjection to supra-national authorities (as with the European Union) restricts the external aspect (see Wilhelmsson 1995). 'The result is that large spheres of human interaction have become progressively detached from purely national regulation' (Albrow 1996: 63). A developing framework of transnational legal institutions and regulations is increasingly restricting the state's former power to control affairs within its borders, leading 'to the lament of "loss of sovereignty" ' (ibid.).

Autonomy in this context 'denotes the actual power a nation-state possesses to articulate and achieve policy goals independently' (Held 1995: 100). Examples of the limitations of state power in this context can be seen in the necessity for multilateral action in the Gulf War and in Bosnia, and for coordinated intervention in financial markets to try to control currency speculation. More dramatic examples of a loss of autonomy can be found in former eastern bloc and developing countries, where the provision of loans by the World Bank and the International Monetary Fund have been conditioned on the implementation of 'structural adjustment' and 'good governance' programmes, which include, *inter alia*, cutting government spending, privatization, eliminating fixed exchange rates for currency, instituting a free market, and implementing the rule of law (see Tamanaha 1995b; Greider 1997: 34–5), policies which have extraordinary internal social, political, economic and legal implications.

Historian Eric Hobsbawn (1994: 576) described recent events in terms of a pincer-like squeeze on the state:

> The nation-state was eroded in two ways, from above and below. It was rapidly losing power and function to various supra-national entities, and, indeed, absolutely, inasmuch as the disintegration of large states and empires produced a multiplicity of smaller ones, too weak to defend themselves in an era of international anarchy. It was also, as we have seen, losing its monopoly of effective power and its historic privileges within its borders, as witness the rise of private security or protection and the rise of private courier services to compete with the post, hitherto virtually everywhere managed by a state ministry.

It might be observed that many of these apparent restrictions on sovereignty and autonomy have been incurred voluntarily, but 'voluntary' is not the same as 'by choice' rather than out of necessity. Martin Albrow (1996: 52–68), a leading theorist of globalization and its effects, argues that the key event that marks the end of the modern epoch and the beginning of the Global Age is precisely the loss of the state's ability to control new forms of social organization, including those related to the economic, political, cultural and legal realms. Circumstances have overcome the nation state's ability to independently determine its own course.

Matching the apparently contradictory notions of a simultaneous coming together and falling apart are two political theories, respectively, 'liberal internationalism' touting the coming of a new unified world order, and the 'new medievalism', which projects 'a shift away from the state—up, down, and sideways—to supra-state, sub-state, and, above all, non-state actors' (Slaughter 1997: 183–4). International and comparative law scholar Anne-Marie Slaughter (p. 184) offers a third model:

> A new world order is emerging, with less fanfare but more substance than either the liberal internationalist or new medievalist visions. The state is not disappearing, it is disaggregating into its separate, functionally distinct parts. These parts—courts, regulatory agencies, executives, and even legislatures—are networking

with their counterparts abroad, creating a dense web of relations that constitutes a new, transgovernmental order. Today's international problems—terrorism, organized crime, environmental degradation, money laundering, bank failure, and securities fraud—created and sustain these relations.

Each of these three models can find support in recent events, and all may well capture an aspect of where we are headed.

As the specific examples cited above reveal, however, the phenomenon of globalization and its influence on law varies by country and by subject-matter. Much of it is occurring predominantly in the West. It is also evident that much of the talk is more so anticipatory, or promotional, than real (see Twining 2000). Academics have sometimes discussed the direct effect of human rights as if it were a fait accompli, but the continuing reality of state oppression and a general lack of enforcement indicates otherwise. The same is true of talk among international law scholars about the New International Economic Order and the Common Heritage of Mankind, themes which advocate a more equitable international economic system and distribution of resources. Power continues to vest decisively in the nation state (though more so with some nations than others), and the international law system is still substantially based on the power and political interests and acquiescence of sovereign states. Although the trends involved in globalization are real enough, especially in the economic realm, it is difficult to know or anticipate their pace or long-term consequences for law and society. Certainly the potential impact is tremendous in a variety of ways large and small.

For the purposes of this study, a particular emphasis will be placed on two aspects of the globalization of law which have been, or are in the process of being, relatively well established: the development of a transnational law of commercial transactions, and of a transnational legal culture.

Transnational Commercial Law

Analysts have increasingly recognized the emergence of a more or less discrete body of law that governs transnational commercial transactions. This body consists of codes like the Vienna Convention on Contracts for the International Sale of Goods, the Convention on the Settlement of Investment Disputes, the UNIDROIT Principles for International Commercial Contracts, and the Uniform Customs and Practice for Documentary Credits; of customs and usages, and general principles, followed by merchants in transnational transactions; of terms or clauses regularly included in standard contracts (especially INCOTERMS, issued by the International Chamber of Commerce); and of the frequent use of international arbitration to resolve disputes, with a small but growing body of arbitration decisions.[9] This sundry collection of economic-related laws constitutes, according to some theorists, 'a kind of trans-national common law' (Friedman 1996: 75).

What makes this body of law especially worthy of note is that, although it takes place on a backdrop of national legal systems and rules, it is autonomous from these systems in several important respects (De Ly 1992: 209, 272–91, 319–20). It has developed over time through the activities and practices of the international community of merchants and their lawyers, constituting a blend of influences from the common law and civil law, and exists in a form not linked to any single national legal system (Trakman 1983: 23–44). To the contrary, the use of international commercial arbitration to resolve disputes is aimed at avoiding national courts and traditional conflict of law rules, and has been a particularly important aspect of the development of this body of law (see Sassen 1996: 37–8; Dezalay and Garth 1996). There may be appeals to national courts, but national courts have often deferred to arbitration decisions (De Ly 1992: 80–131). Transnational commercial practices and the intent of the parties, not state law, provides the primary guidance to the arbitrators' interpretation of the contracts. The result is a 'set of rules with respect to international transactions which are to a certain extent de-politicized and legal system-indifferent' (Grosheide 1994: 74). 'Thus, there emerges a global commercial law independent of any global law giver or enforcer, although dependent on national legal and judicial insti-tutions already long in place' (Shapiro 1993: 39).

Analysts (mostly European)[10] have dubbed this transnational body of law the new *lex mercatoria*. The original *lex mercatoria*, or law of merchants, developed around the seventeenth century (and by some accounts ear-lier) through trading activities around the Mediterranean Sea. Initially it consisted of an independent system of tribunals manned by persons ex-perienced in commercial activities, selected by other merchants, located in fairs or trading centres, disconnected from the state legal or court sys-tems (Trakman 1983: 7–21). Decisions were based upon unwritten rules and practices followed by merchants, with certain Roman law influences. Ultimately the *lex mercatoria* was absorbed into the increasingly powerful

---

[9] For background on this body of law, see De Ly (1992); Trakman (1983); Grosheide (1994); Gessner (1994); Bonell (1992); Jokela (1990).

[10] According to Dezalay and Garth (1996: 39–42), Anglo-American practitioners have tended to oppose resort to the *lex mercatoria*, which they consider too academic.

European states, and many of the rules were incorporated by these states into commercial codes (Merryman 1985: 12–13, 98–9). Although a similar fate may ultimately befall the current *lex mercatoria,* or it may be absorbed into an overarching international (or transnational)[11] legal order with public and private law rules, for now it has an independent and thriving existence.

Transnational Legal Culture

One of the sources contributing to the development of the new *lex mercatoria,* though also an independent development in its own right, is the ongoing creation of a transnational legal culture. Legal culture is a term with many different meanings (see Nelken 1995; Friedman 1969a, 1975). Here I use it to refer to the law-related ideas, knowledge, beliefs, and attitudes of legal specialists.

There are several distinct aspects to the development of a transnational legal culture. A core component has to do with a notable growth in the number of law students, lawyers, and legal academics enhancing their background and credentials by studying at law schools abroad (see Daly1996: 301–9). A good deal of this occurs in LL M. programmes in law schools in the United States, which attract students from around the globe (Wiegand 1991: 230–4; Symposium 1996). 'Graduate study in U.S. law schools is now one of the key items necessary to build a resume for a non-U.S. practitioner' (Dezalay and Garth 1996: 313). Students also go from the United States and elsewhere to Europe, and a pan-European programme designed to help build a common culture has been instituted to allow European students to receive credit for a year of legal study in other European countries (Gessner 1994: 136). So substantial is this phenomenon that some commentators have likened it to the dissemination of a new *ius commune* across Europe, one influenced by American law (Wiegand 1991: 230–1). Another factor contributing to the formulation of a transnational legal culture is the growing academic discipline of comparative law, which has participating scholars from all over the world. Comparative law conferences, professional associations, and journals generate a worldwide community of discourse, creating a baseline of

[11] Although analytical consistency will not necessarily determine what label prevails, the term 'transnational' is preferable to 'international'. Reflecting the background of international law, the term 'international' emphasizes relations between states. Whereas globalization suggests a lessening in the power of states, and the development of relations between a world system and individuals, and among individuals across national borders (see Walker and Fox 1996: 380).

shared knowledge and terminology. Another contributing factor is the hiring of foreign lawyers in domestic firms (see Pardieck 1996), and the growth of international law firms, with branch offices all over the world, though mostly involving US-based law firms (Taylor 1994; Daly 1996: 308–13). Large US law firms, especially, owing to the clients' economic power, have had a notable influence in shaping transnational commercial law, both in its content and its style (Dezalay and Garth 1996: 51–7; Grosheide 1994: 75). Owing to the various mentioned influences of the United States, the transnational legal culture has an 'Americanized' bent, with English serving as the main lingua franca.

A final factor contributing to the development of a transnational legal culture refers back to the point made by Watson, that legal professionals tend to see law as special or apart, which provides a sense of affinity with other lawyers regardless of national borders. Evidence in support of this view can be found in judging:

> Judges are building a global community of law. They share values and interests based upon their belief in law as distinct but not divorced from politics and their view of themselves as professionals who must be insulated from direct political influence. . . . National and international judges are networking, becoming increasingly aware of one another and of their stake in a common enterprise. The most informal level of transnational judicial contact is knowledge of foreign and international judicial decisions and a corresponding willingness to cite them. (Slaughter 1997: 186)

The trend towards citation of the decisions of courts of other nations is a concrete sign of a developing transnational legal culture.

Admittedly, one must be cautious about projecting the creation of a law of transnational commercial transactions and legal culture on a global basis. The above description reveals that they are largely, though not exclusively, located in Anglo-America and Europe. But these are real developments, which have established at least the rudiments of an effective global reach, with the promise of becoming further solidified.

Implications of Globalization for the Law–Society Paradigm

Globalization is relevant for the law–society paradigm in two basic ways.

First, it indicates that important sources of social, political, and (especially) economic-related lawmaking produce direct legal consequences within society, despite the fact that they are in many respects autonomous of that society. An example are commercial rules, like the *lex mercatoria*, which come from outside, generated by actors not accountable to that society. They are based on and determined by external market-based economic interests and concerns, which often purport to be devoid of value underpinnings or implications, yet implicitly carry value presuppositions and have value consequences. Another example are legal, political, and economic reforms routinely forced upon countries seeking economic aid from international lenders and relief agencies. A multitude of other examples exist, more 'voluntary' in nature, ranging from legal reforms necessary for membership in the GATT or the European Union, to the adoption of child and sweatshop labour regulations to satisfy consumer groups from abroad. In each of these cases local conditions, customs, and values have a minimal influence on the creation of the law, though they will experience the consequences of its implementation. More broadly and speculatively speaking, if the trends identified above towards a greater degree of the globalization of law, and towards the development and solidification of a transnational legal culture, are borne out to a significant extent, then a great deal of the law applicable within a society will be born elsewhere and instituted for external reasons.

Secondly, globalization raises doubts about the coherence of the two essential elements of the law–society paradigm: 'law' and 'society'. In both social and legal theory, society has been seen typically in terms of the state-society unit (Albrow 1996: 41–4). Within this unit, law is considered a crucial element that serves to both constitute the state and to integrate society. Legal positivists have conceptually conjoined law and state to be a law-state, with society delimited by the territorial boundaries of the state. The state possesses a monopoly on the legitimate use of force and determines the legal rules operative within society. Globalization, however, suggests that state law no longer exclusively regulates relations within society, but instead different bodies of 'official' law are in play, many of which are generated from outside. Moreover, as alluded to earlier, legal pluralists have made the claim, on a micro scale, that state law is not the only kind of 'law' operative within society, that other manifestations of law coordinate social interaction, often to a greater extent than state law. This challenge to state law from various directions problematizes the very notion of 'law', throwing into doubt the commonly assumed understanding of law's relation to society.

Globalization also throws doubt into the notion of 'society'. From the Greek city-state to the modern territorial state, 'society' has always implied a relatively bounded existence, with the boundaries usually defined in political terms as coextensive with the authority of the state, and often tied to the notion of a nation with a shared culture and language. With globalization—the shrinking of time and space and the increase in transnational transactions and influences, including the media and Internet, which are gradually rendering territorial borders irrelevant; and the removal of national borders for citizens within the European Union—it is becoming increasingly difficult to identify the boundaries of society. Formerly, society was 'significantly delimited by the jurisdictional reach of legal systems' (Cotterrell 1997: 77). '[L]aw and society are almost mutually defining' (ibid.). However, with the problematization of law's claim to exclusivity within society, just identified, law no longer provides a secure means of locating societal boundaries. Talcott Parsons (1966) defined society both in terms of an exclusive government-based legal system with 'final control' (pp. 14–16), and in terms of cultural and normative self-sufficiency (pp. 16–17). It cannot be asserted with confidence that these conditions hold anywhere today. Understandably, social theorists have lately suggested that the concept of society should be discarded (Giddens 1990: 63–4; Bauman 1992: 190).

One possible strategy to maintain the concept of society is to conclude that the process of globalization involves 'the expansion of an international civil society' (Sassen 1996: 40). The globalization of law then is matched by the globalization of society. Attractive as the idea of a global civil society might be, however, under present conditions the links are so attenuated that such a claim stretches the concept of 'society' to the point of all encompassing elasticity, rendering it meaningless. Another suggested possibility is to discard the society paradigm, and talk about a free-standing global legal structure or system attached to transnational economic transactions. As one analyst put it, 'global legal interaction is a social system of its own, with states, enterprises, private citizens and lawyers as its actors and with structural as well as cultural elements as its basic dimensions' (Gessner 1994: 144). Similarly, another commentator combined the aspects within various national legal systems relating to these subjects to constitute a separate subsystem: 'Together these national domains of international business law can be labeled as a legal sub-system in its own right with particular underlying social and economic conditions' (Grosheide 1994: 81). These accounts also smack of stretching—there simply is not enough of a concrete and discrete form to constitute a separate 'structure' or 'system' in any sense other than as a construct of the analyst.

The long-standing, comfortable self-contained law–society paradigm has been rendered obsolete by globalization (Twining 1996: 119–20, 139). Few alternatives have been proposed, and none have gained widespread acceptance.

Revisting the 'Gap Problem'

More than a few socio-legal scholars reading this work will have heard echoes in the discussion of a familiar old theme: the gap problem. At one time the gap problem was 'the central issue for studies about law' (Abel 1973a: 189). A heated controversy raged about two decades ago within socio-legal studies regarding the appropriateness and fruitfulness of this focus (Nelken 1981), although it has since died down as attention has turned to other matters. There are two distinct versions of the gap problem. The first version is the gap between 'law-in-the-books' and 'law-in-action'—the gap between the written law and actual the practices of lawyers and judges. This gap was a favourite subject of the Legal Realists, who made the point that the real law consists of what legal actors do, not the 'paper' law (Llewellyn 1930). The second version is the gap between the legal rules and what people in the community actually do. Studies of the latter gap went under the rubric of the 'inefficacy of law' or efficacy studies. While it is useful to see that there are points of overlap between some of the themes discussed herein and the gap problem, a complete identification of this approach with the gap problem would be more misleading than correct.

The useful aspect of the association is to see that the very point of the second version of the gap problem is that, in each situation in which the gap exists, law is not in fact a mirror of society. Studies of the gap problem revealed that the existence of a gap is a regular feature of Western societies (Abel 1973a, 1978). Inefficacy studies showed that the gap is an even more striking feature of law in developing countries, for many of the reasons indicated in the earlier discussion of transplanted law (see Friedman 1969b). Thus, the findings of these studies can be incorporated into the analysis suggested here.

Another value of these studies is that they help clarify what is at issue in the question of mirroring. Two levels, with a total of four variables, are involved. Level one, comprising law, involves: (a) the law in the books; and (b) the actual practices of legal actors with regard to those laws. Level two, comprising society, involves: (a) the morals and customs espoused by people in social groups; and (b) the actual practices of people in those groups. Further gradations can be made, such as separating customs from morality, depending upon the specific concern at hand. The fullest sense of mirroring occurs when written law and legal practices actually match the morals and customs espoused and actually practised by people. Any study of the degree of mirroring should at least examine whether this is the case. But it is also informative to examine other possible variations and dimensions of mirroring between the first and second levels; for example, observing that the law in the books and espoused morality match, but that the actual practices of legal actors and/or people in the social group do not.

The misleading aspect of the association has to do with the assumption or orientation underlying the formulation of the gap problem. This orientation is reflected in use of the label 'problem' or 'inefficacy'. The underlying assumption is that there is a problem that has to be solved, or that the law has to be made more efficacious. Concomitant with this assumption is the sense that the presence of a gap consists of a deviation, that even if it is a regular occurrence, it is still an aberrant or marginal phenomenon relative to the normal state of law. All such connotations are rejected herein. It may well be that presence of a degree of lack of mirroring is a normal state of relations between law and society (Abel 1973a: 221). Almost by definition, this will be true of all stratified or pluralistic societies. It is certainly the normal state for many formerly colonized countries. It may also be the case that, when a mismatch exists, the proper solution is not to make the law more efficacious, but to abolish the law, or to seek other ways to change society. Or maybe a mismatch is, all things considered, the best solution for a complex social problem, in which it is good that the law espouses certain rules, and it is good that the legal actors take no action to effectuate them, or that people ignore them.

Another misleading aspect of the association is that this work aims at a higher level of generality than gap studies, which were oriented towards specific laws and legal regimes. The mirror thesis that forms the centrepiece of this work is viewed in terms of an idealized theoretical description of the relationship between law and society. Karl Llewellyn (1930: 461) eloquently voices this idealized description:

One matter does need mention here, however: the eternal dilemma of the law, indeed of society; and of the law because the law purports peculiarly among our institutions to 'represent' the whole. There is, amid the welter of self-serving groups, clamoring and struggling over this machine that will give power over others, the recurrent emergence of some wholeness, some sense of responsibility which outruns enlightened self-interest, and results in action apparently headed (often purposefully) for the common good.

That claim—the eternal dilemma—is what this book takes as its concern.

6 A Socio-Legal Positivist Approach to Law

Tracing and challenging the leading theoretical accounts of the relationship between law and society, and juxtaposing them with empirical developments, which has occupied the last four chapters, has both demonstrated the power and pervasiveness of the mirror thesis, and has suggested reasons to be sceptical of it. It has also resulted in the necessity to reconceptualize the very notions of 'law' and 'society'. In this and the following chapter, the notion of law will be taken up. There is no issue more daunting in legal theory. As H. L. A. Hart (1961: 1) noted, 'Few questions concerning human society have been asked with such persistence and answered by serious thinkers in so many diverse, strange, and even paradoxical ways as the question "What is law?" ' Despite its complexity, the question is unavoidable for any attempt at a general jurisprudence.

Hart's analysis of the concept of law and his account of legal positivism will serve as the point of departure for the general jurisprudence constructed here, for two reasons in particular. First, his general jurisprudence and his analysis of the concept of law are the most refined attempts extant. His reduction of law to the union of primary and secondary rules appears to capture a fundamental insight about the basic elements that constitute law, and he applies this reduction to illuminate many longstanding jurisprudential issues. Hart's core analysis has survived relatively unscathed following forty years of critique. With the notable exception of Ronald Dworkin's engagement, much of the discussion today consists of refinements and modifications of Hart's theory, rather than outright repudiations. Yet few would say that we have achieved a general jurisprudence as a result of his work. This failure, despite its extraordinary success in other respects, suggests that his analysis contains debilitating, though perhaps hidden, limitations. A close critical analysis will reveal the limitations located in his approach to the concept of law. In the course of this analysis, I will hold Hart, and myself, to the standards Hart set for himself, both in terms of what he proposed to be the measure of his concepts and in terms of his overall aim.

Concepts that specify what law is are not right or wrong, or testable or falsifiable. Felix Cohen observed, informed by pragmatism, that 'A definition of law is *useful* or *useless*; it is not *true* or *false*' (1935: 835). Its use value is determined by the purposes for which the concept of law is constructed (see Bix 1995). Hart acknowledged that there is more than one way to conceptualize law. 'If we are to make a reasoned choice between these concepts, it must be because one is superior to the other in the way in which it will assist our theoretical inquiries, or advance and clarify our moral deliberations, or both' (pp. 204–5). The ultimate test for the approach to law I set out, consistent with the goals of a general jurisprudence, is whether it enhances our ability to describe, understand, and evaluate legal phenomena across a variety of contexts.

Hart (1994: 239) identified his aim 'to provide a theory of what law is which is both *general* and *descriptive*' (emphasis added). I will argue that he was not general enough and not descriptive enough. Despite his avowed intentions, his concept of law was not capable of accounting for the many variations of legal phenomena in different cultures and times, and his account was not as value neutral has he apparently thought. My argument recognizes that Hart was substantially correct in his identification of primary and secondary rules (though wrong in some of the conditions he attached to them); however, his abstraction from state law provided too limited a base upon which to construct a general jurisprudence. I propose to shift to a higher level of generality, to place Hart's analysis under a broader umbrella and resituate it as one (key) part of what is a more expansive baseline. The non-essentialist version of legal pluralism elaborated in the following chapter will provide the encompassing baseline. This socio-legal positivist approach to law and non-essentialist legal pluralism will provide the conceptualization of law to be utilized in the general jurisprudence.

The second reason for using Hart as a point of departure is programmatic in nature. In a previous work (1997), drawing upon pragmatism at the levels of epistemology and methodology, I systematically argued for, and tried to effectuate, a closer association between legal theory and the cluster of social scientific approaches to law that gather under the label socio-legal studies. Here I take that project a step further. The goal of constructing a general jurisprudence is classically identified with legal positivism. But many socio-legal scholars have set themselves in rigid opposition to legal positivism, despite the fact that Hart's (1961: p. v) self-described aim was to produce a work in 'descriptive sociology'. Conversely, legal theory has traditionally evinced an almost studied disregard for the insights of socio-legal studies. This reciprocal disdain (almost) is mistaken, in my view. Legal theory operates at risk of error and irrelevance if sound findings about the social reality of law are ignored.

Hart's descriptive bent, his emphasis on social practices, and the general legal positivist insistence on the separation of law and morality, are all consistent with the empiricist orientation of the social sciences. My adoption of the label *socio*-legal positivism signals that I encounter legal positivism from the direction of the social scientific study of law in the hope of more closely realizing Hart's aim. A legal positivism reconstructed in the manner I propose provides a framework amenable to the interests and concerns of those engaged in the social scientific study of law, and it provides a bridge which will render this work more relevant to the interests and concerns of legal theorists. These programmatic concerns are secondary, however, to the main point: this merged approach will provide a theoretically sophisticated and empirically informed way to understand law and its relationship with society.

The analysis will begin by describing and criticizing Hart's concept of law, and the conditions he attached to primary and secondary rules. The vehicle for this critical analysis will be an exploration of the tensions contained within his simultaneous resort to conventionalism, essentialism, and functionalism. The analysis of Hart's functionalism is especially relevant because it bears on the argument pressed throughout this book regarding the problematic assumption that the function of law is to maintain social order. Following the critique, the basic elements of the socio-legal positivist approach to law will be set out

The Tensions within Hart's Concept of Law

Conventionalism, Essentialism, and Functionalism

Despite his admirable clarity, it is not easy to pin down precisely the nature of Hart's concept of law. Some theorists label it an 'essentialist' approach to the concept of law (Jules Coleman 1998: 389–90; M. Moore 1998: 313), while others characterize it as 'anti-essentialist' (Green 1996: 1692); some label it functionalist (Dworkin 1977: 347–9; Soper 1998: 363), and others (including Hart (1994: 248–9)) deny that is it function-based (Green 1996: 1709–11). Many theorists also label it a conventionalist approach. The problem with this combination is that conventionalism, functionalism, and essentialism can directly conflict, or pull in different directions. Nonetheless, there is a sense in which each one of these labels is correct when applied to Hart's concept of law.

Hart's approach is *conventionalist* at two different levels. It is conventionalist at the very outset of the enquiry in the sense that he relies upon ordinary usage to identify the social phenomena to which the label 'law' is attached. Having so identified law, it is conventionalist in the further sense that he relies upon the social practices of legal officials to identify the rules of recognition (see Marmor 1998). For the purposes of this analysis, I am primarily concerned with the former resort to conventionalism, whereby he identified—or, more accurately, stipulated—state law to be the central case of what we conventionally mean by 'law' (Hart 1961: 13–17).

Once he located this central or paradigm case, Hart shifted to a predominantly conceptual analysis to discern the *essence* of law. This conceptual analysis consisted of abstracting from the observed characteristics of state legal systems to arrive at the conclusion that, at base, law consists of a system of rules (secondary) about rules (primary). For Hart, this dual rule structure, grounded in social practices, best captures law's institutional character. Jules Coleman (1998: 389–90) described the way in which Hart's concept of law is essentialist: 'It begins by asking whether there are features of law that are essential, or, in an appropriate sense, necessary to law or to our concept of it: essential to our concept in the sense that a social practice that fails to have them could not qualify as law.'

There are a number of respects in which Hart's concept of law can be considered *functional*. First, he explicitly described it in such terms. At several points in *The Concept of Law* he states that law is one among several mechanisms of 'social control' (pp. 165, 188, 208). Early on he asserted that 'law is used to control, to guide, and to plan life out of court' (p. 39). Even when Hart (1994: 249) specifically denied that his account of law is functional, he did so in terms that confirmed that it is: 'In fact I think it is quite vain to seek any more specific purpose which law as such serves beyond providing guides to human conduct and standards of criticism of such conduct.' To state that law is a mechanism of social control, that it controls and guides conduct, is to assert that law has these functions (see Soper 1998: 363–4). Secondly, his (1961: 89–96) discussion of customary societies that contain only primary rules—arguing that they are too static, uncertain, and inefficient—drew the conclusion that they are deficient precisely because they are not ideal in carrying out law's function of maintaining normative order. Thirdly, his (pp. 189–95) acknowledgement that there is a minimum content of natural law was based upon the necessary function that law has in preserving order under conditions of scarcity and limited altruism. Finally, and most importantly, Hart's view that law is functional gave rise to the first of his two necessary conditions

for the existence of a legal system: that the primary rules must be generally obeyed by the populace (p. 113). He observed that it is pointless to
assert that a legal system exists if private citizens do not generally abide
by its rules (pp. 100–1). Hart's account of law is not Functionalist in
Durkheim's sociological sense, in terms of the organic metaphor of law as
a subsystem within society; nor does he characterize law as a functional
kind (see e.g. M. Moore 1992). Rather it is functionalist in the sense that
he characterizes law in (necessarily) functional terms, as an effective
mechanism for the coordination of behaviour and social control, such
that a non-functioning law does not qualify as a legal system. Law is what
it does, in other words, and what it does is carry out these functions.

These various influences give rise to several tensions within Hart's concept of law. The exploration of these tensions will suggest key modifications of his concept.

The Relationship between Essentialism and Functionalism

There is no necessary conflict between essentialism and functionalism.
When the essence of law is defined in functional terms, the two coincide
(see e.g. ibid.). However, when the essence and the function are defined
in different terms, the possibility of two different kinds of divergences
arises. An analysis of how Hart's concept of law relates to these divergences will reveal surprising insights.

1. Implications of Function But Not Essence, and Function and Essence

The first divergence occurs when a phenomenon satisfies the function but
lacks the essential structure. There are many mechanisms that guide conduct and maintain social order, moral norms being a good example, but
also including language, habits, and customs, among others. In social life,
it is often the case that different phenomena can satisfy the same function
(Merton 1968: 86–91). Functionalist theory labels this the existence of
functional equivalents or alternatives. Although various mechanisms satisfy the function of law, it does not follow therefrom that we should
append the label 'law' to all of them. Thus, the question remains of how
to identify the distinctively legal from among these various candidates.
That is where the essential structure comes into play.

Hart uses the presence of secondary rules as the criterion to distinguish
'legal' systems from other means of social control—the distinctive nature
of law entails *institutionalized* norm enforcement (Hart 1994: 249). Hans

Kelsen (1945: 20) described the distinction as follows: 'the reaction of law consists in a measure of coercion enacted by the [legal] order, and socially organized, whereas the moral reaction against immoral conduct is neither provided by the moral order, nor, if provided, socially organized.'[1] As Joseph Raz (1979: 105) observed, 'Many, if not all, legal philosophers have been agreed that one of the defining features of law is that it is an institutionalized normative system.' A majority of social scientists, prominently including Max Weber (1954: 13) and Adamson Hoebel (1954: 28), have similarly pointed to the institutionalized enforcement of norms as the factor that distinguishes legal from non-legal forms of social control, and a number of social scientists have adopted Hart's formulation to provide their test for 'law' (see Galanter 1981; Bohannan 1965).

With this solution, it appeared that Hart was able to match essence (institutionalized structure of secondary and primary rules) with function, eliminating functional equivalents that are lacking this structure. However, Hart's resort to secondary rules was not as effective in distinguishing 'legal' from non-legal systems of social control as he apparently believed. Hart's concept of law has been adopted by many 'legal pluralists', who assert that society consists of a multitude of 'legal' institutions with rule-making and rule-enforcing power, from corporations to universities, to community associations, to sports leagues (see Galanter 1981). All of these institutions exert social control through administering a system of secondary and primary rules. The problematic implications of this view of law will be taken up in greater detail in the following chapter. For the moment the crucial point is that Hart undoubtedly would have rejected the claim that these phenomena are forms of 'law', despite the fact that they technically satisfy his criteria. Indeed social life is thick with phenomena that share law's structural essence and functions, as defined by Hart, phenomena that he would not have wanted to call 'law'. These are essentialist *and* functionalist equivalents, but not conceptual or conventionalist equivalents (in the sense that general usage does not attach the label 'law' to these institutions).

This observation reveals a significant omission in Hart's concept of law. Both Weber and Hoebel emphasized that law consists of the *public* institutionalized enforcement of norms. Hart did not explicitly include this element in his definition because, writing from a jurisprudential

---

[1] For Kelsen (1945: 18–29), the key to distinguishing law from other sources of social order is that law consists of the 'technique' of regulating behaviour as a form of organized coercion. He (1945: 19) declared: 'the law is a coercive order.' And again, 'Law is an organization of force' (p. 21).

standpoint that takes state law as a starting point, he simply presupposed the status of the legal officials as public. Hart repeatedly refers to 'private persons and officials' assuming we know who comprises the latter group. But absent an explicit reference establishing *who* administers the secondary rules—determining who qualifies as legal officials—Hart's concept of law inexorably leads to the legal pluralist position. To put the point summarily, Hart's secondary rules can distinguish 'law' from non-institutionalized forms of normative order (like morals and customs), but it cannot distinguish 'law' from other sorts of institutionalized normative systems (like corporations). Hart paid attention to the former problem but not the latter. He is missing a fundamental feature in the identification of law.

Unlike Hart, Raz explicitly addresses the issue of how to distinguish law from other forms of institutionalized norm enforcement like universities and sports clubs. Raz (1979: 116) asserts that 'We would regard an institutionalized system as a legal one only if it is necessarily in some respect the most important institutionalized system which can exist in that society.' He (pp. 116–20) then identifies three features which characterize legal systems: (1) legal systems are comprehensive in the sense that 'they claim authority to regulate any type of behavior'; (2) legal systems claim supremacy over all other institutionalized normative systems in society; and (3) legal systems are 'open systems' in the sense that they 'maintain and support other forms of social grouping'. As a consequence of these features, according to Raz (p. 121), the 'law provides the general framework within which social life takes place'.

There are serious problems with Raz's account. First, state legal systems are not alone in satisfying his three features. Many systems of religious law, for example, claim comprehensiveness and supremacy, and to provide support for other social groupings (like the family). Raz, however, is reluctant to grant them full status as legal systems.[2] A second, more serious problem is that Raz's strictures would force the conclusion that there were no legal systems throughout much of Europe during the medieval period. During this period several recognized bodies of law co-existed—including ecclesiastical, feudal, merchant, manorial, royal, and municipal—which did not typically claim to regulate all types of behaviour, and did not claim supremacy over all other normative systems (Berman 1983; Ullmann 1969: 71). The notions of comprehensiveness

---

[2] He (1979: 118) grants that religious law might be a 'borderline case'. In an earlier work, *The Concept of a Legal System*, Raz (1980: 207) suggested that religious law could indeed qualify as a 'legal system', though it is not clear that he continues to adhere to this position.

and supremacy are connected to the view that state law possesses a monopoly over the application of force within its jurisdiction, a view also adopted by Kelsen (1945: 21). Although it has been taken for granted for some time, this core legal positivist view gained currency only after—and was an aspect of—the consolidation of the power of the state, which in historical terms is a relatively recent development. A third problem is that it is not clear that even state legal systems today meet Raz's conditions. Many theorists as well as citizens would say that there are protected spheres of private activity which the law has no power over (thus it is not comprehensive), and many would assert that there are normative orders superior to law (like religion or morality). Raz qualifies his account by asserting that what counts is that legal systems *claim* comprehensiveness and supremacy. But it is not obvious that legal systems routinely make such claims, especially those systems understood in terms of limited law-making powers obtained by delegation from the people. The notions of comprehensiveness and supremacy are especially dubious when one considers that in many societies today there are several 'legal' systems asserting authority within the same jurisdictions. Consider, for example, that citizens in European countries are subject to national law, the law of the European Union, public and private international law, as well as the direct effect of human rights (i.e. the International War Crimes Tribunal, and the trials of the East German border guards), not to forget other applicable bodies of law like the *lex mercatoria* and the GATT, as well as various bodies of religious law for adherents. In the context of such various competing and overlapping claims to authority, it makes little sense to give primacy to the features of comprehensiveness and supremacy. Finally, Raz's assertion that the legal system provides the general framework for social life is implausible as an empirical matter. This view of the predominance of law in social life is commonplace among jurisprudence scholars, for whom law looms large, but it is sharply contested by sociologists, who have often demonstrated that law is not the primary source of social order. For all of these reasons, Raz's account of what distinguishes legal systems from other forms of institutionalized normative systems fails.

Weber and Hoebel's use of the 'public' element to make the distinction is also unsatisfactory, as the earlier critique of the public/private distinction made clear. We must return to, and supplement, Hart's analysis to locate the necessary distinction. It might be argued that the identification of legal officials is subsumed within his notion of secondary rules. However, Hart's discussion of primary and secondary rules appears to presuppose the separation of legal officials from private citizens, in the sense that it is the special province of the legal officials to work with secondary rules, especially the rule of recognition, in the identification and application of primary rules. Thus, it would seem that the emergence of the legal officials must be accounted for *before* we can talk about them working with secondary rules to produce and apply primary rules.

Another argument might be that the *first* secondary rule identifies the legal officials, who thereafter go about their task of doing things with secondary rules. Hart (1961: 93) suggested this response when he identified the simplest secondary rule as 'that which empowers an individual or body of persons to introduce new primary rules for the conduct of life of the group, or of some class within it, and to eliminate old rules'. This interpretation, while it works, would not fit precisely within Hart's (p. 92) characterization of secondary rules as being administered by legal officials to identify and apply primary rules. At least one secondary rule, by this account, precedes the existence of legal officials; but then who (and how do we know who?) has the capacity to interpret and apply this primordial rule, and where do they get this authority from (if not the primordial rule itself)? The argument would be that non-legal and/or legal officials follow the primordial rule to identify legal officials, who (thus enfranchised) proceed to apply the rule of recognition to identify and apply primary rules.

A better response would be to avoid the chicken and egg problem by asserting that the recognition of legal officials, and the emergence of secondary rules, are contemporaneous events, both grounded in social practices. An implicit basis for this solution can be found in Hart's (pp. 59–60) discussion of the continuity of a legislature:

Plainly, general acceptance is here a complex phenomenon, in a sense divided between official and ordinary citizens, who contribute to it and so to the *existence* of a legal system in different ways. The officials of the system may be said to acknowledge explicitly such fundamental rules conferring legislative authority: the legislators do this when they make laws in accordance with the rules which empower them to do so: the courts when they identify, as laws to be applied by them, the laws made by those thus qualified, and the experts when they guide the ordinary citizen by reference to the laws so made. The ordinary citizen manifests his acceptance largely by acquiescence in the results of these official operations. He keeps the law which is made and identified in this way, and also makes claims and exercises powers conferred by it.

Consistent with his focus on law as a system of rules and his consequent overlooking of the people whose activities give rise to the rules, in the above passage Hart does not specifically address the status of the legal actors themselves, only their products or 'results'. To make explicit what Hart left implicit, the key to the existence of a legal system is that private citizens and legal officials conventionally act as if the products of certain persons—whom they treat as 'legal officials'—are 'law'.

This view of legal officials and legal institutions is consistent with, and derived from, the theory of the social construction of reality (Berger and Luckmann 1966). As philosopher John Searle (1995: 117) pointed out: 'The secret of understanding the continued existence of institutional facts is simply that the individuals directly involved and a sufficient number of members of the relevant community must continue to recognize the existence of such facts. Because the status is constituted by its collective acceptance, and because the function, in order to be performed, requires the status, it is essential to the functioning that there be continued acceptance of the status.'

Remaining with Hart's resort to social practices, the following additional requirement solves the problem of distinguishing legal from non-legal institutionalized systems of normative order: *A 'legal' official is whomever, as a matter of social practice, members of the group (including legal officials themselves) identify and treat as 'legal' officials.* Owing to their recognized status as legal officials, their products (generated pursuant to the secondary rules) are treated as 'law'. Systems of primary and secondary rules that are administered by legal officials—so identified—are 'legal' systems. Systems of primary and secondary rules that are not administered by legal officials may be institutionalized normative systems, but they are not 'legal'.

For Hart, the *ultimate* rule of recognition is the rule by which the validity of all other rules in the legal system is determined. '[T]he rule of recognition exists only as a complex, but normally concordant, practice of the courts, officials, and private persons in identifying the law by reference to certain criteria. Its existence is a matter of fact' (Hart 1961: 107). A socio-legal positivist approach suggests that Hart's ultimate rule of recognition requires a co-ultimate social convention regarding *whose* actions have the status of law.

2. Implications of Essence But Not Function

The second kind of divergence between essentialism and functionalism occurs when a system consisting of primary and secondary rules (has essence) does not in fact operate to maintain order or guide conduct (lacks function). There are two ways to characterize this divergence, depending on how one's theory of law views the relationship between essentialism and functionalism. If law's essential structure (primary and secondary rules) is *conceptually* joined with its function (maintain order and guide conduct)—that is, the assertion is made as a conceptual matter that all systems of primary and secondary rules also *necessarily* maintain order and guide conduct if they are to qualify as 'law'—then the very possibility of an empirical divergence is conceptually denied, at least for whatever qualifies as 'law'. In the alternative, if the connection between law's essential structure and its function is viewed as a contingent, empirical matter, then it is an open question whether in any given instance the two coincide or diverge. In the latter case, one could say that law exists when its essential characteristics are satisfied (i.e. where a system of primary and secondary rules is present), even if it fails to carry out its primary functions. The legal system might then be evaluated as functionally weak or deficient, but it is a legal system nevertheless.

Which of these two alternatives Hart adopted is not free of dispute. He denied that his account is functionalist in other than a minimal sense, which suggests that he did not link conceptually law's structural essence to a function. On the other hand, one of his two minimum necessary conditions for the existence of a legal system requires that the populace generally abide by the primary rules. This condition, and his comments in support of it, indicates that Hart believed it is fundamental to the nature of a legal system that it functions effectively to guide conduct and maintain order. Particular legal rules may validly exist only on paper, but a legal system that is generally ignored by the group is not a legal system at all. It just does not make much sense, according to Hart, to say that the system exists if it is not effective. This efficacy requirement suggests that Hart indeed conceptually tied law's essence to its function, in that the former without the latter does not qualify as law.

The significance of this position to legal positivism cannot be underestimated. It appears that *all* notable legal positivists impose a condition of efficacy on the existence of a legal system. As manifested in his requirement of habitual obedience by the populace, for John Austin a 'legal system exists if it is generally efficacious' (Raz 1980: 5). It is also a core requirement for Kelsen (1992: 60): 'The validity of a legal system governing the behavior of particular human beings depends in a certain way, then, on the fact that their real behavior corresponds to the legal system—depends in a certain way, as one puts it, on the efficacy of the system.' Efficacy is an essential requirement for Kelsen (1945: 19) because by its nature 'law is a coercive order'. 'The purpose of the legal system is to induce human beings . . . to behave in a certain way' (1992: 29). Thus, to even qualify as law, a normative system must in fact constitute a coercive order, which entails a substantial degree of efficacy. Joseph Raz (1979: 152) also insists that efficacy is essential to the positivist theory of law: 'The view of law as a social fact, as a method of organization and regulation of social life, stands or falls with the two theses mentioned. At its core lie the theses that (1) the existence of a legal system is a function of its social efficacy, and that (2) every law has a source.'

Thus, legal positivists are united in insisting that a legal system exists only if it is generally obeyed by the populace. Underlying, and giving rise to, this unity are two related, already mentioned articles of faith widely shared by legal theorists: that law is fundamentally functional in nature— its function being to coordinate behaviour and maintain social order— and that a legal system has a kind of monopoly or primacy in this respect. Raz's analysis provides a good example of these beliefs and the implications that follow therefrom. When setting out his classification of the 'social functions of law', which revolve around the maintenance of order and coordination of behaviour, Raz (1979: 167) asserts that 'all legal systems *necessarily* perform, at least to a minimal degree, which I am unable to specify, social functions of all the types to be mentioned, and that these are all the main types of social functions they perform.' As mentioned earlier, his monopoly view of a legal system is implied within his assertion of the comprehensiveness and supremacy features of a legal system. The consequences of this monopoly view are revealed in his analysis of the situation in which there are two competing legal systems (for example where a revolution or radical transition has occurred), each with a degree of efficacy. Raz (1980: 208) observes that 'Of the competing legal systems, the *one* that comes out best is *the existing one*.' Informed by the monopoly view of law, rather than conclude that there are two systems one more efficacious than the other, for Raz only one exists while the other is vanquished, wiped away from view.

For legal positivists, then, it is in the nature of a legal system to effectively maintain order and coordinate behaviour, and to be the prime institutionalized force in society so engaged. But why should legal positivists presuppose anything about the nature of law at all, whether about its possible functions, or about its supposed primacy in some respect, or indeed about any other aspect of law, including that it must be institutional? These views about the nature of law are normative (or ideological, to use a more contentious label), no different in principle from the natural law insistence on the inseverable link between law and morality. The founding motto of legal positivism is Austin's (1954: 184–5) aphorism that 'The existence of law is one thing; its merit or demerit another.' Although this slogan was framed in the context of the separation of law from morality, it should also hold in the context of evaluating whether and the extent to which law is functional. Legal positivists consider it crucial to allow us to observe that a legal system is immoral, but they preclude us from observing that a 'legal' system is not obeyed by the general populace (because it would by definition not qualify as a 'legal' system). This is contrary to the spirit of positivism. The existence of law is one thing; whether, to what extent, and which functions it carries out is another.

A compelling defence of the presupposed social order function and the primacy of law, which give rise to the efficacy requirement, is that we must assume certain aspects about the nature of law if we are to identify law, or to have a concept of law at all, and that these particular presuppositions are consistent with widely held (conventional) views of law. The full answer to this response must await a more complete articulation of the conventionalist approach developed in this and the following chapter. For the moment, the argument will focus on demonstrating that legal positivists should not posit efficacy as a condition for the existence of a legal system.

The strongest argument in favour of dropping the requirement of general obedience is that this condition is inconsistent with social reality. An example of this can be found in my study of law in Yap, Micronesia (Tamanaha 1993b). Yap had a legal system, with a legislature, a handful of judges and attorneys, a small police department, and a complete legal code based in its entirety on laws transplanted from the United States. But vast portions of the Code had never been applied, few lay people had any knowledge of the content of the laws or of the operation of the legal system, a large proportion of social problems were dealt with through traditional means without participation of the state legal system, and indeed on most of the islands there was no legal presence at all. The day-to-day behaviour of the people was not governed by state law, but by their own cultural norms. Social order was maintained by sources other than the state law. They did not identify with the legal system in any way. For most Yapese, when confronted with the law, it was like being confronted with the command of an alien sovereign, despite the fact that they were an independent country and this was their own legal system. While they did not routinely act in conflict with the law (with the major exception that their culture perpetuated a thriving caste system, while the law prohibited discrimination), it could not be said that they were obeying or complying with the primary rules in Hart's terms, since they were ignorant of these rules and paid them almost no heed.

Although the overwhelming majority of the populace lived in general disregard of the vast bulk of the rules of the legal system, it is wrong to say that their state legal system did not exist. I worked there as a busy assistant attorney-general for almost two years. They had a full-fledged (though small) legal system, mostly occupied with the affairs of running a government. The existence of state law in Yap was a social fact, based upon the activities of legal officials. Conceivably, Hart (and perhaps other legal positivists) might assert that there are also other culturally generated (non-state) 'legal' systems operative in Yap, which do satisfy his two minimal conditions, but that would not refute the fact that the state legal system did exist despite its failure to meet the efficacy requirement. He could insist that we were confused or wrong, that the legal positivist requirements for the concept of law prevail over our self-identification as state legal actors, but such a position smacks of analytical imperialism. Moreover, this insistence would potentially conflict with the social sources thesis that stands at the core of legal positivism. Our social practices gave rise to the existence of a state legal system, recognized as such by all persons in that social arena, which is what matters, regardless of general efficacy or lack thereof.

Hart might also respond that this counter-example is a rare, relatively unusual one. But the situation in Yap is repeated today in varying ways and degrees in contexts of transplanted law and legal systems around the world, especially in many formerly colonized countries where the language of the law is often not the same as the spoken language(s). During the early period of colonization, the situation was even more extreme. As mentioned in Chapter 5, many early colonial legal systems did not attempt to exert social control or normative authority over the bulk of the populace (at least partially out of recognition that they lacked the power to do so effectively). Yet there is no question that these legal systems existed. Historical (and perhaps current) examples can also be found in the West. Eugen Ehrlich (1975) showed that in the region of Austria he studied substantial aspects of the Austrian Civil Code dealing with social behaviour were generally disregarded by the populace.

In addition to being inconsistent with social reality, the efficacy requirement contains a difficult conceptual problem that legal positivists have acknowledged, yet ignored as they continue to insist upon it. No theorist has proffered criteria to specify how much efficacy is enough.

The most explicit guidance provided on this issue is that there must be 'general' (though not necessarily total) obedience by the populace, or that obedience must not fall below a certain (unidentified) 'minimum' threshold. As a general matter on issues of this kind, especially when there is an underlying consensus, it is not objectionable to leave the precise boundary unspecified—we will know it when we see it—but, as the above examples indicate, given the range and variety of situations involved, it will not in fact be easy to obtain agreement on how much efficacy is enough.

Another set of objections to the efficacy requirement is instrumental in import. With the efficacy requirement as a condition of existence, theorists must describe increases and decreases in efficacy that pass the (unspecified) threshold as a matter of a legal system coming into and going out of existence, rather than the simpler characterization of merely increases and decreases in efficacy. The latter alternative is easily understandable, empirically adequate, avoids the problem of specifying the elusive threshold, and is potentially more informative. To use the example from Raz recited earlier, regarding a society with two competing legal systems, rather than asserting that the more efficacious system exists and the other does not (?),[3] which forces an all or nothing stance, one can observe that two competing legal systems exist, one more efficacious than the other. It is possible to make more refined comparisons and observations, including noting that, for example, the less efficacious system is in certain respects more efficacious than the currently dominant one, which is interesting for its own sake, and might also foretell that it will some day overtake the dominant one, or that it will continue to remain in the shadow of the dominant system as an alternative source of power.

Raz (1979: 104) described the significance of efficacy to the existence of law in the following terms: 'A legal system exists if and only if it is in force. The significance of the point is that it brings out that normative systems are existing legal systems because of their impact on the behavior of individuals, because of their role in the organization of social life.' Ironically, for a legal positivist, these statements are made with the same self-evident quality with which natural lawyers have proclaimed the inherent moral aspect of law. As a legal official in Yap, my activities

---

[3] To even discuss the issue in such terms smacks of a contradiction. To say that the *more* effective system exists necessarily implies that the *less* effective system also exists, otherwise there would be nothing to compare against. Raz uses 'exists' in a technical sense which avoids the contradiction, but again it is not obvious that it makes sense to characterize the situation in terms of existence and non-existence.

ranged from preparing construction contracts with foreign corporations, to drafting various portions of the legal code (which were enacted but remained unused), to advising the Governor on various issues of policy and law, to serving as a symbolic representative of the government at festivities, to dealing with the occasional drunken brawl. Although our role in the organization of social life was marginal at best, to declare as a conceptual matter that under such circumstances the legal system does not exist will prevent legal positivism from coming to an understanding of a complex situation that is more prevalent than legal positivists recognize.

Hart's jurisprudence, and legal positivism more broadly, aspires to be general and descriptive. General obedience of the primary rules by the populace is a *particular* trait common to many Western legal systems (or at least that is the assumption), which coloured the legal positivists' views of what law as such requires. To achieve a general jurisprudence, however, legal positivists must account for and facilitate the study of, not dismiss as exceptional, examples like those described above. Moreover, the conceptual and instrumental problems identified with the efficacy requirement cannot be ignored because they will arise time and again in different ways given the complex situation of legal phenomena today. The efficacy requirement must be dropped. Accordingly, socio-legal positivism holds that a legal system exists whenever there are legal actors (conventionally identified as such) engaged in producing and reproducing a legal system through shared secondary rules, regardless of their efficacy in generating widespread conformity to the primary rules, regardless of their effectiveness, or lack thereof, in maintaining social order. Just as legal positivism allows us to question whether law is moral, socio-legal positivism allows us to question whether law satisfies any functions, and, if so, which ones and to what extent.

The Relationship amongst Conventionalism, Essentialism, and Functionalism

The preceding part examined the tensions between essentialism and functionalism as they relate to Hart's concept of law. Adding conventionalism to the mix introduces several additional revealing tensions.

1. Misfit Between Conventionalism and Functionalism

At the most general level, as Andrei Marmor (1998: 526) argued, 'Conventionalism is markedly at odds with traditional Functionalist explanations of social practices.' Owing to the existence of functional alternatives or equivalents, conventional practices are underdetermined by functional needs. A given function can be satisfied by any number of conceivable conventional practices. While some mechanism(s) must give rise to order if a society is to survive, there are other ways to maintain order besides the activities of an institutionalized legal system (see Ellickson 1991). The emergence of the actual conventional practices that exist in a given situation are the result of many factors—social and historical—besides just functional needs. Relative to the concept of law, this point merely reinforces the argument made in the previous part that the conventions constituting a legal system need have no necessary relationship with the functions of social control or guiding conduct. [4]

2. General Conflict between Conventionalism and Essentialism

Conventionalism and essentialism also potentially conflict. Indeed, Roberto Unger (1975: 80) indicates in the following passage, conventionalism is often offered as an alternative to essentialism:

> If there are no intelligible essences, how do we go about classifying facts and situations, especially social facts and situations? Because facts have no intrinsic identity, everything depends on the names we give them. The conventions of naming, rather than any perceived quality of 'tableness' will determine whether an object will count as a table.

Conventionalism, which is another label for usage or social practice, suggests that law is whatever we attach the label 'law' to. Law is a human social creation that lacks any inherently necessary qualities. Essentialism suggests, directly to the contrary, that law possesses certain necessary characteristics.

Thus, on the surface, these two approaches seem incompatible, but they can with care operate together. Hart reconciled them by using conventionalism in a limited way to locate our shared concept of law, then engaging in conceptual analysis to identify the essential elements of this concept of law (including elements users of the concept were unaware their concept entailed). Hart later reintroduced conventionalism—in the form of social practices of the legal officials—when identifying the rules in a given legal system, but the focus here is his conventionalism in the identification of what law is.

Legal theorists have identified two troublesome questions raised by this approach. Brian Bix (1999: 28 n. 59) asked whether any additional information is conveyed by use of the words 'necessary' or 'essential', or is it just a way of being emphatic. The characteristics of law identified by

---

[4] For a powerful critique of functional analysis, see C. Hempel (1965).

Hart could just as well be labelled 'features (or aspects) of our concept of law' (ibid.). Bix (1995: 468) points out that 'talk about "essences" and the "nature" of items does not fit as comfortably with human artifacts and social institutions as it does, say, with biological species or chemical elements'. The problem is not only that social phenomena are difficult to delimit, but that there is a great deal of variation, and furthermore that social practices change. Given this complex and fluid situation, it is difficult to see how any concepts relating to social phenomena, like law, can make claims about necessary or essential elements. Assuming the term 'necessary' means *necessary*, Stephen Perry (1996: 369–74) asked how one can go from identifying an admittedly contingent concept of law—discerning features which are common but not necessarily universal—to insisting that anything which is to qualify as law must have these features. A large analytical leap, requiring extensive justification, is made from the observation that a usage-derived concept of law has a particular set of elements, to the separate assertion that phenomena without these elements are not law.

The objection I will press raises a different concern. Hart abstracted from state law to come up with *the* concept of law. There are other conventional views of law in circulation as well, as he recognized. Nonetheless, he designated state law as the paradigm case of law, then passed judgement as to whether other phenomena that have gone by the name of law indeed qualify as 'law'; for example, when he (1961: 15, 165, 226–31) characterized customary (or primitive) law and international law to be 'pre-legal' or, at best, borderline instances of law. He came to these conclusions despite acknowledging that usage had for 150 years considered international law to be 'law' (albeit in the face of misgivings from legal theorists). For Hart, essentialism prevailed over conventionalism when the two came into conflict. Users were informed that their usage reflects conceptual confusion—what they call law is not really law, or is a borderline or deficient manifestation of law, since it lacks law's essential elements. Beyond asserting that state law exists in almost every part of the world (without acknowledging that the same can be said of international law), Hart's (pp. 2–3) primary argument in support of establishing state law as the standard case for what law is was that 'most educated people' see this as law.

The problem is not that Hart's privileging of state law is ethnocentric, though it is open to that charge. My objection would be just as strong had he appointed primitive law to be the paradigm case of law. The problem with his approach is that he felt compelled to identify a single concept of law—*the* concept of law—at all. Hart (pp. 4–5) began with what he thought was the standard case—state law—then elaborated on the important features of this standard case. John Finnis (1980: 9–11) labels this procedure the identification of the central case and focal meaning. This manner of identifying key features is not in itself objectionable. The objection is the assumption that there is or there must be a *single* standard or central case; indeed the very terms 'standard' or 'central' case carry that implication. This makes it more difficult to conceive of the possibility that there are several distinct phenomena—several distinctly different standard or central cases—of law, each with its own focal meanings. The monotypic bent of essentialism points us down a single-minded track, foreclosing other ways of conceiving of legal phenomena that conventionalism might otherwise have resulted in if allowed to follow its own course. Even Finnis, a leading proponent of natural law, succumbed to this, which led him (p. 280) to observe that natural law 'is only analogically law'; and he (ibid.) awkwardly explained 'that is why the term has been avoided in this chapter on Law'.

Shorn of its essentialist overtones, another way to view Hart's analysis is that he is really just asserting that primitive law and international law lack some of the core traits state law possesses, and they possess traits that state law lacks. A less misleading title to his classic text *The Concept of Law* would have been 'The Concept of State Law', or 'The Elements of State Law'. Raz, whose central book was entitled *The Concept of a Legal System*, understood this point, but he continued to believe that state law is the epitome of law, and that institutions are essential to law, and thus he made essentialist claims about the nature of law similar to those made by Hart. Discerning the core features of state law is a worthy and monumental task. But it does not provide a suitable foundation for a general jurisprudence, for the simple fact that it is too narrow to account for the complex presence of legal phenomena, especially in (but not limited to) non-Western countries. In effect, Hart constructed his general jurisprudence on a particular, or local, base (see Perry 1998: 432–3). Austin had a similarly debilitating flaw when he built his general jurisprudence around concepts like right and duty, which consequently limited his analysis to the 'maturer' legal systems. In Hart's (1994: 239) own words, a general jurisprudence aspires to be 'not tied to any particular legal system or legal culture'.

Socio-legal positivism recognizes that law is a human social creation. Law is whatever we attach the label 'law' to. It will be unflinchingly conventionalist in the identification of what law is. If law is attached by usage to more than one phenomenon, rather than picking one to serve as the standard by which to evaluate the others, socio-legal positivism will accept that there are different kinds or types of law, each with its own characteristic features. Aside from the social sources thesis and the separation thesis, to be articulated in upcoming sections, it will not assume anything about the nature of these phenomena. In his book, Hart referred to four different types of law: state law, primitive (or customary) law, international law, and natural law. For Hart, the first reigned supreme, the second and third were lacking owing to their underdeveloped or absence of secondary rules, and he never really considered whether the fourth was a form of law. Socio-legal positivism recognizes that each of these kinds of law (and there are others, including religious law and transnational law) has a real social existence that must be investigated.

3. The Problem with the Acceptance Condition

The final conflict that arises between conventionalism and essentialism relates to Hart's second minimum necessary condition for the existence of a legal system: that the legal officials 'accept' the secondary rules. The notion of acceptance was crucial to Hart. He criticized Austin's focus on habits of obedience for its neglect of the internal aspect of rules, and its consequent failure to distinguish law from the 'gunman writ large'. Law is normative in nature, according to Hart, and the way to capture this aspect is by recognizing the internal *acceptance* of rules. 'What is necessary is that there should be a critical reflective attitude to certain patterns of behavior as a common standard, and that this should display itself in criticism (including self-criticism), demands for conformity, and in acknowledgements that such criticism and demands are justified, all of which find their characteristic expression in the normative terminology of "ought," "must", and "should", "right" and "wrong" ' (Hart 1961: 56). It is not necessary, according to Hart, for the citizens to accept the primary rules in this sense, though that would be a healthier society than the one in which the citizens 'obey out of fear of the consequences, or from inertia, without thinking of himself or others having an obligation to do so and without being disposed to criticize either himself or others for deviations' (p. 112).

Hart allowed that the general populace *need not accept* the primary *or* secondary rules, as long as they generally obey the primary rules. But he (pp. 112–13) insisted that it 'is a logically necessary condition of our ability to speak of the existence of a single system' that the legal officials *accept* the rules of recognition as common standards of behaviour, and 'critically appraise their own and each other's deviations'. His strong claim that the acceptance of the secondary rules is a *logical* necessity for the existence of a legal system is what makes it essentialist.

A controversy over the nature of this acceptance requirement ensued from virtually the moment Hart proclaimed it. His description of acceptance in terms of justified demands of compliance, felt obligation, and reflective criticism suggests a rather full-bodied acceptance in the sense of a moral commitment on the part of legal officials to the secondary rules. It is not clear, however, why the unity of a legal system would require such acceptance (ideal though it may be). As long as the legal officials coordinate their actions through shared and interconnected social practices, regardless of why they coordinate their actions or the attitude they have while doing so, a legal system would have sufficient unity to exist. Hart might be resting his claim on an assertion that the system could not hang together for any significant period of time in the absence of such acceptance, but then it is an empirical claim not a logical necessity, and he must produce evidence to support it.

Most problematic, the requirement of acceptance would appear conceptually to rule out the possibility of a corrupt legal system, in which the bulk of the legal officials adhere to the secondary rules out of their own self-interest, or out of fear of the consequences that would follow if they did not cooperate. But we know that such legal systems have existed.[5] Hart's second condition would seem to require that we deny these the title 'legal' system, even though in every other regard they operate and identify themselves, and are conventionally seen by the public as such, however illegitimate they may be considered. To echo Austin, the person around whose neck the hangman fastens the noose pursuant to a judicial order will not be heard to deny the existence of law owing to a pervasively corrupt judiciary. Hart's acceptance requirement has resurrected a variant of precisely the understanding that led legal positivism to react vehemently against natural law theory. This is another instance in which Hart's conventionalism pointed in one direction while his essentialism pointed in another, and he erroneously chose to go with the latter.

Recognizing the problems with the acceptance requirement, others have argued that Hart's view of acceptance is thin (see Shiner 1992),

---

[5] A detailed empirical study of such a system was completed by Sebastian Pompe. He demonstrated in his doctoral dissertation how the judiciary in Indonesia was co-opted by the political apparatus, and suffers from pervasive corruption. The legal system has continued to function despite remaining in this state of affairs for some time. S. Pompe (1996) (doctoral dissertation, on file with author). According to Quigley (1990), the Soviet Union also had a judiciary with decades of questionable credibility.

requiring very little in the way of moral commitment, and there are indications that Hart himself held this view.[6] Interpreted in this way, Hart would require, as the minimum conditions for the existence of a legal system, obedience of the primary rules by the general populace (but not necessarily acceptance), and thin (almost empty) acceptance by the legal officials of the secondary rules. Neither the private citizens nor the legal officials need accept the primary rules under his account (see Payne 1982: 503). A legal system in which no one accepts the legal rules governing conduct, and the officials minimally accept the secondary rules, is a 'gunman writ large' by almost any other name. It is a rapacious legal system that has subjugated its populace.

Socio-legal positivism allows for the possibility that such legal systems might exist. Hart's acceptance requirement must be dropped. If given real content, it is inconsistent with social reality; if given minimal content, there is no reason to keep it. Under a socio-legal positivist view, a legal system will exist when there is a complex of 'legal' actors (conventionally identified as such) who coordinate their actions to do things with norms. The very fact of coordination requires some agreement in their social practices, which would be satisfied by shared adherence to the secondary rules. If, for example, legislators promulgate laws and judges agree about which laws are validly enacted, and take action to apply them, a legal system will exist. This is true without any consideration of the legal officials' attitudes towards the secondary or primary rules, without mention of whether or not they accept them, or without regard to whether the primary rules are generally obeyed. It is also true regardless of whether the law satisfies some function, or is completely dysfunctional.

Hart might have complained that this bare view of law entirely misses law's normative character. The initial retort would be that—when one considers that neither private citizens nor legal officials need accept the primary rules, and that the legal officials must accept the secondary rules in only a minimalist sense—there was very little left of law's normative character in Hart's own account. The more responsive retort is that socio-legal positivism does not deny that law and legal systems often enjoy a substantial degree of acceptance by legal officials; rather, it simply does not build the existence of this normative element into the concept of law. Law often *claims* normative authority, but 'but that does not mean that anyone should [or does] listen' (Schauer 1994: 504). Whether

---

[6] See M. Moore (1998: 308 n. 27) (reprinting private communication from Hart on doubts whether legal officials must believe in justness of their legal system).

the private citizens or the legal officials in fact feel any moral commitment to the primary or secondary rules are empirical questions to be answered in a given case. Hart was correct that the internal point of view must be considered if the normative aspect of law is to be appreciated; he was wrong to presuppose the outcome of the investigation by assuming the existence of acceptance.

The Starting Premisses of Socio-Legal Positivism

Here is a summary of the socio-legal positivist take on Hart's analysis following the above exploration of the tensions underlying his simultaneous resort to conventionalism, essentialism, and functionalism. Socio-legal positivism remains true to Hart's conventionalism and his focus on social practices, but to a greater extent even than Hart did, because it discards the essentialist and functionalist aspects of his approach, which often came into conflict with his conventionalism. To Hart's account, it adds the conventional identification of legal actors qua legal actors. It retains Hart's abstraction of primary and secondary rules at the (most reductive) core of state legal systems. However, it eliminates from Hart's account the requirement that the primary rules must be generally obeyed by the populace, and it eliminates the requirement that the legal officials accept the secondary rules. It makes no presuppositions about the functional effects that law might have, if any. It makes no presuppositions about the normative aspects, if any, that law might possess. It recharacterizes Hart's account to be an abstraction of state law,[7] not a concept of law as such. It is one among several types or kinds of law, and a multitude of specific manifestations of law. Other kinds of law, each of which can be conceptualized in more abstract terms based upon their focal meanings, need not necessarily involve institutions, and they need not necessarily qualify as 'systems'. Finally, the elements discovered in the course of this abstraction are simply features—features that can change, features of which there may be variations within a given kind of law—not essentialist elements.

This bare—some might say impoverished—view of legal phenomena is well suited to achieving the positivist goal of constructing a general

---

[7] In a previous work, I developed what I call a social theory of state law. Hart's primary and secondary rules are retained as key aspects of this approach, but it reaches more broadly to include other social practices and institutions related to law. (See Tamanaha 1997: chaps. 5 and 6). For the purposes of this analysis I will refer only to his primary and secondary rules, though a fuller development of the socio-legal positivist approach I propose would be more expansive in the way described in the earlier work.

jurisprudence. Its great advantage is that it presupposes very little about law, leaving that open to conventional identification, and subsequent conceptual analysis and empirical study. Instead of dictating what law is, it asks how groups of people talk about law. Instead of assuming what law does, it examines what people do with law. It creates a framework for the identification of law, accepting that there may be more than one phenomenon that goes by the name of law, then leaves the rest to be filled in by actually existing social practices. If law is indeed a human social creation, only a flexible, open approach can capture the myriad forms and manifestations that law(s) take(s).

Two Fundamental Theses

1. The Separation Thesis

Socio-legal positivism adheres to the two fundamental theses that unite most legal positivists: the separation thesis and the social sources thesis. The classic separation thesis is that there is no *necessary* connection between law and morality. The genesis of this thesis is in the legal positivist insistence, against natural law theories of law, that moral rectitude is not necessarily a condition of legal validity. Likewise, legal positivists insist a moral norm or principle is not, by virtue of that fact, necessarily awarded the status of law. The separation thesis is a limited, negative thesis, a denial of the natural law position, rather than an affirmative statement of the relationship between law and morality. The separation thesis does not insist that there are no connections between law and morality, only that there is no *necessary* connection. Hart observed that the 'law of every modern state shows at a thousand points the influence of both accepted social morality and wider moral ideals' (1961: 199). Soft (or 'inclusive') legal positivists, like Hart, also recognize that certain legal systems can, through the secondary rules, condition the validity of law upon consistency with moral principles, and award moral principles legal standing (see Jules Coleman 1998).[8] In theory, consistent with inclusive legal positivism's separation thesis, a legal system may even consist of a single rule of recognition: do justice (ibid.). The acknowledgement that many legal systems do in fact have connections with morality, however, does not obviate the possibility—and historical fact—that there are and have been evil laws and evil legal systems which nonetheless qualify as 'legal'.

---

[8] Not all legal positivists would agree with this position. For an overview of the debate, see Bix (1999b); Leiter (1998).

Socio-legal positivism endorses the separation thesis, but further extends it in two important respects. The first respect is that the separation thesis now also applies to functionality as well as morality: there is no necessary connection between law and morality, or functionality. Many forms of law and legal systems may in fact have functional effects, but there is no necessity that these effects entail guiding behaviour or maintaining social order. Furthermore, the socio-legal positivist separation thesis insists that we remain open to the possibility that there are kinds of law and legal systems that are dysfunctional or non-functional, that lead to the disruption of social order.

The second extension of the separation thesis relates to its scope of application. Legal positivists traditionally have applied the separation thesis only to state law, which they took to be the epitome of law. Socio-legal positivism applies the separation thesis to any and all possible manifestations and kinds of law. The reformulated separation thesis reads as follows: *There is no necessary connection between law of whatever manifestation or kind, and morality or functionality.*

While it is easy to envision how the separation thesis might apply to international law and customary law, at first blush it might appear completely inapplicable to natural law theories of law, which define law in moral terms. To give a persuasive explanation of how the separation thesis can apply to natural law theories of law I must complete the discussion of this entire section, which builds the case step-by-step. For the moment, the following observations should establish that this notion not only is conceivable, it is advisable.

There are many stripes of natural law theory.[9] One type, for example, consists of moral realists, who believe that objective moral principles exist independently of human beliefs and conduct. Another type, entertained by Hart, bases natural law on deductions from human nature and the human condition. Another type, represented by the work of John Finnis, is grounded in an argument from rationality or practical reasonableness. Another type involves various religious traditions, especially Catholicism, that consider God to be the source of natural law. Often these accounts make functional as well as moral claims about the nature of natural law. Whichever approach one follows, all face the same fundamental problem: how to identify natural law principles. Various methods have been used to solve this task, from revelation, to rational deduction, to appeals to self-evidence, to evidence based upon prevailing social conventions. As

---

[9] Informative accounts of the various kinds of natural law approaches can be found in Bix (2001); M. Moore (1992).

a result of these efforts, different accounts of the content of natural law principles have been produced, no single one of which has come close to achieving the status of certainty, or even general consensus. This uncertainty, and our lack of confidence that it will ever be resolved, is one of the legacies of the Enlightenment ideas discussed in Chapter 4. Although the possibility of a resolution to this epistemological problem cannot be absolutely ruled out (God may some day descend in dramatic fashion to clear up the matter, though even then there will be doubters—how can we be certain it is really God?), it is safe to assert that we will probably never achieve a foundationalist account of natural law principles, foundationalist in the sense not only that they are true principles, but that we have certain knowledge of their truth.[10] What this means is that even if a particular natural law theory happens to be correct—that is, the principles it espouses indeed reflect objective morality—we will not know for sure. This irrepressible uncertainty creates an opening for the application of the separation thesis. No particular version of natural law principles has a *necessary* connection with morality, or with functionality.

The epistemological problems faced by natural law theory show that it is possible to apply the separation thesis to natural law, but this in itself is not a compelling argument that we should apply it. For that there is a much stronger argument. To the chagrin of natural law theorists, throughout history many iniquitous actions have been committed in the name of natural law[11] (though much good has also been accomplished). 'Indeed,' Weber (1954: 288) observed, 'natural law has also served to legitimate authoritarian powers of the most diverse types.' Being vigilant against this possibility explains why it is essential that the separation thesis also be applied to natural law. The *claim* that one is acting pursuant to natural law does not of itself assure that one's conduct is moral, in precisely the same way that having the status of law is no guarantee of consistency with morality. Durkheim (1993: 94) made the same point with respect to religion: 'Surely the religious ideal is far from being a moral ideal just because it is religious; on the contrary, it contains elements which are immoral or amoral.' If we are to hold state law (and customary law, international law, and religious law) to moral and functional scrutiny and evaluation, the

---

[10] An extraordinary historical overview of moral philosophy in general, and natural law in particular, is Schneewind (1998). It is difficult to read the many varying accounts of the rational deduction and self-evidence in the identification of natural law principles without coming to the conclusion that these issues will never be conclusively resolved.

[11] See Rommen (1998: 134–5) (acknowledging that totalitarian regimes have made claims of acting on behalf of natural law).

same should be true of natural law, since it shares with the others the capacity for accomplishing evil in the name of law.

2. The Social Sources Thesis

The social sources thesis holds that law is the product of a complex of social practices. These practices give rise to law, and through these practices we can identify the existence and content of the law. This is the sense in which law's 'existence is a matter of fact' (Hart 1961: 107). Socio-legal positivism embraces the social sources thesis. Not only is it consistent with the view that law is a human social creation; it fits the empirical, sociological orientation that socio-legal theory brings to the study of law.

Socio-legal positivism modifies the social sources thesis in a manner similar to its modification of the separation thesis. Instead of applying this thesis only to state law, it will be applied to all manifestations and kinds of law, including customary law, international law, transnational law, religious law, and natural law. Their specific shapes and features will not be the same as those discerned by Hart for state law, but whatever distinctive features they do have will be amenable to observation through careful attention to the social practices which constitute them. All of these manifestations and kinds of law are social products. The existence of each is a matter of social fact.

Again, it might be difficult to conceive of natural law in terms of the social sources thesis, especially with regard to those versions of natural law which claim to exist independently of human convention, or those which claim to be derived from God. The key is that while the natural law principles themselves *might* be derived from a non-human source, as adherents believe, natural law is manifested through human social practices. Natural law has a real social existence, consisting of a complex of ideas and a set of social practices comprised by people who believe in and act upon its existence. Unlike state law, it usually does not amount to a concrete system. But it has a social existence and presence nonetheless, one which often interacts in various ways with state law.

Let me offer a few brief examples of the social presence of natural law. There are virulent anti-abortionists who believe that, according to God's natural law, abortion is the murder of innocent lives. Laws that permit abortion are therefore invalid. Doctors who conduct abortions are murderers. Pursuant to this line of reasoning, the execution of abortion doctors is a legitimate defence of others, and perhaps also a justified punishment for their evil behaviour and violation of natural law principles. A more admirable example can be found in the conduct of Dr

Martin Luther King, who protested that segregation laws violated natural law, and urged civil disobedience, which entailed violating the law
but accepting (under protest) the state's imposition of punishment.
Natural law also exists through the activities of natural law theorists, and
general cultural beliefs, that make their way into positive law, like the
incorporation of the notions of liberty and due process into the US
Constitution. These scenarios, all real ones, show the (multifarious) social
existence of natural law, and its interaction with state law, in direct and
consequential ways. As John Finnis (1980: 23) observed, principles of natural law 'are traced out not only in moral philosophy or ethics and "individual" conduct, but also in political philosophy and jurisprudence, in
political action, adjudication, and the life of the citizen'.

It is important to understand precisely the sense in which the social
sources thesis can be applied to natural law. To put the point succinctly,
it can be applied to the social identification and production of natural
law, but not to the truth of natural law principles.[12] Most natural law
philosophers are concerned with the latter, not the former. A distinction
set out by John Finnis will help clarify this point. According to Finnis (p.
24), principles of natural law 'have no history'. They would 'hold good,
as principles, however extensively they were overlooked, misapplied, or
defied in practical thinking, and however little they were recognized'
(ibid.). His book, *Natural Law and Natural Rights*, is about natural law in this
sense, an analysis and exploration of natural law as true principles,
regardless of how or whether they have been manifested in social terms.
In contrast to the perspective he assumes, Finnis (ibid.) also recognizes
that natural law can be understood from a social-historical standpoint:
'there is a history of the opinions or set of opinions, theories, and doctrines which assert that there are principles of natural law, a history of origins, rises, declines and falls, revivals and achievements, and of historical
responsibilities.' Socio-legal positivism applies the social sources thesis to
natural law from this latter perspective, but with a significant difference.
Finnis was concerned, in the above quote, with describing the *study* of
natural law from a social-historical standpoint; whereas, the social
sources thesis as applied here refers to the social *production and identification*
of natural law principles, though the study of this phenomenon is facilitated by and follows immediately therefrom.

The social sources thesis generally holds that 'the existence and content of law is determined by some range of facts about human beings in

[12] I am indebted to Brian Bix for insisting that I address this point, and to Paul Kirgis
for his persistent questioning in a manner which helped me work it out.

a social setting—facts about their behavior, history, institutions, beliefs, and attitudes' (Lyons 1993: 77). There is no question that natural law principles are generated, applied, used, and discussed thtough and in social practices, and thus natural law is subject to the social sources thesis. This application entails the assertion that, in a certain limited sense, natural law principles are also 'posited', hence its amenability to the socio-legal positivist perspective. Although Finnis's book might be *about* natural law in an ahistorical sense, neither he nor his book can escape the fact that they exist in history and participate in the social-historical discourse of natural law.

A natural law theorist might respond that this suggested approach does not suffice because legal positivism is a theory about the *creation* or establishment as well as identification of law. Natural law principles pre-exist or exist entirely apart from the social practices used to help identify them, Finnis might argue; accordingly, they are not created by those practices. The hard-line response to this argument is that natural law simply does not exist in the metaphysical sense claimed. Thus, the creation of natural law principles lies precisely in the social practices that identify them. Nothing exists other than these practices; thus socio-legal positivism captures natural law in its entirety. A softer position, one which abstains from making a determination as to the truth of natural law, would be for socio-legal positivism to examine natural law *as if* the social practices are all that exist. This approach would, in a sense, bracket the issue of truth of natural law principles.

A natural law theorist might further respond that socio-legal positivism cannot bracket truth if it is to encompass the identification of positive law norms, because truth is the ultimate criteria—the rule of recognition— for the validity of natural law principles. However, owing to the epistemological problem described earlier, natural law theorists are themselves in a position of having to identify principles without a decisive determination of truth. Indeed, many who espouse natural law principles, theorists and otherwise, often assume the truth of the principles they posit (a word chosen advisedly), which is itself a kind of bracketing. Socio-legal positivism cannot determine whether or not natural law principles are true, but it can describe how adherents talk about the issue of truth. Socio-legal positivism can and will focus on the social practices of non-theorists and theorists in the identification and production of norms.

A legal positivist might also raise a point of opposition—that this form of identification is too uncertain. One of the demands of legal positivism is that there be a degree of clarity and certainty in the identification of law. This demand, however, was formulated in relation to state law relative to its presumed function of guiding behaviour. It is a characteristic of (the social existence of) natural law that it has continued to thrive as a form of law despite (and perhaps owing to) this fuzzy character. Furthermore, 'soft' or 'inclusive' legal positivists have already recognized that the question of what law is can turn on the resolution of complex moral issues (when so required by the rules of recognition), which is precisely the situation that holds when the social sources thesis is applied to natural law.

Natural law theorists will rightly decry the socio-legal positivist approach as missing a fundamental aspect of natural law, but the perspective it brings to bear on natural law nonetheless promises to generate insights. An empirical perspective will not be able to capture every aspect of natural law, but it can shed interesting light on natural law as a complex of social practices. The same is true of the socio-legal positivist application to religious law, international law, and other kinds of law.

The Social Theory of Law and the Methodology of Socio-Legal Positivism

A previous work developed in detail what I call a 'social theory of law' (Tamanaha 1997: chaps. 5 and 6). This label was chosen to emphasize a focus on the social presence of law, on how social actors give rise to law through their meaningful actions. It recognizes that law is a social construction. Socio-legal positivism adopts the same perspective. The social sources thesis, it should be apparent, provides a natural link with an approach to law that emphasizes its social presence. Several core aspects of the social theory of law and the methodology to be applied to its study will be summarized briefly here.

With regard to methodology, it recognizes, consistent with Hart, that the activities of private citizens and legal officials (if any) cannot be understood without attention to their internal point of view (see Tamanaha 1996). In social science terms this is called interpretivism. Unlike Hart, as argued earlier, socio-legal positivism will not presuppose any aspects of what this internal point of view requires beyond the minimal one that the actors see their conduct as having some connection with law. Also unlike Hart, socio-legal positivism urges application of the external point of view, looking for patterns of behaviour, which can shed light on the understandings of the people involved. These patterns of behaviour can also help establish whether their conduct is consistent with what they claim about their activities, and whether their conduct satisfies their stated goals and purposes, which are relevant inquiries for the purpose of testing the mirror thesis. In social science terms this is called behaviourism. Regardless of the fact that they have often been portrayed in antagonistic terms in the social sciences, the internal and external perspectives, interpretivism and behaviourism, are complementary approaches, not mutually exclusive, and must both be applied when investigating the social presence of law (Tamanaha 1997: chap. 3; 2000).

The social theory of law views social actions in interpretive terms, that is, as meaningfully informed, though often also involving unthinking habits and patterns of behaviour. Shared intersubjective ideas and beliefs, what phenomenologist Alfred Schutz (1962) called social typifications, enable collective action based upon mutual behavioural expectations. Complexes of beliefs and knowledge give rise to interpretive communities and meaning systems that inform the ideas and actions of the people who have gained access to these bodies of knowledge through education, training, and participation in the activities involved (Tamanaha 1997: 142–52). Participants think in terms of the shared intersubjective meaning systems when engaging in the activities. Barry Barnes (1995: 85) provides a summary of the processes involved in contexts of interaction:

Continuing communication in the course of interaction both requires and engenders agreement in cognition and understanding, evident in some degree of shared knowledge, shared culture, shared competence. Constant interaction, with message transmission and reception ongoing as a matter of course between persons, is essential for cognition at the collective level, just as constant interaction with message transmission and reception between neurones is essential for cognition at the individual level.

A key point to recognize is that, although shared norms and knowledge enable social interaction, they do not determine the action. They provide recipes and competences for social actors who are informed by them, and follow them; but, owing to the indeterminacy of norms and openness of knowledge, social actors also frequently use them strategically to further their interests and achieve their desires in particular contexts of interaction. 'Rules, then, do not exist independently of their use. Their precise meaning (their real meaning) is defined in use, as the action unfolds and the situation becomes more clearly defined' (Wilson 1983: 113).

The social theory of law views the existence and presence of law in terms of chains of meaningful action and reaction, based upon law-related significance attached by the actors (lay and legal) involved. Neil MacCormick (1986: 50) provides an example of this perspective on law in the following description of how an act may bring a contract into existence:

What makes it possible is that the act in question belongs to a class of acts whose performance the law treats as operative to make a contract. And what makes that matter is that the law ascribes certain rights and duties to individuals condition- ally upon the existence of contracts. And what makes that matter is that some- times people wish to assert legal rights and enforce legal duties, the procedures for doing which are established by further legal rules. And all that depends on the existence of organized groups of people, the legal profession, the courts, and enforcement officials, whose function is to give effect to such rules and whose actual practice is tolerably consonant with the announced rules.

The social theory of law views institutions in terms of coordinated complexes of human interaction, often supported by a material base (office buildings, etc.). This view of institutions was best articulated by Herbert Blumer (1969: 58), in his account of symbolic interactionism:

It sees [large societal organizations] as arrangements of people who are inter- linked in their respective actions. The organization and interdependency is between such actions of people stationed at different points. At any one point the participants are confronted by the organized activities of other people into which they have to fit their own acts. . . . Instead of accounting for the activity of the organization and its parts in terms of organizational principles or system principles, it seeks explanation in the way in which the participants define, inter- pret, and meet the situation at their respective points. The linking together of this knowledge of the concatenated actions yields a picture of the organized complex.

Another crucial concept is the notion of a social practice. A social prac- tice involves an activity that contains integrated aspects of both meaning and behaviour, linked together by a loosely shared body of (often inter- nally heterogeneous) norms and patterns of action.

To enter into a practice is to accept the authority of those standards and the inadequacy of my own performance as judged by them. It is to subject my own attitudes, choices, preferences and tastes to the standards which currently and partially define the practice. (MacIntyre 1984: 190)

[T]o think within a practice is to have one's very perception and sense of possible and appropriate action issue 'naturally'—without further reflection—from one's position as a deeply situated agent. (Fish 1989: 386–7)

Practices can also be criticized from within, and they have histories and can change. They often contain norms that can point in different direct- ions, and they consist of people who bring different talents and points of view to the practice. A wide range of social activities can be seen in terms of social practices, from playing chess to doing legal theory. Many institutions are internally comprised of complexes of practices, which they support and build around.

As long as one keeps in mind that the notion of a social practice is a heuristic device, a concept that helps frame and isolate activities within the social field for the purposes of study, it provides an excellent starting point for the identification of kinds of law. Law exists whenever there are social practices giving rise to 'law'. Hart said as much.

All of the above aspects of the social theory of law can be approached at several different levels of generality, depending upon the purposes of the enquiry. Institutions, for example, can be seen in terms of a single courthouse or prosecutor's office, or a complex of these taken as a whole. Practices can be approached at the level of being a lawyer (or judge or legal theorist), or at the sub-level of being a criminal defence lawyer, or tax lawyer, or divorce lawyer. The legal meaning system can relate to all persons trained in the law, or be limited more narrowly to particular areas of expertise. The crucial point is that the levels of generality selected must be consistent within the context of a particular study, and across studies when comparisons are made.

Hart's primary and secondary rules, which he took to represent the fundamental elements of state law, look different when construed in the context of the social theory of law. From one standpoint, they represent the constitutive backbone of legal institutions at the most reductive, pared down level (indeed, at this basic level all institutions of any kind might be said to consist of rules, and rules about the generation and application of rules). Viewed from the standpoint of the various practices that constitute law, however, primary and secondary rules can be seen instead as subsets of norms consisting as a part of the practice of judging, or the practice of lawyering, or the practice of legislating, etc., along with many other kinds of norms, as well as attitudes, dispositions, and unthinking habits of behaviour (see Tamanaha 1996). From the latter standpoint, primary and secondary rules are not so much binding dictates but rather aspects in the stream of legal discourse. Depending upon the purposes of the study, one or the other, or both, standpoints—the institutional or the practice-based—can be applied.

The essential ideas behind the social theory of law are to keep a close eye on what people—legal actors and non-legal actors—are actually doing relative to law, and to discover and pay attention to the ideas that inform their actions. These ideas, beliefs, and actions give rise to law, determine the uses to which law is put, and constitute the reactions to, and consequences of, law. The spirit informing this social theory of law was expressed in the following passage by John Dewey, which set out his philosophy of law (1941: 76–7): 'The standpoint taken is that law is through and through a social phenomenon; social in origin, in purpose or end, and in application. . . . [T]his position signifies that law must be viewed both as intervening in the complex of other activities, and as itself a social process[.]'

Conventionalism in the Identification of Law and Category Construction

The question remains of how socio-legal positivism will identify those social practices which involve 'law' as opposed to something else. The answer is provided by Hart's conventionalism stripped of its essentialism: *Law is whatever people identify and treat through their social practices as 'law' (or droit, recht, etc.).*

'For the conventionalist, there are an infinite number of possible ways of dividing the world up and classifying particular things under general words' (Unger 1975: 93). Typically, with regard to law, this involves state law, usually identified at some level of specificity, like the law of New York State or US federal law. But in certain social arenas, especially in post-colonial societies, people also commonly refer to customary law and indigenous law (or specifically, to *adat*, or to Yapese customary law, etc.). And in certain social arenas people refer to religious law (or specifically, to Islamic law, or the *Sharia*, or the Talmud, or canon law), or to natural law. And in some social arenas all of these forms of law are referred to. This list is not exhaustive, as other or new forms of 'law' can be said to exist whenever recognized as such by social actors. Thus, what law *is*, is determined by the people in the social arena through their own usages, not in advance by the social scientist or theorist.

A conventionalist approach to the identification of law raises a number of complex problems and objections. The first problem involves resolving the question of *who* identifies a phenomenon as law through their social practices for it to qualify as such. The answer: *any members of a given group can identify what law is, as long as it constitutes a conventional practice.* It need not (though it can) be legal officials; indeed, a given manifestation of law, as is often the case with natural law, might completely lack legal officials. It also need not be members of the general community; a given manifestation of law may consist of a self-appointed group of 'legal' officials claiming to represent law who attempt to impose their will upon the broader group (which is an abstract way of describing a criminal gang or cult that does things in the name of 'law'). Unlike traditional legal theories bound (or blinded) by the monopoly view of law, this approach accepts the possibility that within a given social arena there may be competing groups who claim to constitute the law. This openness to a multiplicity of kinds of law is required by a rigorous adherence to conventionalism in the identification of what law is.

A related second question that must be resolved is *how many* people must view something as 'law' for it to qualify as such. As a general matter, although other cut-off points may be selected, a minimum threshold to qualify is if *sufficient people with sufficient conviction consider something to be 'law', and act pursuant to this belief, in ways that have an influence in the social arena.* This admittedly vague test is intended to set a low threshold for inclusion. Law, pursuant to this non-essentialist approach, is whatever people recognize and treat as law through their social practices. This general test is formulated to be consistent with this assertion, while screening out the lone lunatic who considers his every wish to be the law. The reliance upon social practices to identify law insures, at least, that there be some minimal degree of continuous social presence; transient or idiosyncratic identifications of law do not amount to social practices.

This relatively low conventionalist standard might be unpalatable to some theorists, first, because it threatens a proliferation of kinds of law in a social arena, and, secondly, because it seems to grant remarkable authority to social actors to give rise to the existence of law. Neither concern has merit. A radical profusion of kinds of law will not occur frequently, since as a matter of general social practice people do not lightly apply the label 'law'. More important, theorists should not shrink from the possibility of a profusion of social practices identifying kinds of law. If such a situation exists, it would be a fascinating social development that must be studied and understood. 'If our concepts do not in some way mime essential reality it is much more important to show how and why we create the concepts we do' (Wachterhauser 1994: 148).

The apparent authority conventionalism grants to social actors to give rise to new kinds of law is also a misplaced concern. Social actors already possess this authority, since law is and has always been a social creation. Conventionalism merely recognizes this reality. Conventionalism is threatening because it challenges the authority of social and legal theorists—the champions of essentialism—to dictate for everyone else what law (properly understood) is. As Zygmunt Bauman (1989: 53) observed, 'Concern with the right to speak with authority is an artifact of academic life.' Appeasing this concern is not a compelling ground to reject a conventionalist approach to the identification of law. Furthermore, the social analyst is still free to develop the second level constructs (or analytical categories), as will be discussed in the next chapter, and free to do the empirical investigation and analytical work.

This relationship between theoretical concepts and lay categories is recognized, if not always acknowledged, in social theory:

Sociological theory piggybacks upon members own knowledge in developing its own concepts and categories: the intersubjectively sustained categories of every-day knowledge of society are the prototypes for sociological theoretical categor-ies, and much of the work required to sustain agreed application for the theoretical categories is actually done by the participants. . . . And it should be recognized further that the concepts and categories employed here by theorists are incompletely differentiated from and in a sense parasitic upon those of the participants themselves. (Barnes 1995: 224)

The socio-legal positivist conventionalist identification of law merely acknowledges what is already a reality.

A conventionalist approach to the identification of law also raises the spectre of two familiar objections attached to linguistic approaches to the identification of law. The first is that there are many references to 'law': 'laws of nature and scientific laws, laws of God and of thought, of logic and of language, etc' (Raz 1994: 180); '"moral law," "sociological law", "international law," "ecclesiastical law," "law of grammar," ' (Finnis 1980: 6). This objection is difficult to surmount for traditional approaches to identifying what law is, but much of its sting is removed here. Unlike the prevailing monotypical, essentialist approach, socio-legal positivism accepts and builds upon the fact that more than one phenomenon is referred to by the term 'law'. Thus, what is a serious hurdle when search-ing for *the* concept of law, is not a problem at all for socio-legal positivism.

Distinctions must still be made to separate those references to law which fall within the interest of social and legal theorists, but that too will often not be a problem in practice. Context and usage sufficiently stabi-lize the meanings of these terms to allow us to make the necessary deter-minations. With regard to the above list, it is beyond dispute that we are not concerned with scientific laws or the laws of nature (as distinct from natural law), or with the laws of thought, logic, language, grammar, or sociology; likewise, it is beyond dispute that we are concerned with moral law, international law, ecclesiastical law, and with the laws of God (if that means natural law). A rough test that can be used to determine what qualifies for the purposes of a general jurisprudence is any phenomena conventionally referred to as 'law' in the sense involving a claim of *author-*

ity (without implying or attaching any necessary normative implications to this claim). That is the minimal shared semantic content of the label 'law' that matters for the purposes of this approach. This broad test cannot be used alone—the 'laws of grammar', for example, might satisfy the test—but the fact that the relevant context is jurisprudence and socio-legal studies will be a sufficient additional consideration to eliminate references to 'law' that fall outside the scope of the general jurisprudence. If there are borderline instances, they should be included because that fact alone makes them interesting and worthy of analysis. This is a pragmatic approach, which takes meaning as the product of usage within communities of discourse, as applied in particular contexts of action.

The second objection has to do with the vagaries of translation. 'Law' is an English term. There will be difficulties in translation when other cultures and societies are studied, in insuring that the same or comparable phenomena will be identified (Bix 1999a: 10–11). Indeed this will be a problem. *Droit* and *recht*, and the multitude of other terms that have been translated to mean 'law', have their own subtle connotations not captured by the English term 'law'. But this is the classic problem of translation among languages, which has been grappled with and overcome (to greater and lesser degrees of success, and with regular misunderstandings) throughout the history of human cross-language interaction. The problems entailed by translation are not a barrier to a conventionalist approach. There will be approximations and misfits, but that just means that care must be used, not that it cannot be done. Furthermore, certain legal phenomena today, like state law and international law, are ubiquitous or widely recognized and can be translated with relative ease.

Although these two problems, especially the first, has led legal theorists to turn to other criteria to identify law, like its supposed purpose, or function, or institutional nature, socio-legal positivism can avoid this fate by accepting the multiplicity of law, and by holding a flexible open attitude towards inclusion. Nothing of great or enduring moment rides on concluding that a particular phenomenon qualifies as law, so socio-legal positivism does not suffer from the high stakes that forced legal theorists to make increasingly difficult to justify determinations about what is or is not law.

A conventionalist approach to law opens up a new way of understanding and observing legal phenomena that promises to generate a host of new insights. The inevitable cost of striking out in a new direction is that a number of complex questions like those above must be confronted, as well as others, including the issue of category construction which will be taken up in the next chapter. These questions should be considered informative and potentially rewarding, rather than as reasons to fall back on the essentialist concept of law.

The essentialist concept of law was appropriate in the period of the rise of the nation state. Ironically, it obtained its purest formulation in the mid-twentieth century, by Hart, during a time in which the monopoly power of the state had already passed its peak. The insights of this concept of law, constructed on a model of state law, have already been plumbed in full. Now it has become a handicap, an approach unsuited for understanding a coming era that portends a proliferation of legal forms.

7   A Non-Essentialist Legal Pluralism

Legal pluralism has become a major theme in social scientific approaches to the study of law. Many of the leading socio-legal scholars in the world today—prominently including Marc Galanter, Peter Fitzpatrick, Roger Cotterrell, Gunther Teubner, Boaventura de Sousa Santos, Sally Engle Merry, and Masaji Chiba—have announced their allegiance to the concept of legal pluralism. It has been called 'the key concept in a post-modern view of law' (Merry 1992: 358), 'a central theme in the reconceptualization of the law/society relation' (Merry 1988: 869), and 'capable of identifying authentic legal phenomena operating on a global level' (Teubner 1997: 3). 'The new paradigm, as far as the social scientific study of law is concerned, is legal pluralism' (Griffiths 1995: 201). Indeed, adherents assert, law everywhere 'is fundamentally pluralist in character', and 'anyone who does not [accept this] is simply out of date and can safely be ignored' (ibid.). 'Today, this pluralism is so commonly accepted that it can be assumed' (Riles 1994: 641).

Two conceptually distinct versions of legal pluralism were introduced in Chapter 5: the older version which refers to the incorporation of customary law regimes in colonial and post-colonial legal systems; and the newer version which refers to the coexistence of more than one 'legal system' in all social arenas. The second, newer version is the one lauded by this ever-growing chorus of theorists. New legal pluralists insist that all societies are characterized by legal pluralism, that it is normal for more than one 'legal' system to coexist in the same social arena.

Its popularity notwithstanding, this dominant conception of legal pluralism is fundamentally flawed. A sign of this can be found in the fact that following almost twenty years of work on the concept of legal pluralism, accompanied by many confident pronouncements, there is little to show by way of concrete results. The core source of the problem is that, as is the case with legal theorists generally, legal pluralists hold essentialist assumptions about the nature of law. Specifically, the dominant approach to legal pluralism contains two essentialist assumptions: it assumes that law consists of a singular phenomenon which can be defined, and it assumes that law is by nature functional. This essentialist approach to law gives rise to unresolvable analytical and instrumental difficulties that inhibit the development of the idea of legal pluralism.

The conventionalist approach to law set out in the preceding chapter also leads to the recognition of legal pluralism, but in a very different way from prevailing approaches. Although the distinction will be made clearer in the course of this chapter, the basic contrast between these alternative ways of approaching legal pluralism can be stated at the outset: an essentialist approach identifies a single phenomenon—law—and points out that several manifestations of this phenomenon often coexist in the same social field; in contrast, a non-essentialist (conventionalist) approach points out that often different kinds and manifestations of law coexist in the same social field. The conventionalist approach, for reasons that will be stated, avoids the most debilitating difficulties that confront the essentialist approach, and provides a superior conceptual apparatus for grappling with the complex situation of legal phenomena in society today, both for legal theorists and for social scientists.

The objectives of this chapter are threefold: to articulate the conventionalist view of legal pluralism for the purposes of the general jurisprudence; to challenge the dominant view of legal pluralism, which is taking socio-legal studies down a fruitless path; and to continue the general programmatic project of integrating legal theory and socio-legal studies, adding this sociologically oriented chapter on top of the legal theory oriented chapter which came before. The first section will provide an overview of the prevailing conception of legal pluralism and the analytical and instrumental problems that bedevil it. The next section will identify the source of these problems in attempts to define law and in functionalist assumptions about law. The two sections thereafter will discuss the two most sophisticated recent elaborations of legal pluralism, by Santos and Teubner, respectively. The following section will elaborate in detail on the conventionalist, non-essentialist approach to legal pluralism. The final section will draw upon the analysis to revisit an old debate within legal anthropology regarding the issue of whether all societies have law.

The Problems with the Concept of Legal Pluralism

The *analytical* problems in the prevailing approach go to the heart of legal pluralism, and consist of two related aspects. While they agree on the initial proposition that there is a plurality of law in all social arenas, legal pluralists immediately diverge on what this assertion entails because there is no agreement on the underlying concept of law. For example, John Griffiths (1986: 38), one of the leading promoters of the concept of legal pluralism, defines law as 'the self-regulation of a "semi-autonomous social field" '; Galanter (1981: 18–19) defines law, following Hart, in terms of the differentiation and reinstitutionalization of norms into primary and secondary rules; Santos (1995: 114–15) defines law in more elaborate terms as 'a body of regularized procedures and normative standards, considered justicable in any given group, which contributes to the creation and prevention of disputes, and to their settlement through an argumentative discourse, coupled with the threat of force'. This lack of underlying agreement is the first aspect of the analytical problem.

Since there are many competing versions of what is meant by 'law', the assertion that law exists in plurality leaves us with a plurality of legal pluralisms. Legal pluralists can hardly be condemned for their failure to come up with an agreed upon concept of law. It is a goal that has eluded legal theorists as well, despite innumerable attempts. Until this problem is resolved, however, the concept of legal pluralism will not have a sound foundation. There is reason to believe that legal pluralists' prospects for successfully resolving this issue are better than those of legal theorists. The latter have typically approached the task in absolute or abstract terms, trying to define law *as such*. Although legal pluralists have also followed this strategy (contributing to their essentialism), they are social scientists who can instead choose to define law in a way designed to facilitate the study of social-legal phenomena of interest, which might provide the basis for an agreement.

Legal pluralists are in agreement on a second proposition, a negative proposition: 'not all the phenomena related to law and not all that are law-like have their source in government' (S. F. Moore 1986: 15). The core credo of legal pluralists is that there are all sorts of normative orders not attached to the state which nevertheless are 'law'. These non-state legal orders, as mentioned earlier, range from pockets within state legal systems where indigenous norms and institutions continue to exert social control, to the rule-making and enforcing power of corporations and universities, to the normative order which exists within small social groups, including, among others, business networks, community associations, factories, sports leagues, and the family. So generous a view of what law is, for reasons I will articulate in greater detail in the next section, raises the imminent danger of sliding to the conclusion that all forms of social control are law. As Sally Engle Merry (1988: 870) put it, 'Where do we stop speaking of law and find ourselves simply describing social life?' This is the second aspect of the analytical problem.

To their credit, legal pluralists have explicitly acknowledged this central difficulty. Aware that social life 'is a vast web of overlapping and reinforcing regulation', Galanter (1981: 18 n. 26) asked, 'How then can we distinguish "indigenous law" from social life generally?' Santos (1995: 429) conceded that 'this very broad conception of law can easily lead to the total trivialization of law—if law is everywhere it is nowhere'. Teubner (1997: 13) observed that it 'has proved hopeless to search for a criterion delineating social norms from legal norms'. The intractable nature of this problem can be seen in the following observation Merry (1988: 870) offered without a sense of contradiction, following a review of the field: 'Recent work defines "legal system" broadly to include the system of courts and judges supported by the state as well as *non-legal* forms of normative ordering' (emphasis added). This description of the 'legal' including the 'non-legal' captures perfectly the dilemma legal pluralists find themselves in. Although she endorsed the concept of legal pluralism, Merry (p. 879) was compelled to conclude that 'calling all forms of ordering that are not state law by the name law confounds the analysis'.

Some legal pluralists have embraced the inability to separate legal from social, insisting that 'all social control is *more* or *less* legal' (Griffiths 1986: 39) or that all normative orders can be seen in legal terms (Macdonald and Kleinhans 1997: 40). This approach attempts to make the best of an insoluble problem, but it generates confusion by doing violence to common understandings. Not only does the term 'law' thereby lose any distinctive meaning, but other forms of normative order, like moral norms, or customs, habits, and even table manners are swallowed up to become law. It also raises the suspicion that, at base, legal pluralism involves an exercise in theoretical relabelling, transforming the commonplace sociological observation that social life is filled with a pluralism of normative orders into the supposedly novel observation that it is filled with a pluralism of legal orders.

The analytical problems, then, are quite serious in both of their primary aspects. First, there is no agreed upon definition of law; and, secondly, the definitions of law proffered by legal pluralists suffer from a persistent inability to distinguish what is legal from what is social.

The *instrumental* problems are a function of the analytical problems. It is difficult to reconceptualize the law–society relationship if there is no agreement on what 'law' is, and if the versions of 'law' adopted share the inability to keep law from swallowing up social life. Without agreement on fundamental concepts that allow for the careful delineation of social phenomena, there can be no cumulative observation and data gathering.

Moreover, current versions of legal pluralism, especially in their con-flation of normative systems and legal systems, flatten and join together distinct phenomena, resulting in less refined categories, leading to less information and a reduction in the ability to engage in careful analysis. Consequently, the use value of the concept is open to serious question.

Despite its flaws, legal pluralists have succeeded in one instrumental respect: combating what they call the ideology of legal centralism. Legal centralism, according to legal pluralists, is the false ideology that 'law is and should be the law of the state, uniform for all persons, exclusive of all other law, and administered by a single set of state institutions' (Griffiths 1986: 4). Galanter (1981: 18) charged that ' "Legal centralism" has impaired our consciousness of "indigenous law" '. Legal pluralism was intended by its proponents to dispel this ideology. Griffiths (1995: 201) described the pursuit of this objective in heroic terms, whereby 'an ini-tially small band of revolutionaries waged an ideological battle against the vested ideology of legal centralism [until] . . . the paradigmatic change was accomplished (at least within legal sociology and anthro-pology of law)'. With the expanding list of social scientists and social the-orists announcing their rejection of legal centralism and adoption of legal pluralism, legal pluralists have reason to exult.

The history of social science and social theory, however, is littered with the remains of theories that claimed victory prematurely. The analytical and instrumental problems identified earlier cannot be suppressed no matter how impressive the list of adherents. The persistent and insur-mountable inability to separate legal from social, in particular, is a warn-ing that the current approach to legal pluralism is ill-fated. The source of the problems can be discovered through a closer look at how law is defined.

The Problems with Defining Law and Functional Analysis

Social scientists and legal theorists have struggled for so long to define what law is that it has been likened to 'the quest for the Holy Grail' (Hoebel 1954: 18). None of these attempts have succeeded in attracting a critical mass of support. The underlying reasons for this failure are involved and have been explored in depth elsewhere (see Tamanaha 1995a), but the problem can be laid out in relatively basic terms.

Virtually all attempts to define law fall into one of two categories: law is either seen in terms of concrete patterns of behaviour within social groups, or in terms of institutionalized norm enforcement. Significantly, both categories are oriented toward law in functional terms—in that both revolve around the maintenance of social order—although with a differ-ence. The former category focuses on the norms and mechanisms embodied within ordered behaviour itself; the latter category focuses on institutional responses to the disruption of ordered behaviour.

Eugene Ehrlich and Bronislaw Malinowski have formulated the most influential examples of the view of law in terms of ordered behaviour. The central insight propounded by both analysts is that law consists of and can be found in the regularized conduct or actual patterns of behav-iour in a community, association, or society. Ehrlich (1975: 24) declared that 'the law is an ordering'. In similar terms, Malinowski (1926: 14) insisted that the law is 'an aspect of . . . tribal life'. Both explicitly deny that law entails the existence of courts or institutions. Rather, the law is to be found in the customary practices that people actually follow in their social behaviour. The mechanisms of enforcement for this behaviour are to be found in their 'social relations' (Ehrlich 1975: 64), in the 'concate-nation of the obligations, in the fact that they are arranged into chains of mutual services, a give and take extending over long periods of time and covering wide aspects of interest and activity' (Malinowski 1926: 67).

The flaw with this approach to law is openly apparent, and by now familiar. Legal Realist Felix Cohen (1960: 187) observed that 'under Ehrlich's terminology, law itself merges with religion, ethical custom, morality, decorum, tact, fashion, and etiquette'. One commentator sug-gested that Ehrlich's view of law as order 'was quite similar to what anthropologists now mean by "culture pattern" ' (Shur 1968: 37). Similarly, anthropologist Sally Falk Moore (1978: 220) concluded that 'the conception of law that Malinowski propounded was so broad that it was virtually indistinguishable from the study of the obligatory aspect of all social relationships'. Owing to this difficulty, most social scientists (though not all legal pluralists) have rejected Ehrlich's and Malinowski's patterns of social order approach to the concept of law.

The genesis of the problem lies in the fact that there are many social mechanisms—in addition to those mentioned by Cohen: language, habits, shared culture, social typifications, and reciprocity, among others—that contribute to the creation and perpetuation of concrete pat-terns of behaviour. Ehrlich and Malinowski defined law in functional terms as that which maintains social order. But when functional equiva-lents or alternatives exist, as is the case with social order, defining some-thing in terms of the function alone inevitably draws in all of the functional equivalents. Niklas Luhmann's Functionalist approach to law provides a modern example of this problem. He (1985: 82) defines law in terms of the function of maintaining behavioural expectations. Luhmann recognizes, however, that it would not be easy to distinguish custom from law under this definition; more dramatically, he acknowledges that 'it is more difficult to establish a clear delineation between law, language and its accessories (e.g. rules of spelling). Although it may be intuitively clear that law is not identical with language, it takes some reflection to find the crucial point of difference' (p. 81). Again, this problem is created by the existence of functional equivalents.

To distinguish law from among other mechanisms that contribute to social order, one must identify the distinguishing characteristics of 'law', indicating what it is that makes law unique unto itself *apart from* any function it might fulfil. That is where concepts focusing upon institutionalized norm enforcement, the second approach to the concept of law, come into play. Many theorists, including Luhmann (p. 83), turned to the second category of the concept of law to avoid the problems created by the first.

The most prominent examples of this second approach have been produced by Adamson Hoebel, Max Weber, and H. L. A. Hart. Hart's view of law in terms of primary rules of obligation and secondary rules that identify and apply the primary rules has already been discussed. Here are Hoebel's and Weber's versions, respectively:

[A] social norm is legal if its neglect or infraction is regularly met, in threat or in fact, by the application of physical force by an individual or group possessing the socially recognized privilege of so acting. (Hoebel 1954: 28)

The term 'guaranteed law' shall be understood to mean that there exists a 'coercive apparatus,' i.e., that there are one or more persons whose special task is to hold themselves ready to apply specially provided means of coercion (legal coercion) for the purposes of norm enforcement. (Weber 1954: 13)

These concepts of law, it must be emphasized, were derived by abstracting the core features of state law. Hart and Hoebel explicitly acknowledged that their definition of law was modelled upon state law, and Weber was trained in law. In effect, all three analysts decided (or assumed) that *state law* is '*law*', which they then pared it down to its basic features.

Two key points of similarity between the two approaches to the concept of law should be noted before moving to the problems with the second approach. To repeat, like the first approach to the concept of law, this approach has a *functional orientation* towards law. The difference is the first approach starts from established patterns of order, and works backwards towards its sources to locate law (finding language, custom, and reciprocity); whereas this second approach takes state law to represent the epitome of law, and assumes that its primary function is to enforce norms, and that it is the primary source of normative order in society. The second point of similarity lies in their assumed view of the way they must satisfy the task at hand: both *define* law in terms of a *single particular set of criteria*— 'generate social order' (first) or 'institutionalized norm enforcement' (second). Both are looking for a single phenomenon to constitute law. Thereafter, for anything to qualify as 'law', it must satisfy these criteria. These two shared elements, I will show in the course of this chapter, are the essentialist characteristics which cannot be overcome.

Although this second approach to the concept of law is the more popular one, different groups of theorists find different aspects objectionable, so it too has failed to garner total support. For some, the emphasis on force and coercion (which Hart lessens) is too narrow, since there are manifestations of law which do not entail this threat. More problematic for many, defining law in terms of institutions engaged in the application of rules results in the conclusion that certain societies lack 'law'. Hart acknowledged that, by his definition, societies without secondary rules were pre-legal. In certain societies a compromise was arranged without the presence of a third party, or the application of rules did not seem to play a primary role, or contests, self-help, or retribution were the responses to disputes. Those social scientists (including many anthropologists) and theorists (including Functionalists) who are committed to the proposition that 'No society is without law' (S. F. Moore 1978: 215) must reject these concepts of law.

A different reason this second approach to defining law is not acceptable to some is that, as indicated in the previous chapter, it would include all kinds of institutionalized norms systems that many people would not consider law; universities and sports leagues, for example, use and consist of primary and secondary rules (see Galanter 1981: 17–18). The 'public' aspect of enforcement contained in Hoebel's definition is too weak and unstable—since many institutions can be considered public or private depending upon how one looks—to provide a distinguishing criterion which will produce consistent results, and which will allow a multitude of institutionalized norm systems that many people would not consider law. It is precisely for this reason that, in the preceding chapter, the identification of legal officials qua legal officials was used in lieu of the 'public' element.

Functionalist analysts, like Malinowski, offer another reason why this second approach must be rejected. The root of the problem is that institutionalized norm enforcement is seldom the dominant source of social order (see Searle 1995: 90–4; Tamanaha 1995a). As the discussion of functional equivalents just indicated, there are many sources of social order, including culture, customs, habits, reciprocity, and language, many of which do not entail the institutionalized enforcement of norms. Hence Malinowski (1926: 14) emphasized that law does 'not consist in any independent institutions'. If law, consistent with functionalist thinking, is whatever is necessary to social order, then law cannot be defined in terms of institutions, since institutions are not (always) necessary to social order.

A final set of reasons exist to challenge the second category of law, still related to functionalism, but now in terms *opposed* to functionalist reasoning. These definitions are crafted to capture the view that the core function of law (in particular, state law) is to enforce norms. But state law often does more things, or is used to do more things, than just maintain social order, including, among other functions or purposes, enabling, facilitative, performative, status conferring, defining, legitimative, distributive, power conferring, and symbolic; or being used as an instrument of harassment, manipulation, revenge, or vindication, or as a resource of raw power. Most of these uses are hidden from view by a concept of law that focuses on the enforcement of norms, which views the law from the societal standpoint, and in terms of disruptions. Hart's approach was more open to some of these non-functional aspects, but as argued earlier he fundamentally viewed law in terms of the function of social control. Perhaps the greatest blind spot of this approach is the deeply held assumption that law is always functional—the presence of and resort to law can, under many circumstances, actually lead to or perpetuate a disruption of social order (see Schur 1968: 84).

Hence all kinds of reasons, from various quarters, have conspired to prevent a consensus from forming in support of any particular definition or concept of law within either category. Not only do both general approaches to the concept of law fail individually; they cannot be combined because the first approach denies the necessity for institutions while the second approach insists upon it. These alternative approaches identify different criteria of existence (Tamanaha 1993a: 205–11).

The two analytical problems that have plagued legal pluralists can now be explained. Their inability to agree upon a concept of law is a consequence of the fact that the scholars involved have approached from different starting points, with different requirements, that force them to accept or reject one or the other category. In particular, those who start with the belief that all societies have law must reject the second category; those who believe that state law is the standard case for law must reject the first category. The second category has proven more popular for the plain reason that more people hold the latter belief.

Legal pluralists' inability to sharply distinguish legal from non-legal is a result of the fact that both categories suffer, in different ways, from this problem. The first category cannot distinguish law from the other functional equivalents that contribute to social order, like language, customs, moral norms, and etiquette. The second category cannot distinguish those forms of institutionalized norm enforcement which are 'legal' (like state law) from forms of institutionalized norm enforcement like sports leagues.

Given the logic of the dispute and the starting assumptions about law that are involved, *this impasse cannot be broken*. The only way out is to discard the two essentialist assumptions that have constructed the impasse. All functionalist assumptions about law must be dropped. And the assumption that law constitutes a single phenomenon that can be defined must be dropped. The argument in this section has established the reasons the first assumption must be dropped; the next three sections will show why the second must be dropped. A conventionalist approach to law is free of both assumptions.

One final point must be made about legal pluralists who adopt the second category of the concept of law, which includes most adherents. Recall that a major goal of legal pluralists is to combat legal centralism. What legal pluralists fail to recognize is that defining law in terms of the institutionalized enforcement of norms is itself a product of legal centralist beliefs. This conception of law is an abstraction of state law, as Hart and Hoebel acknowledged, and it reflects the notion that law can be reduced to a single phenomenon that state law epitomizes. Even as they strive to get away from state law, therefore, legal pluralists do so in a manner that perpetuates its influence.

Consider the fact that during the medieval period in Western Europe, prior to the consolidation of state power (and even after), there was a radical state of legal pluralism. In many areas there existed, simultaneously, local customary law, Germanic (or barbarian) customary law, vestiges of Roman law, canon law of the Roman Catholic Church, the law of merchants, law of the cities, and the law of local or provincial Chiefs, Warlords, or Kings, as well as other bodies of law (see Berman 1983; Ullmann 1969). Customary law, in particular, was multifarious. 'It was common to find many different codes of customary law in force in the same kingdom, town or village, even in the same house, if the ninth-century bishop Agobard of Lyons is to be believed when he says, "It often happened that five men were present or sitting together, and not one of them had the same law as another" ' (Morrall 1980). These various kinds and bodies of law cannot all be reduced to institutionalized norm enforcement, and thus would not qualify as 'law' under this definition, even though the people involved considered them to represent 'law'. Application of this legal pluralist definition of law would therefore have the effect of *reducing* the factual plurality of law, favouring only those forms that satisfy the abstracted characteristics of state law. The same effect occurs today. Natural law in its entirety, and substantial aspects of international law, for example, would not qualify as law under a standard having the institutionalized enforcement of norms as its touchstone. Without realizing it, and contrary to their expressed intentions, legal pluralists who adopt this approach in effect privilege the legal centralist model.

Santos's Concept of Law and Legal Pluralism

Using concrete examples can better establish the difficulties with essentialist, function-based approaches to the concept of law and legal pluralism. Boaventura de Sousa Santos has produced one of the most nuanced accounts of legal pluralism to date, especially as it relates to globalization. Santos (1995: 428–9) defines law as 'a body of regularized procedures and normative standards, considered justicable in any given group, which contributes to the creation and prevention of disputes, and to their settlement through an argumentative discourse, coupled with the threat of force'. With its emphasis on regularized procedures, normative standards, and the threat of force, his definition falls in the category of the institutionalized enforcement of norms, resembling the definitions put forth by Weber and Hoebel, except that the latter emphasized the *public* production and enforcement of norms. Santos's definition is functionalist in orientation, grounded in the idea that the function of law is to maintain the normative order of a group by enforcing norms and resolving disputes. His definition is essentialist in the sense that it specifies what he believes to be the characteristics essential to law—any social practice lacking in the characteristics he describes would not qualify as law.

Santos (p. 429) acknowledges that this broad definition 'could easily lead to the total trivialization of law' because if literally applied it would suggest that law is everywhere. He (ibid.) accepts that under his definition there are 'a great variety of legal orders circulating in society', but reduces this surplus by focusing particularly on 'six structural clusters of social relations in capitalist societies integrating the world system'. First is *domestic law*: 'the set of rules, normative standards and dispute settlement mechanisms both resulting from and in the sedimentation of social relations in the household' (ibid.). Second is *production law*: 'the law of the factory, the law of the corporation, the set of regulations and normative standards that rule the everyday life of wage labor relations (both relations of production and relations in production), factory codes, shop floor regulations, codes of conduct for employees and so on' (p. 432). Third is *exchange law*: 'the law of the marketplace, trade customs, rules and normative standards that regulate market exchanges among producers, between producers and merchants, among merchants, and between producers and merchants on the one side, and consumers on the other' (p. 434). Fourth is *community law* ('one of the most complex legal forms'): 'It may be invoked either by hegemonic or oppressed groups, may legitimize and strengthen imperial aggressive identities or, on the contrary, subaltern, defensive identities, may arise out of fixed, unbridgeable asymmetries of power or regulate social fields in which such asymmetries are almost nonexistent or merely situational' (ibid.). Fifth is *territorial* or *state law*: 'the law of the citizenplace and, in modern societies, it is central to most constellations of legalities' (p. 435). Finally, sixth is *systemic law*: 'the legal form of the worldplace, the sum total of rules and normative standards that organize the core/periphery hierarchy and the relations among nation-states in the interstate system' (p. 436). Although he sets them out in terms of separate clusters, Santos recognizes that the law from each of these clusters often overlaps with and interpenetrates law from the other clusters. State law, in particular, operates in each of the other clusters. It tends to be more spread out, and it 'is the only self reflexive legal form, that is, the only legal form that thinks of itself as law[.]' (p. 429).

Santos's account is exceedingly elaborate and can neither be fully reproduced, nor adequately critiqued, here. Instead I will rest upon a few observations. Ultimately, as with all alternatives, including the one I propose, the validity of his approach must be measured by its value in illuminating the situation of law in society. Santos's scheme suffers from an immediate weakness in this respect. It indeed appears to construe law as virtually everywhere. Society is a thick complex of legal regulation. In response to the question repeatedly asked of legal pluralism—'Where do we stop speaking of law and find ourselves simply describing social life?' (Merry 1988: 878)—Santos answers, in effect, much of social life *is* law.

By comprehensive relabelling, Santos has in effect juridified the social world. Contributing to this all-encompassing quality, the outlines of each cluster are exceedingly fuzzy. His community law category, in particular, appears devoid of any specific identifying content. It is as difficult to say what falls within this cluster as it is to identify what would not. More generally, it is difficult to say where each cluster ends and the others begin, intensifying the sense produced by his scheme that law is omnipresent, even overlapping and doubling up on itself.

In addition to these general objections, there are several evident specific difficulties raised by his approach. Santos is not troubled by the problem of including social norms within the 'legal', as revealed in his (1995: 429) use of the notion of domestic law, which he describes as 'very informal, nonwritten, so deeply embedded in family relations that it is hardly conceivable as an autonomous dimension thereof'. Reiterating this complaint would thus be redundant. But that does not obviate questions of conceptual consistency and use value. It is not clear that the normative relations within the family satisfy, or fit within, his explicit criteria for law as consisting of regularized procedures and normative standards backed by the threat of force. Informal, unwritten, deeply embedded family relations sounds like the first category of the concept of law described earlier, which focuses on concrete patterns of behaviour, while Santos's explicit definition of law focused on the second category of the concept of law. Santos's approach to law cannot, without pain of incoherence, straddle both categories of the concept of law, because they refer to ontologically distinct phenomena (see Tamanaha 1997: 111–14).

It is also not clear what is gained, either analytically or instrumentally, by appending the label 'law' to the informal, unwritten normative relations within the family. Use of this label does not facilitate the analysis of the normative relations within the family; to the contrary, it leads to confusion owing to an unfamiliar usage of terms. More important, there is a political cost. Consider the society where the culture tacitly approves of wife beating, while the state law makes it illegal, a situation that until relatively recently prevailed in many communities in the United States. Following Santos's view, one could assert that wife beating is prohibited under 'state law' but acceptable under 'domestic law'. Indeed, the claim that physical abuse is a form of 'domestic law' is almost required, since Santos defines law in terms of the threat of force, and physical abuse is the most obvious instance of the threat of force within the family. This phraseology should give discomfort to opponents of domestic violence, for the reason that the term 'law' often possesses symbolic connotations of right. The man who defends his conduct as legitimate according to 'domestic law' has much greater rhetorical authority than the man who claims that his father, and many of his pals, consider it appropriate for him to beat his wife, regardless of what the state law says.

As this example demonstrates, many patterns of behaviour are *bad*. Many legal pluralists are anti-state law by inclination—as reflected in their attack on legal centralism—and consequently have a tendency to romanticize non-state normative systems. In terms of Santos's own assertion that every concept of law and legal pluralism must be adjudged by its political value, especially in its capacity to relieve oppression, his concept is found susceptible to abuse. In fairness, Santos recognizes the romanticist tendency within legal pluralism (see Twining 2000: 228). He is well aware that forms of non-state 'law' can be bad. The problem is that categories of law cannot be constructed and evaluated according to political criteria, as he suggests they should be, precisely because political implications are always contingent upon particular situations; and thus are neither consistent across circumstances, nor can they be known in advance when constructing the scheme. Legal pluralists who engage in a blanket attack of legal centralism for political reasons make this error, because there are many situations in which state law does good, in which state law serves to relieve oppression brought about by oppressive social norms and practices.

There are more difficulties. The possibility that, under Santos's account, one body of rules can belong to more than one cluster leads to substantial confusions. This is not a problem at the borders only, but rather involves core instances of law. *Lex mercatoria* provides a good example. Santos (1995: 434) explicitly mentions *lex mercatoria* as an example of exchange law. However, it is clearly a prime example of global law, and thus also falls in his systemic law category. His (p. 436) comments on the status of *lex mercatoria* do not help clarify matters: '*Lex mercatoria* operates, in general, either as a mixture of exchange law and production law or as a mixture of exchange law and systemic law.' But according to Santos, *lex mercatoria is* exchange law and *is* systemic law, so what does it mean to call it a *mixture* of the two? Mixture implies a combination of two different elements, whereas the way he has constructed the categories suggests that *lex mercatoria* is simultaneously both. And his use of a disjunction raises even more questions. *Lex mercatoria* by its nature would seem to *always* be a form of systemic law, since it operates on the global level; by interjecting an 'either/or' in the above statement, however, Santos implies that when *lex mercatoria* is a mixture of exchange law and production law, it is not still a form of systemic law. With effort, Santos can probably clear up these confusions. These examples, however, and each additional one, merely re-raise the issue of whether the benefits of seeing law in this way are worth the trouble.

Indeed, what are the benefits of squeezing together all of the following under the rubric 'law': the sedimented social relations within the household, the 'law' of the corporation, the regulations and normative standards that rule the everyday life of wage labour relations, the 'law' of the marketplace, the rules invoked by hegemonic or oppressed groups or by imperial aggressive identities, the 'legal' form of the worldplace, state law, and much more? In their various and complex manifestations, these phenomena are far more unlike than alike one another. The one—narrow but fundamental—characteristic these myriad phenomena share is that they involve rules. This common element is captured most precisely by calling them *rule systems*, with the concomitant assertion that social arenas are characterized by *rule system pluralism*. No information is lost in this formulation because being involved with rules is exactly what they have in common. Instead of leading to the counter-intuitive assertion that much of social life is law, this will result in the uncontroversial assertion that rule systems are pervasive in social life (see Winch 1958).

Santos (1995: 115) contemplated, and flippantly dismissed, this obvious critique of his position: 'It may be asked: why should these competing or complementary forms of social ordering be designated as law and not rather as "rule systems," "private governments," and so on? Posed in these terms, this question can only be answered by another question: Why not?' The answer is that the latter designations allow for more subtle discriminations to be made, and thus they generate more information and facilitate more careful analysis than lumping all of this under the label 'law'.

The primary value Santos (ibid.) cites in support of his view is that 'a broad conception of law and the idea of a plurality of legal orders coexisting in different ways in contemporary society serve the analytical needs of a cultural political strategy aimed at revealing the full range of social regulation made possible by modern law (once reduced to state law) as well as the emancipatory potential of law, once it is reconceptualized in postmodern terms.' If emancipatory potential is the primary consideration, if it is about successful politics, then a premium must be placed upon the clarity and persuasiveness of the analysis and the analytical tools and resources it provides. On this score, Santos's version of legal pluralism is wanting.

Teubner's Autopoietic Approach to Legal Pluralism

Gunther Teubner recognized two basic flaws of legal pluralist attempts to define law: their inability to distinguish law from other kinds of social norms, and the limiting effect of defining law in terms of a single function. His solution to both problems was to follow the 'linguistic turn'. According to autopoietic theory, law consists of all discourse that invokes the binary communicative code of legal/illegal. This approach to identifying what law is excludes 'merely social conventions and moral norms since they are not based on the binary code legal/illegal' (Teubner 1992: 1451).

Teubner's (1997: 14–15) version of legal pluralism bears quoting at length:

Now, if we follow the linguistic turn we would not only shift the focus from structure to process, from norm to action, from unity to difference but most important for identifying legal propruim, from function to code. This move brings forward the dynamic character of a world-wide legal pluralism and at the same time delineates clearly the 'legal' from other types of social action. *Legal pluralism is then defined no longer as a set of conflicting social norms in a given social field but as a multiplicity of diverse communicative processes that observe social action under the binary code of legal/illegal.* Purely economic calculations are excluded from it as are sheer pressures of power and merely conventional or moral norms, transactional patterns or organizational routines. But whenever such non-legal phenomena are communicatively observed under the *distinction directrice* legal/illegal, then they play a part in the game of legal pluralism. It is the implicit or explicit invocation of the legal code which constitutes phenomena of legal pluralism, ranging from the official law of the State to the unofficial laws of world markets.

To avoid misunderstanding, I hasten to add that the binary code legal/illegal is not peculiar to the law of the nation-state. This is in no way a view of 'legal centralism.' It refutes categorically any claim that the official law of the nation-states, of the United Nations or of international institutions enjoy any hierarchically superior position. It creates instead the imagery of a heterarchy of diverse legal discourses.

A global merchant's law would belong to the multitude of fragmented legal discourses, whether the discourse is of state law, or rules of private justice or regulations of private government that play a part in the dynamic process of the mutual constitution of actions and structures in the global social field. Nor is it the law of nation-states but a symbolic representation of validity claims that determines their local, national or global nature. The multiple of orders of legal pluralism always produce normative expectations, excluding, however, merely social conventions and moral norms since they are not based on the binary code legal/illegal. And they may serve many functions: social control, conflict regulation, reaffirmation of expectations, social regulation, coordination of behavior or the disciplining of bodies and souls. It is neither structure nor function but the binary code which defines what is the 'legal propruim' in local or global legal pluralism.

Teubner's account of law and legal pluralism advances over previous formulations in precisely the respects he identifies. It provides a sharper means to distinguish law from non-law than heretofore available, and it allows for a broader view of the various functions of law. It is not essentialist in the same way as concepts that identify or define the essential characteristics of law (although, as I will show, it is essentialist in the different sense that it contains a thick set of functionalist and autopoietic assumptions about the nature of law). Teubner merely says law is whatever people discuss in terms of the binary code of legal/illegal.

This novel way of understanding law and legal pluralism produces interesting insights, but it contains several debilitating drawbacks. First I will point out the problems in relation to functional analysis, then the problems in relation to his way of distinguishing law from non-law, and finally the problems which follow from viewing law exclusively in terms of communication. Most of these problems, it should be noted, derive more from his autopoietic theory than from his particular approach to the identification of law.

Autopoiesis, initially developed by Niklas Luhmann, is fundamentally functionalist in nature. The term 'functionalism' has been described and used throughout this work in various contexts. To avoid confusion, and at risk of repetition, it is important to clearly separate two different versions of functionalism. The first version is Functionalism (with a capital F) from the field of sociology. Durkheim is the acknowledged progenitor of this version. Its basic postulate is that society should be viewed as an organism with interdependent subparts. Each subpart satisfies an essential function that contributes to the survival of the whole. The second version of functionalism (with a small f) refers to those (many) concepts that see law in terms of the function of social control and the coordination of behaviour. Or to put it differently, functionalism says that law is what law does, and what it does is maintain order. All Functionalists (F) have functionalist (f) views about law; but theorists who have functionalist views about law are not necessarily Functionalists, and indeed most are not. The categories of the concept of law do not break down along these lines. For example, Malinowski was a Functionalist, while Ehrlich was a functionalist.

Luhmann is the most prominent current Functionalist theorist (see Barnes 1995: 37). Law is an autonomous, differentiated subsystem within society, according to Luhmann (1985; 1982). Law, he asserted, involves the facilitation of normative behavioural expectations, and in serving this function it coordinates social order (1985: 82). Although Teubner's version of autopoiesis differs in certain respects from Luhmann's, it does not substantially differ in this view of the tight, functional relationship between law and society. Teubner (1988: 212) remarks: 'the historical relationship of "law and society" must, in my view, be defined as a co-evolution of structurally coupled autopoietic systems.' Consequently, although Teubner is more generous than most legal pluralists about the possible range of functions law might serve—'social control, conflict regulation, coordination of behavior, or disciplining bodies and souls' (Teubner 1992: 1451–2)—and (significantly) he does not use any particular function as a means to *identify or define* law, he still sees law as fundamentally functional in nature. He states this in the clearest terms when asserting in the above quotation that the 'multiple of orders of legal pluralism *always* produce normative expectations', and when all of the functions he recites revolve around the control and coordination of behaviour.

Under autopoietic theory, as in classical Functionalist theory, law is essential to the survival and functioning of the overall social system that provides its environment. Thus, Teubner's approach suffers from the same limitations of all function-based approaches. It eliminates from view the effects or consequences of law which are not functional in nature. 'A functionalist account mentions *only* those operations, and those consequences thereof, that help us understand the equilibrium of the system' (Barnes 1995: 40). Moreover, while it does allow for the possibility that specific instances of law might be dysfunctional or non-functional, it cannot accept the possibility that law in its totality is dysfunctional without necessarily resulting in societal collapse. As with all Functionalist accounts, the very notions of societal collapse, or normal and abnormal states, or equilibrium and disequilibrium, are problematic and difficult to specify (see Maniacs 1987: 158–60). The view that law is crucial to the equilibrium of society is what makes this an essentialist concept of law; the theory posits fundamental aspects of the relationship between law and society as a part of the nature of law (as an autopoietic system) and its relationship to its environment.

Beneath the surface, Teubner's approach to law contains a tension grounded in the fact that he relies upon conventionalism to identify law—law is whatever people code as law—while at the same time having a function-based view of the relationship between law and society. This combination harbours a potentially serious internal schism for Teubner because, as discussed in connection with Hart, 'Conventionalism is markedly at odds with traditional Functionalist explanations of social practices' (Marmor 1998: 526). Owing to the existence of functional alternatives or equivalents, conventional practices are underdetermined by functional needs. A given function can be satisfied by any number of conceivable conventional practices, regardless of whether they happen to be coded as 'law'. Nor is there any reason to assume that the social practices that are coded in this way in fact serve the function autopoiesis designates for law in society. The emergence of the actual conventional practices that exist in a given situation, and the terms in which they happen to be encoded, are the result of many factors—social, cultural, and historical—besides just functional needs. Teubner makes the precarious assumption that a conventional coding will correctly identify as 'law' phenomena that will take part in a function-based 'structural coupling' with society.

The problems with Teubner's version of law extend beyond its functionalism. While his method of separating law from non-law provides a sharper distinction between law and other social mechanisms than previous attempts, it nevertheless gives rise to serious objections of a different kind with regard to delimitation. The first problem is that his manner of line-drawing produces shifting and overlapping boundaries, even within a single conversation or within a single sentence. Imagine the following dialogue between two stock traders considering whether to use insider information:

SMITH. 'The value of NEWCORP's stock will increase by at least 50%, and perhaps 100%, when this takeover bid is made public tomorrow. If we buy now we will make millions.'

JONES. 'You're right, we could easily double our assets. But it's illegal, and we might get caught. We could go to prison.'

SMITH. 'Sure it's illegal, but the risk of being prosecuted is small. We'll be rich if we do it, so it's worth taking the chance.'

JONES. 'Okay, we probably won't go to prison, but it's still illegal, and furthermore it's immoral. It's wrong to break the law, and even if it weren't illegal it would be wrong and unfair to everyone else to use this information. Crime and immorality never pay.'

Perhaps aside from the exaggerated moral sensibilities expressed by Jones, this dialogue is realistic. The question is how Teubner would break down the communicative codes involved in this conversation. Before addressing this, it must be said, those readers whose initial reaction is that this conversation has nothing to do with being a part of law do not appreciate the radical nature of autopoiesis's grounding in communication.

Any act or utterance that codes social acts according to this binary code of lawful/unlawful may be regarded as part of the legal system, *no matter where it was made and no matter who made it.* The legal system in this sense is not confined, therefore, to the activities of formal legal institutions. (M. King 1993: 223–24, emphasis added)

In the above dialogue, the participants are invoking the binary code of legal/illegal, and thus according to autopoiesis this communication is a part of the legal system.

Smith's first observation is a purely economic calculation, so it would involve economics, not law. Jones's response is first economic, then legal, so the first sentence is not a part of the legal subsystem while the second and third are.

Smith's second observation begins as legal, then ends as economic. But it is a bit more complicated than that, because even his invocation of illegality is made in the context of an economic calculation. He discusses the illegality in terms of a transaction cost, which would appear to render it simultaneously economic in nature.

Jones's second response is similarly complicated. In the first sentence he invokes both law and morality. Moreover, in the second sentence, he makes the compound assertion that it is *immoral to break the law,* intertwining the moral and legal codes of communication in a single expression. Similarly, the third sentence, that crime and immorality never pay, intertwines the moral, legal, and economic.

To build a further twist into this already messy scenario, let us modify it to assume that Smith was actually an undercover investigator for the Securities and Exchange Commission, and this conversation was a part of a sting operation designed to catch Jones, who was suspected of being a dirty dealer. Furthermore, assume that Jones was aware of Smith's true identify and purpose (which explains Jones's sanctimonious stance), and he was merely playing along. Recall that Teubner includes the implicit as well as explicit invocation of the legal code as a part of law. Since both Jones and Smith would have legal/illegal in the back of their minds during the entire conversation, it would seem that it could be considered law in its entirety.

What appears to be a rather simple conversation is extraordinarily complex when analysed from an autopoietic standpoint. How each of these utterances is to be characterized—whether they are a part of 'law' or not—is debatable. Theorists of autopoiesis recognize that 'one communication may exist and have meaning in more than one system' (p. 224); so they would not necessarily be troubled by this analysis. But it does lead one to wonder what legal pluralists would gain by travelling down this path. Teubner has provided a relatively clear criterion for separating the legal from non-legal but in the process created other equally difficult analytical problems, and also ends up including aspects—like the above conversation, or subparts thereof—which most people would not consider 'law'.

The final problem with Teubner's approach to legal pluralism has to do with the autopoietic isolation upon communication as the embodiment of law. Characterizing law exclusively in terms of communication loses direct touch with the material power and effects of law. As Teubner (1997: 12) puts it, with the shift to communication as the locus of law, sanction recedes 'into the background', 'losing the place it once had as the central concept for the definition of law'. One may agree that sanction need not be the touchstone of law without going to the opposite extreme of banishing it from law. Integral to the authority of state law often lies the threat and application of force. Reducing law to communication, as autopoiesis does, eliminates raw physical violence from within law—thereafter it may at most be considered an effect or consequence of law as communication, or a part of law's environment. It would be more true to the social reality of certain manifestations of law, certainly at least state law, to formulate an analytical apparatus which would include the material power of law as central to its existence while excluding such marginal phenomena as the private conversation between two individuals contemplating a criminal course of action.

The foregoing objections to Teubner's account are all linked to its autopoietic and Functionalist intellectual underpinnings. These can be bracketed, however, to uncover an important insight alluded to earlier contained within Teubner's version of law. He delimited law in terms of how the social actors themselves identified law—law includes all instances of communication invoking the binary code of legal/illegal. Although Teubner called his formulation a 'definition' (ibid.), a better way to view it is that he articulated a criterion for the identification of law. His criterion is parasitic. In effect, it identifies as law whatever social actors themselves discuss in legal terms. The non-essentialist, conventionalist approach to law is based on the same insight.

A Conventionalist Version of Legal Pluralism

Essentialism and the Conventionalist Alternative

For more than a century, legal theorists and social scientists have conceptualized law by asserting that 'law is . . .,' usually filling in the remainder of the phrase with some variation of an institutionalized, function-based abstraction of law, such as: law is institutionalized norm enforcement, law is institutionalized dispute resolution, law maintains social order, law coordinates behavioural expectations, law integrates society, law is governmental social control, and so forth. This approach implicitly presupposes an essentialist view of law because it assumes that law is some particular phenomenon that can be captured in a formulaic description. From these efforts, socio-legal scholars have learned that there are many kinds of norms and rule systems, that many kinds of institutions enforce norms, that there are many ways of resolving disputes, and that a variety of sources coordinate behaviour, integrate society, and contribute to the maintenance of social order.

Each formula, though intended to define law, is instead best understood to create a function-based category. This can be observed by simply deleting the words 'law is . . .' from each proffered definition. That move immediately transforms the definitions into categories, like: 'institutionalized norm enforcement' (which includes everything from baseball leagues, to corporations, to state law); or 'institutionalized dispute resolution' (everything from community mediation, to business arbitration, to state law); or the 'coordination of behavioural expectations' (everything from habits, to language, to state law); or 'maintains social order' (everything from socialization, to language, to customs and morality, to state law); or 'governmental social control' (everything from government-sponsored education and advertising, to selectively subsidizing or cost increasing tax regimes, to state law). It is correct that each category includes state law as one of its members. But that is merely evidence of the versatile nature of state law, and it is a product of the fact that state law served as the model for most theorists when formulating their abstract concept of law. While each category may contain one or more members which overlaps with those of other categories (like state law), no overlap is complete, and other than state law no single member falls in every category. Each category consists of a different set of members. These findings demonstrate that each category goes beyond state law, while at the same time no single category encompasses every facet of state law (keeping in mind that state law does and is used to do many things that fall outside the categories recited above).

The essential points, which have already been made in several different ways, are that every attempt to define law in functional terms has suffered from being either too broad or too narrow. They have been too broad by including phenomena like the normative regulation within a corporation or the family, ultimately expanding to encompass virtually all social regulation and institutionalized norm enforcement within the term 'law'. They have been too narrow in two respects. First, when law is defined in terms of a particular function, like social control, everything else law does (or is used for) falls outside the scope of that definition, artificially constricting our ability to study and observe these other activities and functions. Secondly, it is too narrow in the sense that these definitions often exclude what many people would think should qualify as law. Natural law, for example, as well as certain manifestations of religious law or customary law which do not involve institutions, or are not focused on social order, would not qualify as 'law' under most of these definitions despite the fact that the people involved see them as such.

The long history of failed attempts at articulating an essentialist concept of law should be taken as instructive—there is something wrong with the ways in which the question of what law is has been posed and answered. The source of the intractable difficulty lies in the fact that law is a thoroughly cultural construct. What law is and what law does cannot be captured in any single concept, or by any single definition. Law *is* whatever we attach the label *law* to, and we have attached it to a variety of multifaceted, multifunctional phenomena: natural law, international law, state law, religious law, and customary law on the general level, and an almost infinite variety on the specific level, from *lex mercatoria* to the state law of Massachusetts and the law of the Barotse, from the law of Nazi Germany to the Nuremberg trials, to the Universal Declaration of Human Rights and the International Court of Justice. Despite the shared label 'law', these are diverse phenomena, not variations of a single phenomenon, and each one of these does many different things and/or is used to do many things. There is no law *is* . . .; there are these kinds of law and those kinds of law; there are these phenomena called law and those phenomena called law; there are these manifestations of law and those manifestations of law.

No wonder, then, that the multitude of concepts of law circulating in the literature have failed to capture the essence of law—it has no essence. A non-essentialist concept of law thus requires that law be conceived in a way that is empty, or that at least does not presuppose any particular content or nature. But that is impossible—a concept with no content is not a concept at all. Formulating a concept of law, therefore, will not work. Instead what is needed is a way to *identify* law that is not itself a concept of law, but rather, like Teubner's approach, the specification of criteria for the identification and delimitation of law. That is what the conventionalist approach to law provides. To repeat: *Law is whatever people identify and treat through their social practices as 'law' (or recht, or droit, etc.).* If this approach to law seems odd, it is because the essentialist approach to law has such a strong hold on our thinking. Readers might react negatively that law must be something more concrete and distinct. In fact, law in its various kinds and manifestations is *always* concrete and distinct. But the distinctive content of particular manifestations of law are determined by the social actors who give rise to them, not by theorists legislating for others based upon an abstract conception of the essential requirements of a singular phenomenon they designate as law.

A state of 'legal pluralism', then, exists whenever more than one kind of 'law' is recognized through the social practices of a group in a given social arena, which is a relatively common situation. This approach is different from most approaches to legal pluralism in a fundamental respect, already stated at the outset of this chapter. In the typical legal pluralist approach—say, defining law as the institutionalized enforcement of norms, or as the self-regulation of the semi-autonomous social field—law is 'plural' because in a given social arena there are many manifestations of institutionalized norm enforcement (corporations, sports leagues) or many self-regulated semi-autonomous social fields (the garment industry, a university, a family). This kind of plurality involves the coexistence of more than one manifestation of a single basic phenomenon. This is the implication of using a definition with a singular set of necessary criteria. In contrast, I assume that the label 'law' is applied to what are often quite different phenomena—sometimes involving institutions or systems, sometimes not; sometimes connected to concrete patterns of behaviour, sometimes not; sometimes using force, sometimes not. Thus, the plurality I refer to involves different phenomena going by the label 'law', whereas legal pluralism as typically conceived involves a multiplicity of one basic phenomenon, 'law' (as defined).

Category Construction

A complicated implication of this conventionalist approach to the identification of what law is must now be addressed. Up to this point, for the sake
of convenience, following Hart, I have referred to primitive or customary
law, international law, state law, religious law, and natural law as if they
were kinds of law. This shorthand reference is improper in so far as it creates the impression that they comprise separate categories based upon
shared characteristics. They can indeed be considered categories, but categories by virtue of shared labels, not shared characteristics. Investigation
of conventions within social arenas will reveal that various phenomena
that go by these labels can have little in common with one another. Some
manifestations of primitive law consisted of the institutionalized enforcement of norms, while others lacked this characteristic. The situation is
more complicated than that, since no group has ever identified their own
law as 'primitive law'. That is a label used by legal and social theorists.
'Customary law' has many different manifestations as well, one primary
form of which exists only in the context of recognition by state law. The
internal variation of what goes by the name of natural law is also substantial. Finally, international law arguably does not constitute a category at
all, but represents a single manifestation of law (a category of one). These
observations reflect significant concerns. The danger is not only that we
might be comparing apples and oranges, but that inconsistencies of usage
may give rise to categories with members sharing little in common.

A key analytical distinction will help navigate around these problems.
Two different levels in the analysis must be kept in mind: the concepts of
the people being studied, and the concepts of the social scientists or theorists doing the study. In interpretive theory, as articulated by Alfred
Schutz (1962: 5–7) and Clifford Geertz (1983: 57–8), the latter are 'second level' or 'experience far' constructs, which are constructed by social
scientists and theorists in a way designed to meet their interests and concerns. These second level constructs are built upon, but not limited to, the
'first level' or 'experience near' conceptions of the social actors being
studied.

The general jurisprudence proposed here will involve the construction
of two (at least) qualitatively different sets of categories relative to law: one
based on conventionally applied labels; the second based on abstracted
features. Both sets of categories are second level constructs in the sense that
both are created by theorists. They are simply constructed in different
ways, the first by theorists hewing more closely to the identifications of lay

people, and the second oriented more toward the interests of theorists in locating fundamental features. Both have the same starting point in that both begin with conventionalist identifications of law. From that shared beginning, however, they go in completely different directions, which will be indicated below. Other kinds of categories based upon second level constructs are also possible. These two are elaborated here because up until now theorists have been typically constructing categories of the second kind, which is a valuable exercise, but the general jurisprudence suggests that the first kind must also be considered.

The first set of categories consists of conventionally applied labels of law: i.e. state law, natural law, customary law, indigenous law, international law, transnational law, religious law, and any others that might exist. All those phenomena recognized as state law fall in the state law category, all those recognized as natural law fall in the natural law category, all those recognized as religious law fall in the religious law category, and so forth. These are conventionalist categories. It should be understood from the outset that the members of each of these categories will not necessarily share characteristics in common beyond the fact that the same label (at the general level) has been applied, and indeed they may have features in common with members of other conventionalist categories. Nonetheless, it is still necessary to recognize and study the fact that the general label has been appended, for that fact alone has significant implications, especially comparative ones.

The second set of categories consists of complexes of shared fundamental features abstracted from phenomena to which the label 'law' has been conventionally attached. These feature-based categories can be formulated by theorists only after investigations of the various social practices and phenomena to which convention attaches the name 'law'. When sufficiently developed, these categories may be organized as a typology. Typologies and categories based upon abstracted characteristics are analytical devices that are designed to meet the purposes of the theoretician who constructs them. The grounding in social practices, and the abstraction of core features, insures that the categories created will be comparable on the same level. This second kind of category construction may well give rise to a category encompassing publicly institutionalized norm enforcement, for example, but it will now be viewed in much different terms than those of Hart, Hoebel, and Weber. It will not be a concept or definition of law as such. It will merely represent a category for the purposes of analysis, based upon the abstracted features of one conventional version of law (state law), constituting just one category among others.

At the end of this process, there will be a set of label-based categories and a set of abstracted feature-based categories. Both sets must remain open to new members, because social actors are always free to create new labels using the term 'law', and because social actors are always free to attach the label 'law' to social phenomena with different core features (an example being the relatively recent development of the label 'indigenous law', which appears to have a mostly rhetorical existence in the arena of minority rights discourse), and because the features abstracted for the second category are determined by the interests of theorists, which can change. The possibilities of making fruitful comparisons and contrasts within and between these two categories, and for examining specific instantiations of law relative to both categories, are literally endless. For example, specific empirical investigations will reveal that certain manifestations of what are called state law might lack the features of the category derived from state law. Administrative law in many Western states, to provide one such instance, often involves balancing of interests and instrumental reasoning for the purposes of achieving policy initiatives, and thus does not obviously fit the description of primary and secondary rules or institutionalized norm enforcement.

Advantages over Existing Approaches to Legal Pluralism

This version immediately overcomes the primary defect that plagues other accounts of legal pluralism—the inability to distinguish legal from social norms. Law is whatever people in a social arena conventionally recognize as law through their social practices. Anything not so identified is not law. Under this account, the normative relations within the family or a private conversation between two people regarding illegal conduct, for example, will be considered 'law' only if existing social practices within that social arena conventionally characterize them in terms of 'law'. Indeed, the problem that completely debilitates current versions of legal pluralism is not even an issue under this conventionalist approach, because it does not resort to a definition that encompasses other kinds of social phenomena. Instead it contains a criterion for the identification of law that is parasitic upon how people in a social arena identify law. A related benefit of this approach is that it is neither too narrow, because it does not exclude phenomena people consider to be law, nor too broad, because it only includes what people consider to be law, in the ways identified relative to existing legal pluralists accounts (though it may be too broad for some in a different way to be mentioned later).

The conventionalist approach is superior in another important respect: it allows for more refined distinctions to be made within the field of study. Many legal pluralists are unable to speak simultaneously about rule system pluralism or normative pluralism *as well as* about legal pluralism, because they conflate the latter with the former. This conflation is reflected in Santos's acknowledgement that 'legal' pluralism could also be called 'rule system' pluralism, and in frequent suggestions by legal pluralists that legal pluralism is equivalent to 'normative' pluralism: 'the coexistence of plural *legal or normative* orders is a universal fact of the modern world' (C. Fuller 1994: 10). The inability to distinguish law from rule system and from normative regulation, however, results in a less nuanced view of the various phenomena at play in the social arena.

Pursuant to the conventionalist approach, law is identified in terms of an entirely different axis. For example, certain kinds of law (such as natural law and versions of customary law) often do not amount to rule 'systems' but still qualify as 'law'; and rules systems that are not conventionally identified as 'law' (and the overwhelming majority, including universities and sports leagues, are not so identified) are rule systems but not 'law'. Law can thus be distinguished from rule system. Likewise, many kinds of norms, like most moral norms, do not exist in what would be called 'systems'. So norms are distinct from rule systems, which are distinct from law. Social analysts can thus identify normative pluralism, rule system pluralism, and legal pluralism in terms of separate criteria, talk about them together, and observe where they overlap or intersect and how they interact. Applying the conventionalist approach to law, one can say not only that there is a pluralism of kinds of law, but also a pluralism of kinds of rule systems, as well as a pluralism of kinds of normative regulation (which ranges from social disapprobation, to rule systems, to most manifestations of 'law'). A much richer picture of the social situation is available under this approach.

This approach to law and legal pluralism reopens old questions from new angles. For example, an informative question will be to ask *why*, in a given social arena, the label 'law' has been appended to a particular social phenomenon—that is, what political, moral, rhetorical, symbolic, power, and so on, benefits follow from the label—and what relationship it has to other phenomena going by the same name. A rich example of this is the notion of customary law. In post-colonial societies, it is common for state courts to draw upon what they call 'customary law'. As described in Chapter 5, legal anthropologists have pointed out that, at least in certain instances, 'customary law' norms often are inventions made up in the context of colonial legal systems. People in these societies also often refer to certain bodies of norms as 'customary law', which are not always the same bodies of norms as those recognized by the state legal system. In addition, there are also lived customs within these societies that have not been identified as forms of customary law by anyone. Legal pluralists have labelled the recognition of customary law by the state as old legal pluralism, the study of which they reject in favour of the study of new legal pluralism (the version critiqued here). This artificial separation of kinds of legal pluralism limits the phenomena to be studied and the kinds of questions that can be asked. The non-essentialist version of legal pluralism reopens all of these questions in a way that cuts across the old/new dichotomy. Social investigators can ask *who* (which group in society, which social practices) identifies *what* as 'customary law', *why*, and under what circumstances? What is its interaction with state law, and what relationship does it have, if any, with actual customs circulating within society? The same kinds of investigations can occur in a social arena with regard to religious law, natural law, the *lex mercatoria*, and so forth.

Religious law provides another instructive example. Recall that Santos's typology of six clusters of legal pluralism does not specifically account for religious law despite its prevalence in many different societies today. In certain societies (theocracies like Iran and Afghanistan), religious law *is* state law; in other societies, state law incorporates from religious law selected bodies of norms (like in the Republic of Ireland), or even complete institutions (as in Israel); in many societies, religious law stands entirely apart from state law (as with canon law in the past and today), as a separate and sometimes competing source of legal authority for the populace. The approach to legal pluralism I suggest recognizes all of these as forms of law—assuming existing social practices within the social arena treats them as such—and urges that they be studied in their specific manifestation, in their relations with other kinds of law in that social arena, and as they compare to general categories of kinds of law or manifestations of law in other social arenas.

Finally, this approach to legal pluralism, as with existing approaches, continues to challenge the notion that 'law' is exclusively the law of the state. The non-essentialist version of legal pluralism easily recognizes forms of law that may have little or no connection to the state. No one version of law is placed in a hierarchy above any other—the degree of actual influence in a given social arena can be determined only following investigation, based upon the results of the inquiry. No presuppositions are made about the normative merit or demerit of a particular kind of law, or about its efficacy or functional or dysfunctional tendencies or capacities (if any).

Indeed, one merit of this approach—what makes it non-essentialist— is that it is entirely free of presuppositions about law (beyond the negative one that it has no essence), or, stated more precisely, free of presuppositions about the phenomena to which people attach the label 'law' to. Everything is left open to empirical investigation, and category construction and analysis following such investigation. Another significant merit of this approach is that its lack of content and presuppositions regarding law creates a critical distance that facilitates study as well as evaluation. It directs an equally sharp-eyed, unsentimental view at all manifestations and kinds of law. Whether the claims of a particular social practice regarding 'law' are made by a criminal gang, a band of revolutionary zealots, a group of religious fundamentalists enforcing 'God's law', or the state legal apparatus, each will be subjected to the same scrutiny, which includes examining what is gained by use of the label 'law'. Owing to its lack of presuppositions and its distance, this equalizing approach to all claims about law enables and facilitates critical evaluation, which is a key reason for, and justification behind, engaging in the project of a general jurisprudence.

Breaking the Impasse—A Look Back at Legal Anthropology

The conventionalist approach to the identification of law avoids the main characteristics that led to the impasse in the attempt to achieve a consensus over how to conceptualize law. That does not, however, mean it will be successful in breaking the impasse. Given the history of the problem, it would be foolish to think otherwise. As with any approach, this one has weaknesses, and will generate opposition. Several of the most serious possible points of contention were addressed in the previous chapter, regarding who and how many people must consider a phenomenon to be law for it to qualify, regarding determining which usages of the term 'law' qualify for inclusion under the conventionalist approach, and regarding the difficulties of translation. Whether the answers given are satisfactory cannot be determined fully until the suggested approach is implemented and its success evaluated.

Another point of opposition will come from legal theorists and others who believe that law has an inherently moral aspect to it. They will resist with fervour any suggestion that, for example, a criminal gang claiming to be 'law' could have the status of law. The best response to this opposition is to point out that it is entirely appropriate for a legal theorist to be committed to a moral view of law; socio-legal positivism, however, consistent with its background in socio-legal studies, takes a descriptive approach to legal phenomena. As an empirical matter it is undeniable that many manifestations of law (including instances of state law) have claimed a moral component but not lived up to it; accordingly, it would be inappropriate, or at least a mistake, from the standpoint of the empirical study of law, to build a moral requirement into the definition of law.

From within the social sciences, opposition will come from two different quarters (at least). Functionalists (capital F) cannot accept the conventionalist approach because it empties out all of the many presuppositions Functionalism builds into the concept of law. In a variety of different ways and contexts, this book has raised criticisms of Functionalist theory, and has tried to demonstrate several of its drawbacks as an analytical framework. Rapprochement between Functionalists and this conventionalist approach is therefore impossible. Many others with a functionalist (lower case f) understanding of law will also have hesitation, because the view that law is functional in nature runs deep, but here there is a reasonable prospect of gaining acceptance for conventionalism. As emphasized in the preceding chapter, the argument pressed here does not deny that manifestations of law (state law in particular) often carry out significant functions. Rather, the argument is that such functions should not be built into the definition of law, and that law should not be seen exclusively in terms of functions. These functionalists, it is hoped, will see the benefits of coming over to the conventionalist view, which is congenial to many other beliefs about law and legal pluralism they may hold.

The second quarter within the social sciences that will likely oppose the conventionalist approach is those, primarily legal anthropologists, who believe that all societies have law. One of the implications of a conventionalist approach is that if no group within a society refers to 'law', then there is no law in that society. Thus, it is conceivable that there will be societies without law. This possibility is heightened, and made more complicated, by threshold puzzles regarding how to translate the term 'law' into traditional societies. Responding to this potential source of opposition is necessary, not just for its own sake, but because the answer will point back to an earlier stage in the development of legal anthropology that, in key respects, arrived at the same place as conventionalism. The elaboration of this (unseen) connection will help solidify the argument on behalf of the conventionalist approach.

A few preliminary remarks must be said about the assertion that 'No society is without law' (S. F. Moore 1978: 215). When made outside the context of Functionalist theory—which includes law a priori as a necessary subpart of all social systems—this assertion is a political belief, even when made by social scientists. Whether law exists in all societies is a combined conceptual/empirical question: it depends upon first identifying a concept of law, then applying this concept to examine whether the phenomenon it captures is always present. However, the assertion that law exists in all societies is usually made *prior* to the formulation or adoption of a concept of law. Starting with this (political) belief has significant conceptual consequences: when attempting to define law the believer is forced to come up with criteria that will identify phenomena which are indeed present in all societies, otherwise the starting commitment will be falsified. This places a heavy demand, since the theorist is then restricted to looking for phenomena that are universally shared, which is not easy given the diversity of societies and the many changes that have occurred in the course of history.

There was a time not long ago, especially during the early development of anthropology, when it was important politically to assert that all societies have law. In the nineteenth-century heyday of evolutionary theory, as indicated in Chapter 3, self-congratulatory exaltation of the Enlightened West, by way of contrast to savages, was common, and law was touted as one of its key marking achievements: 'Without [law] there could be no civilization and no order' (Field 1995: 713). Given views like this, which were widespread, it is understandable that anthropologists would find it necessary to demonstrate that 'primitive' societies also have law. This agenda is on open display in Malinowski's classic *Crime and Custom in Savage Society*.

This time has passed, however, and few people (outside of sanguine legal theorists) still identify law with civilization. Against those that do, rather than insist that law exists everywhere, which by implication perpetuates the equating of civilization with law, a better response would be to suggest a more appropriate measure of civilization, such as how generously a society treats it least well off members. For the most part, anyway, the attempt to measure civilization is now widely condemned as an inevitably ethnocentric, useless exercise, and has been largely abandoned. Thus, there is little political justification to continue to assert that all societies have law.

With this background, it is now possible to confront directly the classic question of whether law exists in 'primitive' societies, and the related issue of translation. Every nation in the world today has state law, and the term 'law' has already been translated in most languages in the world. Whatever translations there are for 'law', including whatever indigenous terms are used to designate the existing state legal apparatus, will satisfy the requirements of the conventionalist approach. Thus, existing translations of the term 'law' will have already done most the necessary work for the identification of 'law' in non-English contexts (keeping in mind that disputes and borderline cases will remain, with the default rule being inclusion).

This is not the case, however, with the study of no longer existing historical societies, or so-called 'primitive' societies, in relation to which any translations for the term 'law' must be done in hindsight. To translate or locate 'law' in such societies one must have a definition of law that identifies what shape law takes or what function law fills. Otherwise it will be impossible to identify any parallel terms or phenomena within the indigenous language. The conventionalist approach, therefore, will not work in such contexts.

Although this limitation might at first blush appear to expose a flaw in the conventionalist approach, it actually demonstrates its coherence, in so far as it arrives at precisely the point legal anthropologists came to two decades ago. During the 1950s and 1960s it was de rigueur for every legal anthropologist to begin a major work either formulating a definition of law or adopting one already formulated. This definition was thought to be necessary as a means to identify the appropriate subject-matter to be studied in the context of *legal* anthropology. After many attempts (see S. F. Moore 1978: 218–23), and no signs of agreement, the debate over the concept of law came to be seen as a wasteful exercise which has 'not borne much fruit' (Nader 1965: 5). By the mid-1970s, the consensus in the field was that 'for the time being, at least, it seems clear that we must displace law from the center of our conceptual focus' (Abel 1973b: 224). Thereafter, eschewing the claim to focus on 'law' as such, 'legal' anthropologists explicitly identified their focus of attention to be on phenomena such as dispute processing institutions or on the various mechanisms that maintain social order. A striking example of this is Simon Roberts's text *Order and Dispute: An Introduction to Legal Anthropology* (1979: 9), which states in the preface that 'Despite the sub-title, it must be said that this is not a book about law'. An entire chapter in the book was dedicated to explaining 'Why Not Law'. By this time the debate within the field over the concept of law had all but expired (until later revived again by the discussion surrounding legal pluralism).

It is essential to recognize that, although legal anthropologists quit the debate over the concept of law, they continued to study precisely the same phenomena they had before (e.g. institutionalized norm enforcement, institutionalized dispute processing, sources of social order), only now without making the claim that what they were studying was 'law' (as Roberts indicated), even as they still identified their field as 'legal' anthropology (as Roberts did). Legal anthropologists thus found themselves trapped in a peculiar box involving a kind of forced self-denial.

Earlier I suggested that theorists should simply drop the 'law is . . .' off the front of attempts to define law, and keep what remains as function-based categories. Without describing it in such terms, in effect that is what these legal anthropologists did. The dilemma they were forced into reveals this: asking whether primitive societies have 'law' is the *wrong question*. It is a question that can be answered correctly in more that one way, which means that it is poorly constructed. We can ask whether a given primitive society has institutionalized dispute resolution, because that is a social phenomenon described in functional terms, which can be compared across different languages, cultures, and forms of social organization.

But the term 'law', *our* term 'law', is not like that. Like many terms, we have applied it to more than one phenomenon; we have used it in different ways and for different purposes, sometimes inconsistently; we have attached it to certain phenomena which have not been present in all societies, and to certain phenomena which have; and political considerations often play a significant role (for lay people as well as social scientists and theorists) in determining whether the label 'law' is applied to a given phenomenon. Or to make the fundamental point again: the term 'law' has no essence. Every dictionary of the English language will contain a lengthy entry for the term 'law', including such phenomena as customs, state imposed rules, general principles, and religious laws, among others. Each of these entries is recognizable as law and correct in its own way. Furthermore, they have distinct criteria of existence (as elaborated in terms of the two categories at the outset of this chapter) which cannot be combined at a more abstract level. Law might have begun with a single meaning (though the Greek *nomos* and *nomoi* already had ambiguous references), but whether by metaphor or analogy or direct extension its usages expanded to point of being identified (in a non-metaphorical sense) with several different phenomena. Conventionalism, and legal pluralism in conventionalist terms, is thus forced upon us as the way to identify and understand law.

The conventionalism argued for here cannot be applied to identify law in primitive societies, then, for precisely the same reasons that forced 'legal' anthropologists to drop claims that they were studying 'law'. Some theorists saw 'law' in terms of patterns of order, and some saw 'law' in terms of institutionalized norm enforcement, and given their starting points there was no way to overcome this divide. Legal pluralists revived all the same old problems when they resorted, once again, to attempts to define law, and did so in essentialist, functionalist terms. The only way to break out of the cycle is to adopt the conventionalist approach to law, and to stop asking the question whether primitive societies had law. The political concerns that prompted legal pluralists to make the claim that they have identified 'legal' phenomena are not furthered by this claim. And the political concerns that initially prompted the question of whether primitive societies had law are no longer present, so there is no reason to ask the question.

8   Elements of a General Jurisprudence

Delineating the Field of Study—Social Arena

At the completion of Chapter 5 the concepts law and society had both become problematized. The articulation of a conventionalist approach in Chapters 6 and 7 provided a reconstruction of law that left us with a pluralism of legal phenomena. No attempt will be made to reconstruct the concept of society. The literature on the subject makes clear that it is not serviceable as an analytical device. The notion of society serves as shorthand for a discrete group or community unified in certain essential respects, usually including language, culture, politics, geography, tied at the broadest level to the state. The modern condition, with the penetration of almost every corner of the globe by external influences, combined with internal pluralism of some kind in most social arenas, renders it impossible to confidently identify discrete groups of any kind. Formerly distinct boundaries have become fuzzy at best. This is not necessarily a new condition. The holistic or unitary view of a society has perhaps always been a dubious notion that is more a projection by social theorists than a reflection of reality (see Wrong 1994: 223–6). Yet another problem with the notion of society, specifically for purposes of this work, is that its boundaries are tied to groups. Intra-group and trans-group relations, which are essential to any attempt to understand law, are not easily taken account of within a study that centres upon societies.

I reject society as an analytical concept with full awareness—and a tinge of embarrassment—that this work has been entitled, and pitched throughout, as a general jurisprudence of law and *society*. Appreciating the unparalleled value of the term in conveying a central idea, I will continue to refer to society in its common usage, while creating a more acceptable technical substitute as one of the elements of the general jurisprudence.

The starting point of the general jurisprudence is an orienting concept to identify the boundaries of the study. There is no shortage of possible candidates for such a concept in the theoretical literature. Sally Falk Moore's semi-autonomous social field (SASF) is one option. Pierre Bourdieu's conception of the *field* is another possibility, as is Norbert Elias's figuration theory. The problem with all of these, as well as with other available possibilities, is that each is a part of a well-developed theory and comes with a thick set of already built-in characteristics that presuppose certain aspects of the arena to be studied. For example, according to their respective creators, SASFs have rule-generating capabilities, fields have a kind of autonomy, and figurations consist of networks of interdependencies with shifting power balances. To put the objection more bluntly, each alternative is weighted down with a lot of baggage that limits what can be observed, which is the negative side of their strengths.

For the purposes of the general jurisprudence, the orienting concept is merely a way of drawing lines to delimit the field of study. It should be able to operate at many different levels and in many different contexts. Using the plainest terminology possible—to avoid any theoretical pretensions or connotations—I will call it a *social arena*. The boundaries of the social arena in any given study can be drawn in *any way desired*, as determined by the purposes of the study, with only one condition: when moving from the first context to the next in the course of a single study (or follow-up studies) care must be taken that the boundaries in each instance are drawn in precisely the same way. Otherwise one will not be able to accumulate and produce information on comparable social arenas.

Deciding how the boundaries are to be drawn requires careful thought, but will not always prove so difficult. One may, for example, decide that the social arena studied will be coextensive with the nation state. The boundaries of the nation state are already relatively clearly located. The same is also true of sub-states or principalities, districts, municipalities, or local villages. All of these have identifiable political or geographical boundaries that can be used to delimit the social arena. A more complicated situation will involve social arenas with less sharp pre-existing boundaries. One might define the social arena in terms of, for example, a local ranching community (e.g. Ellickson 1991), or a local business community (e.g. Macaulay 1963), or the sweatshops in a major city (e.g. Moore 1978), or the whaling industry (e.g. Ellickson 1989), or the international group of merchants involved in wholesale diamond trade (e.g. Bernstein 1992), or in terms of businesses which resort to the *lex mercatoria*, or in terms of gypsies, or the mafia, or the Mormons, either as local communities or as transnational communities. Some social arenas will be defined in terms of geography, or type of activity, or type of group, or a mixture of all three, or some other mixture; some will be localized, while others will traverse, or operate outside of, nation-state boundaries; some will be tied to groups, while others will encompass several groups, or cut across groups.

The primary considerations when defining a particular social arena are the purposes of the study at hand. To state the obvious, the boundaries should be drawn in a manner that includes what is of interest and excludes the irrelevant. Keep in mind that there are many different possible levels of generality or abstraction. When gathering cumulative information, for example, one can study only sweatshops in major Western cities, sweatshops in major Western and non-Western cities, sweatshops regardless of rural or urban settings, close-knit labour-intensive business communities operating in the shadow of state regulation including but not limited to sweatshops, and so forth.

To repeat, the basic orienting and boundary-delimiting device of the general jurisprudence is the social arena. It is avowedly devoid of content and presuppositions. Its strength is its flexibility. The primary considerations in determining how the boundaries are to be drawn are the purposes of the inquiry. The only restrictions when drawing the boundaries are clarity and consistency. If this all sounds vague, that is the result of a concept intentionally designed to leave the details and control up to the field investigators, without predetermining anything of substance in advance of the actual study. The concept of a social arena should not be reified. Unlike fields and figurations, there is no theory of social arenas. It is just a heuristic tool.

Typology of the Sources of Social Order

The Problem of Order

'The "problem of order" has come to be widely recognized as a major, often as *the* major, perennial issue of social theory' (Wrong 1994: 37). Sociology from its inception has been oriented to understanding the sources of social order, as have, to differing degrees, political science and anthropology. It has been called '*the* fundamental question of all social science' (Rule 1988: 224). It is also central to theoretical discussions of law.

Chapter 1 established that law is identified universally with order, though the point is so evident that the string of citations may have been superfluous. The 'social order problematic' has dominated understandings about the relationship between law and society for centuries, at least since Hobbes's vivid and frightening imagery. His most enduring legacy might well be our inability to easily imagine that life without law can be orderly. The powerful move he made was to instate disorder as normal in the state of nature. Disorder thereby came to be seen as a problem that had to be solved if society were to survive and, following Hobbes, law became the most often touted solution. The view that law is essential to social order is now taken for granted.

A persistent thread running through this book has been an attempt to shake the hold of the assumed association between law and order. The formidable burden that this attempt faces can be felt by reflecting upon how comfortable, natural, and correct the very phrase *law and order* feels; the two terms go together like hammer and nail. But hammers can be put to other uses beside pounding nails; many of the people who use hammers cannot pound nails very well; hammers regularly bend or destroy nails; hammers have many symbolic and metaphorical uses; and nails can be pounded by other things besides hammers (unless one asserts that whatever pounds a nail is by definition a hammer). Analogous objections have been raised in the course of this book about the assumed connection between law and order. I have argued that this view of law blinds us from seeing the many other things that law (in all of its various kinds) does and is used to do. I have argued that many manifestations of law have marginal or no role in the maintenance of social order. I have argued that in order to function law(s) actually depends upon the presence of an already cohesive pre-existing social order. I have argued that manifestations of law can sometimes lead to a disruption of social order. And I have argued, for all of these reasons, that the Functionalist a priori identification of law with order is ill-advised. I have not, emphatically not, denied that law in fact regularly does play a role in social order; rather the argument is that the connection should not be assumed as a necessary one, and that the role is often not as great as routinely thought.

But the power of the assumed association between law and order— there is that wonderful phrase again—will not be easily shaken. In recognition of this reality, in this section I will set out a typology of the sources of social order to help fill in the context within which law(s) operates when it does in fact function relative to social order. This abbreviated typology will compress what is a vast literature on the subject into a handful of basic generalizations.

This entire discussion, I must point out, is a concession to the powerful hold of the association between law and social order. The approach I prefer would be to sidestep the issue of order altogether, much as Weber did. Unique in this respect among major social theorists since Hobbes, Weber did not offer a general theory of social order:

He saw that societies over the sweep of history were always coming together and falling apart, shifting and changing from one set of institutions to another. History shows nothing permanent but continual war, conflict and change: states conquering and disintegrating, trade and finance spreading and shrinking, religion and arts slowly shifting from one theme to its opposite. What does remain beneath the change, the concrete basis of human society, are groups of people bound by ties of common feeling and belief: families, households, kinsmen, church and cult members, friends, communities. The core of Weber's theory of stratification is thus a theory of group formation, a set of hypotheses about the conditions that bring men together into solidary groups. These conditions are found in the way men relate to the institutional orders that link groups together into a society. (Collins and Makowsky, quoted in Wrong 1994: 222)

When looked at in these terms, keying on the 'problem of order', rather than on what brings people together and sets them apart, is the wrong focus: order and disorder (partner concepts) do not capture the situation well. But the collective discussion surrounding the problem of order has gone on too long to be avoided, though the typology of order offered here will be constructed in a manner that nudges the discussion in the direction taken by Weber.

Preliminary Issues Regarding the Notion of Order

Before embarking on the typology, two preliminary, complex and ultimately contestable issues must be addressed regarding the notion of order, and a key distinction regarding levels of analysis must be made. All of these issues derive from a deceptively difficult question: What does it mean to say that a social arena is ordered? In classical Hobbsean terms, order means a lack of conflict. This approach to the issue, however, is not very productive. A pure state of absence of conflict, or the opposite state of total conflict, seldom if ever occur, and if they do they are strictly local and transitory conditions.

In both legal and sociological approaches to this question, the answer is often given in terms of regularity of conduct, patterns of behaviour, predictability and stability. Talcott Parsons (1937: 91) labelled this 'factual order'. The antithesis of this kind of order is randomness, chance, unpredictability, and chaos. This approach to order is analogous to the focus of the natural sciences on observable regularities. Parsons contrasted 'factual order' with 'normative order', an order 'relative to a system of norms' (ibid.). Normative order exists when the order is generated by conformity to a shared body of norms. As he points out, a social arena that manifests normative chaos can still exhibit factual regularities. Patterns can be found, for example, in the actions and reactions between a mob and police in outbreaks of mass violence. He considered normative order, not factual order, to be the key to social order.

Both approaches to order are unsatisfactory. Factual order includes too much and normative order rules out too much. Bare factual regularities, like patterns of eating and sleeping, are not difficult to identify as one moves to more general levels of observation. As chaos theory informs us, patterns of order are even to be found amidst chaos. 'One might say that there is order in disorder' (Davies 1992: 193). Often the regularities found at these levels, however, have little information value, in the sense that they are not meaningful to social investigators. A focus on normative order is also flawed. It excludes important sources of order that are not normative in nature. Equally problematic, it takes an overly conformist view of human conduct, and an overly homogeneous view of norms within societies, and it rules out the possibility that the presence of conflict (including normative conflict) is a normal social state of cohesively functioning societies. 'The most familiar criticism of Parsons has always been that in accounting for social order he gave insufficient weight both to the domination of some by others and to the rational adjustments of their interests negotiated by individuals and groups as against the overriding priority he ascribed to the presence within a group of normative consensus, or shared values and moralities, profoundly shaping its members' conduct' (Wrong 1994: 38).

To benefit from the strengths of both yet avoid their weaknesses, while not being trapped in the antinomy of factual order and normative order, the notion of order adopted here will, in a manner of speaking, approach from the side. In the barest terms, to say that a social arena is 'ordered' is to assert that that arena reflects *a substantial coordination of behaviour*. This approach has the benefit of more closely matching the concerns of legal theorists and social theorists interested in law, many of whom take the coordination of behavioural expectations to be the key social order function of law. A focus on the coordination of behaviour eliminates many irrelevant factual regularities, while not being narrowly limited to normative conformity. It focuses on the ways in which what people are doing in a social arena matches up with the actions of others. Understood in this minimalist sense, beyond the basic point that social behaviour is more effective when coordinated than when it is not, to say that a social arena is ordered does not entail any necessary normative implications. One cannot assert, in other words, that a social arena that exhibits a state of order is *therefore* good. The outcome of coordinated behaviour may be to inflict evil on others in that social arena, or the coordination may be achieved through the sustained application of remorseless and unconscionable force. Whether a given social order is *good* or just is a separate question. This approach also does not rule out the presence of a sustained degree of underlying conflict within a social arena, though if the conflict erupts to the point where the coordination of behaviour collapses it will no longer be ordered.

This last observation raises the second complex issue: at what precise point can it be said that a social arena is indeed *ordered*? How much coordination of behaviour is required? At what precise point can it be said that the social arena is disordered, or in a state of breakdown? As posed, these questions cannot be answered. Functionalist theory and economic theory often refer to the notion of equilibrium—a steady or stable state— to identify when a particular context is ordered. But for three reasons the notion of equilibrium is unsatisfactory. First, there are infinite possible states in which social arenas can stabilize and continue to survive. Even a steady state of relative disorder is imaginable. Short of an absolute collapse of the social arena, functional analysis can almost always offer an analysis to identify any particular state as reflecting equilibrium, which suggests that equilibrium can represent whatever one wants it to. Secondly, there is indeterminacy in the requisite level of generality one uses to identify a state of equilibrium. Consider the social arena in which everyone understands that it is safe to go about during daylight hours, but evening ventures are high risk (or where one area of town is safe but another dangerous). One might say that the daytime is ordered and the evening disordered; but one might also say, stepping back, that the entire situation taken as a whole is ordered, since there are clear and predictable safe periods (or areas), which allows people to coordinate and conduct their activities. Thirdly, the notion of equilibrium implies some sort of tipping point, the moment at which there is a shift from one state to the other. But the messiness of social reality makes it impossible to identify any such point. Owing to the above problems, it is prudent to eschew making the assertion that a social arena is ordered, or disordered, except when an extreme case of one or the other is at hand.

The final point to be made before embarking on the typology has to do with distinguishing among levels when addressing the issue of order. In a comprehensive analysis of the problem of order, Dennis Wrong (1994: chaps. 6 and 7) pointed out that many theorists have failed to recognize that there are two distinct problems of order, what he dubs the 'hobbesian problem' and the 'marxian problem'.[1] Hobbes's war of all against all highlighted the problem of the relations *among individuals* within a society. Marx's class warfare highlighted conflict *between groups* within society, which can be extrapolated to conflict or war among and between societies. Although we tend to think of social order in Hobbesian terms, the vast bulk of social conflict and disorder consists of conflict between groups (including racial, ethnic, religious, political, community, and state conflict). It is important to keep the distinction in mind because the sources of order and disorder at each level may differ, including in one and the same situation. As Wrong (p. 209) points out, 'conflict between groups cannot exist unless there is consensus within groups'. Capable political leaders throughout history intuit and act upon this fundamental point whenever they generate external conflicts as a way of creating internal solidarity. In the typology that follows, I will focus mostly (though not exclusively) on the sources of order among individuals within groups and societies, which is consistent with the primary orientation of law; but one must be cognizant of the distinction, and pay attention to relations between groups within and across social arenas.

A Typology

The following typology of the sources of social order,[2] then, focuses on what contributes to the coordination of behaviour among individuals in contexts of social action. It is broken down into six different categories, with the first category consisting of two subcategories. The categories are set out in *presumptive* descending order of their contribution to the coordination of behaviour, though with regard to any particular context of social action the mix and proportion of these elements will vary greatly. As will become clear in the presentation, these categories artificially separate aspects which are integrated in contexts of social behaviour, so the discreteness of the categories cannot be pressed too hard. In preparing this typology a premium has been placed on simplicity. Perhaps except for the first category, all of the categories are quite familiar and do not require substantial elaboration.

---

[1] Following Wrong, I have used the lower-case designation of these problems, respecting his desire to indicate that Hobbes and Marx did not themselves set the problem out in these terms.

[2] A typology of the sources of social order can be constructed in a variety of ways. Though it differs considerably from the one set out here, an informative alternative can be found in Ellickson (1991: 123–36).

1. The Unarticulated Substrate

This category consists of those elements that exist and operate *beneath awareness* while contributing to the coordination of behaviour. In one sense, they *enable* behaviour; in another sense, they *are* behaviour just being carried on. Whichever sense is used, their distinguishing characteristic is that they often remain unarticulated, unthematized, unknown to—or at least not present to the consciousness of—those actors whose behaviour they generate or constitute. There are two basic variants of this unarticulated substrate, roughly divisible as one more behaviouristic in orientation and the other more interpretive in orientation.

The more behaviouristic version holds that much behaviour is constituted and coordinated through shared habits, modes of action, customs, practices, and unthinking rule following. As Hayek (1973: 18) put it: 'Man acted before he thought and did not understand before he acted. What we call understanding is in the last resort simply his capacity to respond to his environment with a pattern of action that helps him persist.' Learning follows from experience and the spread of successful practices. 'The result of this development will in the first instance not be articulated knowledge but a knowledge which, although it can be described in terms of rules, the individual cannot state in words but is merely able to honour in practice' (ibid.). Especially through the influence of Wittgenstein (Hayek's relative and contemporary), of late there has been an increased emphasis on the significance and prevalence of unthinking, routine rule-following behaviour, and shared practices. '[T]here is a way of grasping a rule which is *not* an *interpretation*,' Wittgenstein (1958: s. 201) observed. 'And hence also "obeying a rule" is a practice' (s. 202). Much of social life consists of shared, rule-governed activities, under this view.

The more interpretive version holds that much of behaviour is constituted and coordinated through shared language, interpretive schemes or constructs, social typifications, ideas, concepts and beliefs, the totality of which has been called the background of the intersubjective lifeworld.[3] This is the phenomenological approach to social action. Habermas (1996: 22) described it in terms directly parallel to Hayek's more behaviouristic account above: 'This all penetrating, yet latent and unnoticed

---

[3] An excellent phenomenological exploration of the lifeworld can be found in the work of Alfred Schutz (1962, 1967). For an overview of interpretive theory, see Tamanaha (1993b: 76–103).

presence of the background of communicative action can be described as a more intense yet deficient form of knowledge and ability. To begin with, we make use of this knowledge involuntarily, without reflectively knowing *that* we possess it at all.' This more interpretive version emphasizes the extent to which shared language and concepts enable, shape, and determine the way in which we see and act in the world.

Although they have different emphases, the separateness of these two versions of the unarticulated substrate should not be pushed too strongly. Hayek and Wittgenstein recognized the significance of language in constituting and coordinating behaviour—language is itself a form of behaviour—and Habermas recognized the significance of practices. In most accounts, practices contain integrated aspects of meaning and doing (Tamanaha 1997: 168–75). Thus, most theorists who tout one version do not do so to the complete exclusion of the other. Regardless of which version one would give priority to, both are complementary contributors and inseverable at a deep level. Thus, I will highlight what they have in common.

Both versions emphasize that they (practices, interpretive constructs) enable actions and perception, that they are socially shared and conveyed, that they are pervasive, underlying and giving rise to many of our routine activities, and that they operate beneath our awareness, automatically and unthinkingly reiterated time and again. Much of what they refer to can be described as 'rule governed', though these rules have not been consciously articulated or followed. These practices and interpretive schemes can be thematized by concertedly focusing our attention on them; in such moments they can be brought to conscious contemplation in a way that might never have occurred previously. But short of that, we do not think about them; we just do them, or think through them. Combined, these qualities make the unarticulated substrate the very foundation of coordinated behaviour. They form the behavioural and ideational background of all intentional conduct, and of all social behaviour.[4] They generate widely shared patterns of conduct which facilitate the (unthinking) anticipation of one another's actions and reactions in contexts of social action. Without the contributions they make, there would be no coordinated behaviour.

---

[4] John Searle (1995: 129–47) develops the notion of the 'background' that has strong parallels to what I mean here by unarticulated substrate. The basic difference is that he encompasses more in his notion of background than I do.

2. Shared Norms and Roles

Shared norms make a major contribution to the coordination of behaviour. Many social theorists, prominently including Durkheim and Parsons, have identified this element as the key to social order. An element of shared norms is already contained within both the more behaviourist version and the more interpretive version of the unarticulated substrate, in the sense that norms are socially generated and shared and emerge from a genesis in the unarticulated substrate. Wrong (1994: 48) describes the connection between 'habit-expectation-norm' as 'a sequence emerging in the course of time'. 'In short, interaction generates habits; perceived, they become reciprocal expectations; in addition to their purely predictive and anticipatory nature, sensitivity to them endows them with a constraining or even an obligatory character' (ibid.). The practices described in the preceding category are a form of rule-following behaviour; rules have a normative quality. Thus, this category cannot be sharply distinguished from the preceding one.

Nevertheless, the contribution to coordination that norms make qua norms is significant enough to warrant separate mention. This category focuses on the degree to which behaviour is influenced specifically owing to the sense of *ought* attached to the norms involved. Or viewed another way: a sense of guilt or social disapprobation is experienced when the norm is disobeyed or when non-compliance is contemplated; or a sense of social approbation is experienced when it is complied with. In this sense, it can be distinguished from the preceding category because here there is at least a minimum level of awareness (at some point) that a particular course of action is obligatory in some sense. Like the preceding category, the particular quality that makes values so effective in co-ordinating behaviour is the fact that they are widely shared. Sharing implies a higher degree of similarity of behaviour, at least under similar circumstances or constraining conditions. Shared norms generate more predictability, and thus allow for greater anticipation of behaviour by others, which facilitates coordination. Note that the coordination benefits of shared norms are present without regard to the content of the norms; there are also norms which specifically make coordination and cooperation socially obligatory.

Although there are distinctions between norms and roles, they are sufficiently connected and similar enough to be combined in one category. They are both socially generated and shared; they both carry obligatory connotations; they both allow for predictability of action; and they both allow for and generate a coordination of behaviour among social actors. Roles can be understood as clusters of norms and patterns of action linked to particular positions or contexts of actions that guide conduct in generally expected and understood ways.

At this point, it is again necessary to guard against perpetuating an overly conformist view of norms and roles, and against the overly practice and rule-oriented emphasis in the preceding category:

As Robert Edgerton points out, there are many different types of rules, rules with exceptions, rules enforced without exceptions, rules about the exceptions to rules. Winch's view belongs to the older conformist models of rule following. As Edgerton describes this conformist 'normative theory,' 'people everywhere not only followed the rules of their societies—but also made these rules a part of themselves and became, almost literally, inseparable from them.' But theories challenged this view based upon the indeterminacy of rules—that is, the fact that that people often do not follow them, do not incorporate them and frequently use them strategically to further their own interests. Under the new perspective of strategic interactionism, embodied in the works of theorists like Erving Goffman, rules are treated as flexible, negotiable and subject to exceptions. (Bohman 1991: 64–5)

James Bohman, in the above passage, issues an important reminder about the ever-present possibility of a strategic approach by actors towards norms and rules. A different but related point is that practices and bodies of norms are often internally heterogeneous, which makes it possible for contrary courses of action to arise from a single normative context or practice, either because different sets of available norms have been internalized, or they have been selected strategically by the actors to achieve a desired course of action. Social conformity must not be over-emphasized to the exclusion of individual strategic behaviour.

3. Self-Interested Instrumental Behaviour

Although normative and instrumental approaches to action are often presented as alternative or competitor theories, they are clearly both equally significant influences in social action (see Rule 1997: 114), and can therefore exchange positions in this typology. Instrumental behaviour in general terms means acting to achieve a particular end, acting in a goal-oriented way. Because goals or ends will often be normatively coloured or determined, this category is also difficult to separate sharply from the preceding one (as well as from the one that follows). Furthermore, when 'large numbers of individuals solve co-ordination problems, the resulting patterns of activity involve the following of *conventions*, and it is in the interest of [rationally maximizing] individuals to continue to follow such conventions' (Barnes 1995: 18), which connects this category with the first category.

For analytical purposes, the distinction can be heightened by emphasizing the aspect of self-interested instrumental behaviour, or what is also known as rational maximizing or economic behaviour. In this more restricted sense, this category centres specifically upon behaviour motivated by, and designed to, maximize the interests (wealth or welfare) of the individual actor. Several compelling critiques of the view of people as rational maximizers have been pressed, including that much behaviour is not in fact rational, that people are affected by biases and make decisions relying upon heuristics and formulae, that there are knowledge and time constraints which render decision-making bounded at best, that they are not always motivated to maximize wealth or welfare, and that this view of social action is based upon overly simplified one-dimensional models which have limited application to reality. All of these criticisms can be accepted without denying that self-interested instrumental behaviour constitutes a major category of behaviour (though rejecting the view that all behaviour is instrumental in the self-interested sense).

The core idea behind the link between instrumental behaviour and social order is that, in the absence of an ongoing perfect match between the distribution of resources and individual desires, instrumental behaviour inevitably leads to transfers which result in a better match between what people possess and what they desire (James Coleman 1990: chap. 2). A multitude of individual transactions across a society results in an unplanned complex of ordered exchanges, operating continually to the benefit of all those involved. Market theory is based upon this assumption. Hayek (1973) suggested that unfettered instrumental behaviour cumulatively gives rise to spontaneous order—as an unintended product—which in turn provides the environment most conducive for further successful instrumental behaviour. This is the 'invisible hand' version of the emergence of order. In a related but more conscious sense that shades into the next category, instrumental behaviour contributes to coordination because one of the most effective ways to achieve desired ends is to cooperate with others also seeking to obtain their own ends, giving rise to (self-interested) reciprocity and mutually supportive conduct (including the formulation of alliances) alongside consensual exchanges. In this sense, all individuals have a (shared) self-interest in coordination.

It should not be forgotten that instrumental behaviour also generates conflict, as when two individuals desire the same scarce good, whether material or glory. Economic theory asserts that people try to exchange where possible; when not possible, they compete for the goods within the bounds of the rules. But people also go beyond the rules in the pursuit of their desires. From the economic standpoint, the rules (customary, moral, and legal) and the consequences that follow from a breach (real and anticipated) are considered in terms of costs of courses of action. Conflicts occasionally break out, but, according to the theory, overall enlightened self-interest (including fear of the consequences) keeps rationally maximizing individuals pursuing their interests within peaceful bounds generally. It should also be remembered that under certain circumstances instrumental behaviour can inhibit cooperation and lead to sub-optimal outcomes. The often cited demonstration of this is the 'Prisoner's Dilemma', in which individual interests point towards non-cooperation when cooperation would more optimal.

4. Consent

Consent entails agreement. When consent is involved, the resultant behaviour is intentionally and often explicitly coordinated (though agreement maybe be implicitly understood). Consent results in a mutually agreed upon course of action, which constitutes a good deal of our social behaviour. Consent is grounded on shared values (the felt obligation to live up to an agreement, trust) as well as instrumental behaviour (the mutually beneficial results of reliance upon agreements), so it too builds on earlier categories. Although a consensual exchange is the epitome of consent, it does not exhaust the category. Consent includes everything from making a luncheon appointment to an engagement to wed, to agreeing (even implicitly) who walks first into an unlighted room. A repeated course of action that is initiated through an agreement can over time become habitual, and later become normative apart from its origin in the initial agreement. A great deal of social behaviour, mundane as well as monumental, is coordinated through consent.

5. Love, Altruism, Sympathy, Group Identification, Social Instinct

This is unabashedly a catch-all category that can best be described as including any emotive sense outside of strict self-interest, regardless of source or genesis, which generates a need or desire to be with others, to do for others, and to identify as a part of a group. This can be considered a naturalistic factor in the sense that it suggests that being members of a society is in some sense natural to the human social make-up. It contributes to the coordination of behaviour because it places people in continual proximity with others, and for this need to be satisfied it requires that behaviour be coordinated successfully. A good deal of this is often considered in normative terms, but that is too limited to capture what is involved. Sociobiologists argue that these feelings are genetically programmed into us and reflect natural selection, a kind of cooperative instinct like that possessed by bees and ants; psychological theory points instead to a genesis in the utter dependence of infants upon adults. Whatever the source of these feelings or impulses, that they exist is undeniable. Specific manifestations of this category may also lead to disruptions in social order—think of the love triangle that turns violent, or rabid ethnocentrism that leads to conflict with other groups—but overall the effect is to bring people together.

As emphasized at the outset, all of the above categories are interpenetrating, and all contribute together to the coordination of behaviour. Discussing them separately is artificial and potentially misleading. To correct this, before articulating the final category, it is helpful to read the following observations by Adam Smith from *The Theory of Moral Sentiments* (1759):

It is thus that man, who can subsist only in society, was fitted by nature to that situation for which he was made. All the members of human society stand in need of each others assistance, and are likewise exposed to mutual injuries. Where the necessary assistance is reciprocally afforded from love, from gratitude, from friendship, and esteem, the society flourishes and is happy. All the different members of it are bound together by the agreeable bonds of love and affection, and are, as it were, drawn to one common centre of mutual good offices.

But though the necessary assistance should not be afforded from such generous and disinterested motives, though among the different members of the society there should be no mutual love and affection, the society, though less happy and agreeable, will not necessarily be dissolved. Society may subsist, among different men, as among different merchants, from a sense of its utility, without any mutual love or affection; and though no man in it should owe any obligation, or be bound in gratitude to any other, it may still be upheld by a mercenary exchange of good offices according to an agreed valuation. (quoted in Rule 1997: 14)

Smith mentions, at least implicitly, a contribution to the social bond from each of the above categories except the first.

6. Coercion and Threat of Coercion

The final category refers to coercion and the threat of coercion as mechanisms leading to or resulting in the coordination of behaviour. Coercion involves one or more actors exerting pressure to compel others to act in a desired fashion. Coercion and the threat of coercion can be applied before or after the behaviour. Coercion in the form of a sanction, is often, though not always, applied after the desired behaviour has failed to materialize (though before future instances of the behaviour). When this occurs, coercion differs from the other categories, and from the threat of coercion, which usually precede and give rise to the coordinated behaviour. Another difference is that the earlier categories, except for the first, all give rise to coordinated behaviour in a more or less voluntary way (the unarticulated substrate cannot be considered 'voluntary' or 'involuntary'), while coercion or the threat of coercion work involuntarily; the former are 'internal' sources of coordinating behaviour, the latter 'external' (Tamanaha 1997: 115). Possible forms of coercion and threats of coercion applied to social action range from self-help, including directly administered threats or revenge, to uncoordinated or coordinated social disapprobation, including an arched eyebrow, gossip, and shunning, to the organized application of force, including the imposition of fines, exile, imprisonment, and death. These sanctions are applied by various parties, from family, friends, and colleagues, to immediately formed temporary groups (lynch mobs and posses), to the state legal apparatus.

The Fixity of the Mundane and Reversing Hobbes's Presumption

Many theorists identify groups of various kinds—especially including stable, organized complexes of action like institutions—as the key components of social order, as reflected in the theories of Weber and Ehrlich. Civil society, it is commonly thought, is organized around social associations, clubs, unions, business associations, factories, universities, corporations, the family, the neighbourhood, the state, and so forth. Society can be understood as the totality of a multitude of vast and small complexes of separate, overlapping, cross-cutting, and interacting social networks and instances of social action. The typology set out above specifies the elements that both give rise to and coordinate behaviour within such groups and institutions, but also those elements that operate between groups and institutions, and that operate between individuals interacting outside of groups and institutions. They are the various bonds underlying the coordination of social behavior. They have all been described at a superficial level, without pretending to get beneath them, or to explain how or why they exist, or to say anything else in great detail about them. And it should be evident that additional categories or an entirely different set of categories could have been devised (including 'culture', 'socialization', etc.). Nonetheless, the categories identified adequately convey the basic sources that contribute to social order.

There is one more operative factor that must be mentioned. The cumulative effect of the above sources of social order is to create an emergent phenomenon that perhaps more than anything else—and in combination with everything else—contributes to the stability of social order. For lack of a better term, I will label this emergent phenomenon the fixity of the mundane. People in modern urban societies are linked in endless webs of interdependencies from which they cannot extricate themselves short of living alone under harsh conditions in the wilderness. These constitute the mundane aspects of our daily existence, the conditions within which we exist but about which we rarely think. 'Dependence on heat and light supplied by electricity, on plumbing linked to water supply systems, on automobiles and the unobstructed roadways they require, on telephonic communications, on regular garbage collection and disposal, to mention only the most obvious examples long antedating the products of recent electronic technology, binds people to myriads of others in far-flung systemic networks' (Wrong 1994: 233). Each of us participates in the creation of these networks, and all of us live within the networks we collectively create. We fill up and pay for gas; the gas was delivered to the station by a truck driver, who got it from a large tanker, which got it from a refinery, which in turn had it delivered by a truck, which got it from a ship that came overseas; the ship got it from a tank, which got it from a pipeline, which got it from an oil pump; the oil pump is sunken deep into the ground; the oil pump was constructed half-a-world away; and on and on. Groceries at the market, the clothes we wear, the water delivered to our houses, the abodes we live in, and much more, can similarly be traced back in long (often transnational) chains to their points of origin. All along the way there are people doing routine daily work, and earning and spending money. Many of these networks, despite perpetual changes in personnel and material equipment, have a continuous historical, factual existence that spans centuries (surviving wars and other serious disruptions). The very pervasiveness of these networks, our role in creating them and our abject dependence upon them, generates a kind of general inertia that effectively resists massive social disorder. Each network is at every point dependent upon and overlaid upon a vast complex of other networks. Tear at any small part of this fabric, as localized (labour, interpersonal, religious, economic, racial, etc.) conflict regularly does, and the rest of it is still there to hold.

Either it collapses whole, or it remains to generate and insure relative stability. The more solid the network—that is, the longer it has been in existence, the further its reach, the greater our dependence upon it, the more it is supported by other networks—the more stable it is (though the vulnerability of the Internet, and riots which follow blackouts, suggests that certain kinds of dependencies create additional risks of temporary social disorder).

A total societal collapse, which must overcome the fixity of the mundane, is no easy task, one which occurs only following massive physical destruction caused by intense inter-group conflict. However, since inter-group conflict requires a high level of the coordination of behaviour *within* each of the combative groups, even this scenario does not amount to total social collapse, although that will be the outcome if the combatants continue the conflict to the point of mutual annihilation. Although the phenomenon of the fixity of the mundane has been described in relation to modern urban societies, the effects it describes exist in other kinds of social contexts as well, albeit with varying degrees of influence. Life within a family or within a small village also have their own kinds of interdependencies, their own kinds of fixity of the mundane that resist social disorder.

If the typology of the sources of social order set out above and the notion of the fixity of the mundane is correct, then Hobbes was flatly wrong. 'Always and everywhere, the relations between human beings are linguistically and cognitively, culturally and practically ordered' (Barnes 1995: 67). The natural social state is far more ordered than disordered. To state the point more affirmatively: *the natural social condition is one of order, permeated at various levels with regular episodes of conflict.* Hayek (1973) developed a naturalistic theory of spontaneous order that evolves and exists owing to the adaptive superiority it supplies to the groups that possess it (see Grey 1986). Unlike the intentionally created order of the social contract tradition, Hayek's spontaneous order is not created purposively by humans; it arises as an effect or outcome of the multitude of purposive actions of the individuals within society. Hayek's account must be supplemented with the contributions made by the sources of social order mentioned above, including the unarticulated substrate, the fixity of the mundane, and allowing for the substantial presence of ordered interactions which are intentionally created. The result of all of this is relative order coexisting with a degree of conflict. Were it otherwise, theorists would not be free to discuss the issue in abstract terms under such luxurious conditions.

What about Law?

The preceding discussion of the sources of social order was completed with nary a mention of law. In setting out the above typology of sources of social order, law—or specifically state law—was referred to only once, and even in that context it was mentioned as just one example of a much broader category of coercion. Imagine a social arena without state law, yet with the full panoply of other sources of social order still available, and it is easier to perceive that law—at least state law—is often not in fact necessary to social order in many social arenas. Even when it is a necessary component, it is seldom the key one.

The traditionally assumed relationship gets things precisely upside down. It is state law that is dependent on these other sources of social order if it is to have a chance of exerting an influence. The state legal system would not even exist—could not be constructed—were it not for an already stable and effective baseline provided by the unarticulated substrate, shared norms, instrumental behaviour, and consent. Stated more strongly: law (of whatever kind) can exist only where there is already a significant degree of order. Even when legal officials can effectively coordinate their behaviour, the law is often impotent against general social disorder, as is plainly evident in any riot situation. 'Once the number of lawbreakers reaches critical mass, the police force is largely for show' (Searle 1995: 91). Finally, with regard to the vast bulk of everyday social conduct, people act with seldom a thought about law and its proscriptions, which suggests that it has little role in the coordination of routine behaviour. At the most fundamental level, then, in several different respects, law (of whatever kind) does not substantially *generate* social order, but rather presupposes it, though it may also help contribute to it.

Typology of Kinds of Law by *Label*

The articulation of a typology based upon essential characteristics must await the study and abstraction of the various manifestations of law with the care and attention that Hart committed to the abstraction of state law, a process that has not yet begun in earnest because, owing to the essentialist view of the law and the dominance of the state law model, heretofore the existence of other kinds of law has not been taken seriously. In this section, I will set out a typology of the most prevalent general categories of kinds of law by label that would be found in a conventionalist approach. Consistent with the preceding typology, the emphasis here is on simplicity. By their nature, conventionalist approaches draw from common understandings, and various aspects of many of these categories have already been touched upon in the course of this book. Thus, the categories will require little elaboration.

The seven categories set out below are neither permanent nor exhaustive, for two reasons, respectively: (1) conventions change, and thus the label 'law' may be attached to new or different phenomena, and old uses may lapse; and (2) there are obscure usages of the label 'law', ones applied in a limited community (like 'gypsy law', 'mafia law', or the gang 'law' of the 'bloods' and 'crips') which I have left out, but should be included when present in the social arena being investigated. The emphasis in this list is on those kinds of law regularly found operative in social arenas. Although by necessity this discussion will be a general one, these kinds of law should not be considered in abstract terms, but rather in relation to their ability to exert an influence in given social arenas; what matters most is their actual social presence.

State Law

State law is ubiquitous today, though on a historical scale the ascension of state law as a kind of law is a relatively recent development. It serves as the paradigm example of law in many social arenas, especially in the West, where it is often (though not always) the most powerful or dominant kind of law. It is the law identified with the state and its legal officials. There are different levels and divisions of authority among state legal systems, the most familiar being federal, state, provincial, and municipal. Traditionally state law has been identified with the nation state, but the situation need not remain so. Often manifestations of state law will not be called literally 'state law', but rather will have specific labels like the US Supreme Court, the Revised Statutes of the State of New York, and so forth. What makes them a part of this category is their connection to, and place within, the state legal apparatus. Each state legal system is different in nature: in its degree of penetration or the scope of its reach, in the strength of the legal tradition, in the power of its legal institutions, in the kinds of matters and activities it occupies itself with, in its degree of autonomy from political actors, in the size and solidarity of its legal professionals, in the source of its norms, in whether it has a rule of law orientation, and so forth.

Customary Law

Customary law is a controversial and contested idea, as I indicated in earlier Chapters. Legal anthropologists cannot agree on a definition of customary law, and some have argued that it is a political creation to further the interests of colonization. Many legal and social theorists define 'customary law', like Lon Fuller (1975: 92) did, as 'the rules of conduct that arise directly out of the interaction of human beings, rules that enable men to anticipate the interactional behavior of their fellows in future encounters'. The problem with this approach, I have demonstrated, is that it is incapable of distinguishing custom from customary law, and has an irresistible tendency to draw in much of social life under the ambit of law.

The conventionalist approach does not need a definition of customary law; nor is the fact that it might be a recently invented doctrine make any difference in whether it qualifies for consideration as a kind of 'law'. The only question is whether the people in a given social arena refer to the notion of customary law (and *not* whether the theorists who study it might consider it customary law). Such references are not unusual in former colonized countries (see Tamanaha 1989). Usually this reference, as with the preceding category, will be with some degree of specificity, like Yapese customary law, or Adat, and often the actual label 'customary law' (or its translation) will be used because that is what accords it status under the state law regimes which recognize customary law. Sometimes customary law in a given social arena operates independently of the state legal system, constituted by social actors at various degrees of informalization or institutionalization. Often customary law has its primary existence as a category or source of norms recognized and incorporated by the state legal system. Sometimes in a social arena both forms and uses of customary law exist.

Under the conventionalist approach adopted herein, a customary body of norms and practices operative in a social arena does not, by virtue of this fact alone, constitute a form of 'customary law'. It will not be customary law for the purposes of a conventionalist approach if it is dubbed 'customary law' by an anthropologist or legal theorist because it satisfied their criteria, though it may later qualify as such if this understanding is related back to the social arena and is conventionally taken up (which has in fact occurred). It qualifies as a 'customary law' if the people in that social arena refer to it using the term 'customary law' (or its translation in that language), even when it may also have a more specific label, like Adat. Otherwise it will be a custom or customary norm, but not 'law'. This assertion holds even if these customs are strong and widely adhered to, more so even than the norms of state law. The significance of this point is that it demonstrates again how the conventionalist approach solves the most dogged problem faced by legal pluralists of distinguishing law from custom and morality. The question which arises here is not whether a particular custom is 'law' as such, but rather whether a particular complex of norms is 'customary law' or 'custom', and the answer depends upon the terms and understandings applied conventionally by the people in that social arena. A question may arise when certain people in the social arena claim that a given collection of norms are customary law, while others argue that they are just customs not amounting to customary law. But this dispute is not an analytical problem for the conventionalist approach. Rather, it is an interesting dispute in the social arena—one to be investigated—which will reveal the political and symbolic significance attached to this distinction by the people themselves.

These observations highlight, once again, that an important aspect of the conventionalist approach is to examine *why* people attach the label 'law' to certain phenomena, to uncover what strategic or other benefits are gained thereby. This entails approaching use of the label 'law' from a rhetorical standpoint.

Religious Law

This category refers to those bodies of law that are directly associated with a religion. Obvious examples of this are Islamic law, Hebrew law, and the canon law of Catholicism.[5] Again, the key for inclusion to this category is that people in the social arena see the particular religious norms at issue as a 'law'. Turn the other cheek may be a Christian value, but it is not ordinarily thought of as a 'law'. A law under Catholicism is that one may not divorce (albeit with several escape clauses) or take a life. As with the previous category, when there is a disagreement in a given social arena regarding whether something constitutes a religious value or a religious law, that is not an analytical problem but rather an

---

[5] A preliminary issue that might arise is whether something—like Scientology—qualifies as a religion. The answer, consistent with conventionalism, is to allow the understandings of the people involved to decide. If sufficient people use the label 'scientology law' to describe certain norms, then those norms qualify as a form of religious law.

informative dispute. Like the relationship between state law and customary law, religious law often has its own independent institutional existence; also it is often intertwined with and incorporated into the state legal system; and occasionally it is the state legal system (as in a theocracy).

International Law

This category is arguably unlike the others in the sense that the others are general categories made up of specific examples, but international law is a specific case, or at least it originated that way. International law is widely thought of as a single system, albeit a diffuse and uncertain one. However, it might also be argued that international law is a general category that consists of disconnected or poorly integrated elements, including, but not limited to, private international law, public international law, and human rights law, and a mix of institutions like the War Crimes Tribunal, the International Court of Justice, and so forth. Whatever the characterization, international law is clearly a kind of law, conventionally understood as such for the last couple of centuries, albeit one with a weak (though growing) institutional presence. Similar to customary law and religious law, it too stands independent of, and is also sometimes incorporated into, particular state legal systems. Conversely, international law also sometimes incorporates norms and institutions from state law, as well as customs and (its own version of) customary international law.

Although human rights are considered an aspect of international law, they bear separate mention because they have a separate identity, which in some senses takes them beyond the normal ambit of international law. A separate institutional presence is developing to support human rights, but the more interesting developments are the influence of non-governmental organizations (NGOs), like Amnesty International or consumers groups, which have begun to pressure both governments and corporations to eliminate human rights abuses. In many of these contexts the sanction applied and the institutions that apply them do not involve kinds of law. Shaming and economic boycotts (Nike, Levi Strauss, Disney) are the forms of coercion most frequently applied, sometimes to great effect. And voluntary private organizations, like the Fair Labor Association, are developing their own set of regulations and standards and means of enforcement. These are not aspects of international law, though they may later be incorporated as such, and thereby acquire the status of law.

Transnational Law

Transnational law is a relatively new category that is gaining increasing recognition as such, proportional to its accelerating development, a development which is connected directly to the process of globalization, especially in its commercial aspects. Transnational law is distinct from international law in two main respects. Transnational law cuts across national boundaries, unlike international law which is grounded in the sovereign state system; and it developed independently, outside of the international law tradition, and thus does not draw extensively from the existing body of international law doctrines. Having said that, there is a real possibility that, as conventional understandings change, at some point the two categories will merge under a global law umbrella. The best existing example of transnational law is the *lex mercatoria*. The *lex mercatoria* has its own independent system (though its institutionalized presence is extremely weak), but it also interacts in various ways with state legal systems, with international law, and also with customs within particular social arenas (among business communities).

Indigenous Law

Indigenous law, as a label, has sometimes been used interchangeably with customary law, and has sometimes been used in the context of legal pluralism to refer to private systems of normative order. Both usages, especially the latter, are relatively infrequent. In prevailing usages the term 'indigenous law' is most closely attached to movements of ethnic or national minorities seeking political independence from the majority in a nation state. Thus, indigenous law entails a rejection of the state legal system rather than integration. In many contexts its existence is largely a rhetorical or symbolic one—that is, it exists primarily in the form of an argument or claim pressed in the context of international, national, and local political discourse—without any concrete institutional presence. Significantly, this observation is not meant to deny the existence of indigenous law, but rather the opposite, to point out its very real existence in a form completely unlike the typical understanding of what law entails. In certain social arenas there may be references to both customary law and indigenous law; then both will be present, and their interaction with one another and with the state legal system (and with any other kind of law) should prove informative.

Natural Law

Of all of the kinds of law set out herein, this is the most inchoate and diverse in its specific manifestations. Unlike the others (except indigenous law), it often has no institutional presence, though it may be supported and perpetuated by institutions (like academic philosophy departments and Church taught Sunday school). In many social arenas, natural law is believed and acted upon, and thus it has a measurable influence, a social presence. In the past, natural law was quite closely tied to religious law, especially Catholicism, and there is still an overlap in many social arenas, but natural law also has a tradition independent of specifically religious law. Its most powerful presence most often arises in two situations. First, when people refuse to abide by the dictates of other bodies of law (like state law), or of custom or morality, based upon the perceived dictates of natural law, as in instances of civil disobedience. Secondly, when natural law principles qua natural law are expressly incorporated into state law. On occasion, natural law takes on a more active and powerful presence, as occurred when the Nuremberg trials cited offences against natural law principles as punishable offences.

The Core *Initial* Focus of the General Jurisprudence

Two Questions, Two Standards

Most of the starting elements of the general jurisprudence of law and society are now in place. The final key elements to be supplied are the presentation of standards that provide it with universal application, that will allow its findings to be integrated into traditional work in legal and social theory, and that will allow its products to be cumulative. To complete this task we must return to the framework and themes set out at the beginning of this book.

At the outset, I asserted that a common presupposition is pervasive in theories about law and society: *that law is a mirror of society, which functions to maintain social order.* This presupposition consists of two separate but connected ideas: the fact that law is a mirror of society—particularly of its customs and morality—is what makes it effective in accomplishing its social order function. The background in Chapter 1 and the survey in Chapter 2 were intended to demonstrate the strength and pervasiveness of these two ideas in a variety of different traditions and forms. Chapters

3, 4, and 5 discussed theories and developments that should have raised doubts about the assumption that these two ideas, especially the mirror thesis, are universally true. The discussion in Chapter 6 extended the separation thesis to functionality, and the discussion about the sources of social order in this chapter further questioned assumptions about the primary role that law plays in maintaining social order. The cumulative effect of this sustained argument should have been to open up a critical distance from the assumption that law is a mirror of society and the notion that the function of law is to maintain social order. Both ideas can now be held at arm's length, and be scrutinized rather than assumed as true for any given manifestation of law.

For its core initial inquiries, the general jurisprudence takes the two ideas underlying the presupposition about law and flips them from assumptions into questions; also, separately, it turns them into standards. For a given social arena, the core initial questions posed will be: (1) *to what extent is (state, customary, international, religious, natural, indigenous, etc.) law a mirror of prevailing customs and morals?* and (2) *to what extent does (state, customary, international, religious, natural, indigenous, etc.) law contribute to the maintenance of social order?* These two inquiries can (and should) be directed at any and all kinds of law that are present in a given social arena.

It will be impossible to come up with precise quantitative measures for the extent or degree of mirroring and the extent or degree of contribution to the maintenance of social order, but it should be feasible to produce reliable findings on a broad scale, such as: none, low, moderate, high, and extremely high. This is more a qualitative than a quantitative judgement.

A number of concomitant issues and questions should be examined along with the questions of the degree of mirroring and extent of social order function. Obviously a crucial enquiry is whether the degree of mirroring has any relationship with the extent of social order function, which is a way of testing the assumed causal connection between the two ideas. Many additional questions may be inquired into, such as: What are the social consequences (to the law and to the social arena) connected to low or high degrees of mirroring? What does law (of whatever kind) do, or what is it used to do, when its social order function is low? Does the law (of whatever kind) mirror society in certain respects or subject matters but not others? Is there a relationship between degrees of mirroring and prevailing views of the legitimacy of law (of whatever kind)? Or between the degrees of social order function and views of legitimacy? What relationship is there, if any, between degrees of mirroring and the presence of a monopolizing group of legal professionals? Why in a given social arena are certain phenomena given the label 'law'? What rhetorical, symbolic, or other benefits are attached thereto? What are the relationships among the various phenomena called law in a given social arena? How do they compare with one another on mirroring and social order function relative to the social arena? Which, if any, kinds of law are the closest reflection of customs and values within that social arena and why? A multitude of such questions are possible; the ones to be asked depend upon the purposes of the enquiry, and on the issues of interest to legal and social theorists regarding the law–society relationship.

When examining the extent of the social order function of law, the various sources of social order identified in the typology set out earlier should also be examined and taken into consideration, as they interact with the kinds of law present in a social arena. It will then be possible to learn whether and in what respects the presence of the various sources of social order has an effect on, and interacts with, the various kinds of law. Looking in these two directions—at the typology of sources of social order and the typology of kinds of law—and combining their findings, should result in more sophisticated understandings of the relationship between law and society with regard to social order in specific social arenas.

In addition to serving as core questions, as I indicated, a central component of the general jurisprudence is to use these two ideas to formulate standards. A broad scale can be created along a continuum ranging from none, to low, to moderate, to high, to extremely high, which will constitute such standards. There will be a standard for the degree of mirroring, and a standard for the extent of contribution to the maintenance of social order. The significance of these standards is that they will permit the accumulation of information from various social arenas along a single scale. The standards will serve as a baseline of comparison when moving from one social arena to the next. The questions asked in each social arena will provide information about that social arena. The two standards will provide information about how that particular social arena compares with other social arenas, and, considered as a whole, the information accumulated relative to the standards will present a portrait of how all (or a diverse variety of) social arenas stack up in terms of the mirroring and social order function of law (of whatever kind), and the consequences that follow therefrom.

The ability to gather information on *all* kinds of social arenas, on *all* state legal systems as well as on other kinds of law, is precisely what qualifies this proposal as a *general* jurisprudence. Unlike other attempts, it is not limited to particular systems, or to only Western systems. Indeed it is specifically designed to provide a way of accounting for the kaleido-scopic manifestations of law around the world, especially in non-Western countries with a history of legal transplantation, which have been all but ignored by legal theorists. For the first time it will be possible to situate, and understand, all of these myriad manifestations of law relative to a sin-gle theoretical framework. This univeral application is possible because, unlike the approaches of Austin and Hart, it is not based upon concepts or commonalities, which inevitably render them too narrow. Rather the aim is to identify differences against a common standard, then observe the consequences and implications of these differences. Observing the differences and their attendant consequences promises to be at least as informative as the commonalities.

As data is collected on more and more social arenas, patterns might begin to emerge on various consequences relating to the degree of mir-roring and the degree of social order function relative to the different kinds of law, many of which we do not now recognize. Following the accumulation of the results of studies, it might be possible to formulate reliable broadly applicable generalizations regarding the relationship between law and society, generalizations which recognize that different relationships exist and that these differences have systematic implica-tions. At the very least, even if no significant patterns or reliable general-izations are found, using this framework will produce an unmatched comparative portrait of the relationship between law and society. Presently, without a unifying scheme, the situation is so unruly that it has been impossible to build a cumulative body of knowledge on which to ground theory.

Another implication of the standards and enquiries suggested here should be made explicit, in case it is not apparent. Contrary to prevailing views, it should become evident that there is no such thing as a 'normal' or 'abnormal', or a 'proper' or 'deficient', relationship between law and society. What is normal is that law (of all kinds) has an extraordinary range of relationships with society with all kinds of consequences good and bad. Those tempted to turn the standards into modern versions of the old evolutionary scale—placing themselves at the privileged end (wherever they decide that might be)—will have missed the point.

The Implications of this Proposed Inquiry and Some Tentative Hypotheses

Flipping the assumptions into questions, and turning them into standards, is a simple idea, but powerful nonetheless. Its power derives from the fact that so many legal and social theories have constructed their theoretical edifice upon these assumptions.

Consider the descriptive/prescriptive axis. Many of these theories held that law *is* as well as *should be* a mirror of society, and that law *is* as well as *should be* a key mechanism in the maintenance of social order. Assume we discover after extensive study that in many social arenas state law is at most a moderate mirror of the customs and morals, and that regularly it is a low mirror. Theories that assume a high degree of mirroring will be proven empirically inadequate, or at least of limited application, and their value thrown into doubt. Assume we discover in many social arenas that state law has a medium to low role in the maintenance of social order. Theories that assume state law has a central role in maintaining order will be proven empirically inadequate. Those are a couple of the possible theoretical consequences on the descriptive side. Assume, further, we discover social arenas where the degree of mirroring is low, and the role played in social order is low, yet state law nonetheless functions quite effectively and provides other important services. Conversely, assume we discover that often when state law exerts a high role in maintaining social order, the populace is alienated from the law. Findings of these sorts will give us reasons to question the validity or desirability of the prescriptive link. Findings that point in the opposite directions will help validate the claimed descriptive and prescriptive links.

Remember that, for many theorists, the primary value of touting the mirror idea and the social order function of law was the service these ideas provided in legitimating law. These ideas perpetuate the beliefs, respectively, that the law is law of the people, and it saves the people from the frightful ravages of disorder always lurking just around the bend. If the descriptive and prescriptive claims of these two pervasive ideas are undercut, the dominant theoretical forms of legitimation of Western legal and social theory will be exposed, like the two dominant myths about the origins of law discussed in Chapter 3, as largely rationalizations on behalf of law (state law especially).

Based upon the information provided in Chapters 3 through 5, a number of preliminary hypotheses can be offered about what might be found in the course of the enquiry proposed by this general jurisprudence, suggesting a few of the issues that might be investigated. These are:

- It would seem obvious that the degree of mirroring will be higher when the legal system (whether state law or customary law, etc.) and its norms have been substantially homegrown, as compared to situations in which the legal systems and its norms have been substantially transplanted from elsewhere (though the length of time since the initial transplantation, and the tradition in which the legal professionals have been trained, will be additional contributing factors in the extent of mirroring).
- In situations of low mirroring, the role of law (of whatever kind) in the maintenance of social order will be relatively lower than in situations of high mirroring. Ironically, when mirroring is high, there will actually be less of a need for the intervention of law (of whatever kind) because people will be doing what the law requires anyway, owing to the influence of the other sources of social order.
- When legal actors have come to specialize and monopolize knowledge about law (of whatever kind), the degree of mirroring will be lower relative to those situations without such monopolization of knowledge.
- When *state* legal actors have come to specialize and monopolize knowledge about law, over time the law they produce will tend to be borrowed from or influenced (through the transnational legal culture) by legal traditions elsewhere.
- When monopolization is high, non-legal (or lay) social actors will have relatively lower access to and control over the law (regardless of what kind); when low mirroring is combined with high monopolization, access and control by lay social actors will be even lower still.
- When mirroring is low and monopolization is high, people in the social arena will have a limited knowledge and understanding of the law (of whatever kind), they will not be normatively committed to the law, they will not identify with the law, and they will tend to ignore or avoid the law.
- When mirroring is low and monopolization is high, the law (of whatever kind) will be more subject to capture and instrumental use by select groups, especially the economic or political elite (often including the legal professionals) within in the social arena.
- When monopolization is high, law (of any kind) will increasingly attempt or claim to be self-legitimating, pointing to its own nature (especially if it is a formal rationality version of law), and drawing upon the general symbolic authority that attaches to law.
- When more than one kind of law (of any kind) exists in a social arena people will consider the co-existence in instrumental terms; that is, one or the other (or both) kinds of law will be resorted to, and they will be played

off against one another, for strategic reasons, to further the goals of people involved (legal actors as well as lay people); and the degree of mirroring (whether low or high) will be one of the considerations in the strategic choice, as well as one of the arguments used in the ensuing conflict.

As this perfunctory and abbreviated list of hypotheses should indicate, the general jurisprudence urged here implicates a range of serious social and political issues, and has substantial critical potential. What makes the suggested inquiry powerful is that it puts the central claims of legal and social theorists directly to the test.

Beyond the Initial Inquiry

Although an extensive and systematic investigation of these subjects has barely begun, enough studies have already been completed to indicate that, with regard to many social arenas and many subject-matters, state law (and possibly other forms of law) will prove to rate low on both mirroring and social order function.[6] There will, of course, also be situations in which mirroring and social order function is high. In many situations a moderate to high degree of mirroring will hold in certain respects or for subject-matters with a low degree in others. A significant bulk of state law in many societies originates from elsewhere, and even those aspects generated locally pass through a filter of legal knowledge and legal professionals. Usually primacy for maintaining social order lies in the other sources of social order identified in the typology above, a fact that social scientists know but legal theorists perpetually ignore or forget. If these assertions are correct, as an empirical and theoretical matter the significance of the mirror thesis and the social order function of law should to some extent recede. That is why I have indicated that these two questions should serve only as the core *initial* inquiries, though ones of substantial magnitude.

These two ideas about law emerged centuries ago and have dominated ever since, shaping (and limiting) our views of the nature of law and its relationship to society. But society has changed. Law, in all of its various kinds, has changed, and what people do with law and use law for has changed. Even if it were true that when societies were small law (of whatever kind) often did mirror and often was primarily concerned with matters related to social order, there are many signs that this comfortable old

---

[6] For a study that demonstrates both points in a modern setting, see Ellickson (1991).

description no longer fits. As long as the time-worn mirror thesis and social order function thesis dominate theories about law, theorists will be blind to these changes.

Following the first stage, the enquiry should develop a new understanding of each kind of law and its relationship to society. Until the actual investigation occurs, it is impossible to anticipate precisely what the new questions will be. When attention is pried away from the social order function, new realms of investigation will open up that promise to alter our understandings of the phenomena which go by the name of law.

The discussions in Chapters 2, 3, 4, and 5 suggest that the relationship between law and society may have undergone a profound transformation that has yet to be adequately accounted for in theoretical terms. Three separate developments—the formalization and proceduralization of state law, the incredible growth and development of the state apparatus and of the market, and the spread of both around the globe—appear to have altered state law (in particular) and its relationship with society.

With regard to the market, reliability and predictability of transactions, the ability to possess and dispose of property, the development of new commodity forms, and a means to adjust relations in cases of conflict, are the primary concerns of law (of several kinds). This is *law as the formal infrastructure underlying the market and transactions* (although it should be remembered that even in this context law is still often secondary in influence to the other sources of social order). If current trends continue, it would seem reasonable to project a coming global commercial legal system, with unification both in terms of legal rules and systems, achieved through borrowing, imitation, and imposition, which will spread around the world on the tail of the advancing market and the expanding power and reach of transnational corporations. In this respect, the law (of most kinds) will follow and be determined by the dictates and needs of such corporations and the market. The kinds of law related to the market and transactions will have little to do with general social order. And, unless there is active intervention by political and influential non-governmental authorities, the only customs and morals they will reflect will be those of the merchants and businesses involved in the transactions. The notion of consent seems entirely out of place with regard to market driven law, since the imperatives of the market are what have final say. Deals are done by agreement, but the legal forms the deals take generally are not. Often it is less important how things are done than that they be done the same way in a recognizable manner. Often tax consequences in base countries will determine the forms deals take. The key tests for this kind of law will be whether they maximize wealth and efficiency, and reduce transaction costs. If these projections come about, then from a theoretical standpoint market-related law (of most kinds) must be looked at differently and accounted for differently. Law in the realm of the global market, while there are points of overlap, is not the same animal—in impetus, use, or function—as law relating to everyday social life.

With regard to the growth of the state apparatus, state law has come to serve a new role and purpose, especially in social welfare states. State law has increasingly served to *construct the infrastructure of the government bureaucracy*, and it has become *a way of doing things*. When the government engages in activities in the social arena alongside other private actors it acts through law—this is *law as a form of instrumental action*, which is distinctly different in operation from law as the enforcement of norms. In its social order role state law primarily operates in negative terms, by enforcing prohibitions directed at social behaviour. But in this new form and role, state law acts positively to achieve goals; and its attention is not directed at social behaviour, but rather the government itself is doing things through law. Administrative law in particular has this quality and is in this respect quite unlike traditional understandings of law. Custom, consent, morality, and reason have little to do with this process, and institutionalized rule application and enforcement, which is the classical view of law, poorly describes this process. Instrumental success (the achievement of policy directives) and interest balancing are more often what is involved. As governmental bureaucracies at all levels increase in size and expand the scope of their activities, this form of law as action will also increase, and current theoretical understandings of state law account for it almost not at all. Law as the means and form of government action is a different animal—in purpose, use, and function—from law governing everyday social life.

The third development—the proceduralization and formalization of law—as I argued earlier, is closely tied with the increased distancing of state law from custom and morality. With the assistance of expatriate lawyers and local legal specialists trained in the West (members of the transnational legal culture), Western derived legal systems and norms (state law, international law, and transnational law), especially the rule of law and formal democracy, are being transplanted around the globe, oblivious to local cultural and institutional conditions. Formalization and proceduralization are peculiarly Western ways of doing law, which are substantively empty in nature; and like the market, the rule of law carries its own internal imperatives, implications, and consequences. In many locations where this form of legality and formal democracy is spread, there could hardly be a greater gap between the state law and local customs and morality; and the entire process could hardly be less consensual. Moreover, state law's instrumental capacity will be available to any group able to capture the political selection process, and/or able to co-opt legal officials, legal specialists, or the lawmaking and legal proces. Formal and procedural law perpetuated by legal professionals carries special dangers of distancing law and its output from common understandings of social arenas. These problems, it must be emphasized, are not limited to the non-West. Western societies are becoming increasingly pluralistic and internally riven. The law is becoming an increasingly detached expert system. Whether procedural law can continue to credibly maintain its stance of neutrality is open to serious doubt. Recent trends towards greater consideration of substantive justice in rule of law regimes suggest that state law has already begun to swing in a less formal direction, which portends the appearance of new problems for state law in the context of a divided society.

These three developments suggest that state law (and perhaps other kinds as well) is changing, separating into three distinct realms (market, governmental/administrative, social relations) at least, and undergoing changes in all of these realms. This is neither good nor bad in itself. The problem is that our theoretical understandings have yet to catch up with these developments. Old ways of viewing the relationship between law and society—the mirror thesis and the social order thesis—continue to comfort us while law has moved on.

Perhaps the biggest change in theories relating to law that must take place, however, is not the result of changes in the kinds of things that (state) law does. Rather it will involve a flip in perspective of theorists, which could have been made long ago. The mirror thesis and the social order function of law privilege the societal standpoint in orientation and approach. But that is only half the picture, and perhaps the less revealing half. Law (of every kind) is a social creation and has a real social existence. The vast bulk of the people who resort to the law (of whatever kind) have no interest in or concern about social order in the context of their use, and this is also true of many legal actors (especially lawyers) when engaged in legal activities. From the lay standpoint, (state) law is often seen in terms of a resource of power; from a lawyer standpoint (state) law is seen as their arena of business, and the rules are approached in purely instrumental terms (as a barrier or tool) relative to their strategic goals. The disjunction between the theoretical view, which focuses obsessively on social order, and the intentions and motivations of people when they resort to or participate in law, could not be greater. Resort to law, and the way law operates, often creates and perpetuates conflict. This does not necessarily suggest that there is an inconsistency between the two points of view: law (of whatever kind) may be created and perpetuated by some social actors in a manner which facilitates social order by providing a background framework for others engaging in their everyday activities with other things on their mind; and law may (as Functionalists suggest) have a latent effect that contributes to social order regardless of whether any individual has that as their purpose. All of this, however, remains to be seen, and cannot be established nor understood well until the motivations and actions of social actors in their resort to law is more carefully explored. The process school of legal anthropology is the only approach that covers this perspective, though it is small and perhaps past its high point. The instrumental tradition described in Chapter 2 saw law as an instrument, but primarily in terms of an instrument to achieve social purposes. To make the final step, theories about law and society must create an integral place for understanding and incorporating the strategic approach of individuals (lay and legal actors) toward law (of every kind).

The mirroring and social order function ideas about law appear quaint and one-sided in the modern context. Law (of every kind) should be demystified and understood as a tool or instrument, a resource of power and way of doing things that draws upon symbolic connotations of right or good, but with no necessary connection to custom, consent, morality, reason, or functionality in a social arena. Understood in these terms, there would be nothing sacred about law (of every kind). Despite the impression it might provide, the approach suggested here is not cynical about law, though admittedly it is cynical about theories about law. The motivation that drives this general jurisprudence is to produce a more realistic understanding of the social existence of law.

Abstaining from the Legitimation Enterprise

The history of legal and social theory is replete with discussions of the legitimacy of law, or, more correctly stated, with attempts to portray law as legitimate. This is the legitimation enterprise. Many legal and social theorists might protest that their objective in setting up standards against which to test the legitimacy of law is to provide for a critique of law, to prompt improvement of the law by demonstrating its illegitimacy, not to rationalize the law. But it has seldom worked out that way. Natural law theory, for example, has the most critical edge of any form of legitimation enquiry, because it conditions the validity of positive law on conformity to a higher standard. Far too often, however, natural law has been enlisted to bolster the legitimacy of state law regimes. Odes to the consistency of state law or international law with customary law, or with customs, morality, reason, or natural principle, have been made with regularity. These practices merit suspicion about the legitimation enterprise. Legitimation theory can serve as a critique, or it can rationalize the status quo. More often than not in the hands of legal and social theorists, for whatever reasons, the critical potential of the legitimation enterprise has been sublimated in favour of serving as an apologist for the existing system of law. Exposure to this history suggests that the legitimation enterprise should be abandoned.

This conclusion is drawn with full awareness that it flies in the face of beliefs widely held among legal and social theorists. Indeed it would not be an exaggeration to say that, the selective mirror tradition and instrumental tradition notwithstanding, the single most dominant theme in legal theory throughout its history has been the legitimation of law. My point is not to deny that law should in fact *be* legitimate. My point is rather that it is not obvious that theoretical musings about the legitimacy of law have advanced this cause (see Tamanaha 1999). For this reason, and owing to its descriptive orientation to law (of whatever kind), the general jurisprudence I propose affirmatively abstains from participation in the legitimation enterprise. Other theorists might apply the findings from this general jurisprudence to serve the ends of their own legitimation discussions. That use, however, will form no part of the general jurisprudence itself.

The term 'law' carries symbolic connotations of authority, of rightful power. That is bolstering enough. Law, in all of its various kinds, need not be supplied with further theoretical justifications for its claims of legitimacy. Every specific manifestation or instance of law, every legal rule, every system, every legal practice, every legal claim, of every kind of law, must always answer directly to the question of whether it is in fact good or right. Every application of law or action in the name of law that increases human misery must be carefully scrutinized, regardless of whether it does or does not mirror society or enhance social order, and must stand up to a test of rightness. The answer in each instance is to be found in the particular circumstances at hand. The question of rightness is always a particular one. The most the general jurisprudence can do is help to place a given particular circumstance within a broader context.

The general jurisprudence can help us understand the reality of law (of whatever kind) in society. Whether that reality lives up to our desires, or accords with justice, is a decision that cannot be made by the general jurisprudence.

The Beginning

A general jurisprudence has not been completed by this work. It is, again, a necessary prolegomenon towards this end. This book has engaged in a close study of the terrain to uncover why past attempts to understand the relationship between law and society, and to construct a general jurisprudence, have fallen short. The theories discussed in this work convey valuable insights about the relationship between law and society. The hope of this work is to build on the strengths and avoid the weaknesses of past and existing theories.

Socio-legal positivism, the conventionalist approach to law and legal pluralism, the notion of the social arena, the two core inquiries and standards, are all in a sense empty. They do not provide significant details about what the relationship between law (of all kinds) and society is actually like; rather they identify key features, and suggest what to look for and how to look. Much hard work remains to be done.

Bibliography

Abel, R. (1973a), 'Law Books and Books about Law', *Stanford Law Review* 26: 175–228.

—— (1973b), 'A Comparative Theory of Dispute Institutions in Society', *Law and Society Review* 8: 217–347.

—— (1978), 'From the Editor', *Law and Society Review* 12: 489–98.

Ajani, G. (1995), 'By Chance and Prestige: Legal Transplants in Russia and Eastern Europe', *American Journal of Comparative Law* 43: 93–117.

Akers, R., and Hawkins, R. (eds.) (1975), *Law and Control in Society* (Englewood Cliffs, NJ: Prentice Hall).

Albrow, M. (1996), *The Global Age: State and Society Beyond Modernity* (Stanford, Calif.: Stanford University Press).

Allott, A., and Woodman, G. (eds.) (1985), *People's Law and State Law: The Bellagio Papers* (Dordrecht: Foris Pub.).

Aquinas, T. (1993), *Summa Theologiae*, trans. R. J. Henle (South Bend, Ind.: University of Notre Dame Press).

Aristotle (1985), *Nicomachean Ethics*, trans. T. Irwin (Indianapolis: Hackett Publishing Company).

—— (1988), *The Politics*, trans. E. Barker (Cambridge: Cambridge University Press).

Austin, J. (1913), *Lectures on Jurisprudence* (R. Campbell edition) (London: John Murray).

—— (1954), *The Uses of the Study of Jurisprudence*, ed. H. L. A. Hart (London: Weidenfeld & Nicolson).

—— (1995), *The Province of Jurisprudence Determined*, ed. W. Rumble (Cambridge: Cambridge University Press).

Barber, B. (1993), 'Global Democracy or Global War: Which Comes First?', *Indiana Journal of Global Legal Studies* 1: 119–37.

Barberis, M. (1996), 'Universal Legal Concepts: A Criticism of "General" Legal Theory', *Ratio Juris* 9: 1–14.

Barnes, B. (1995), *The Elements of Social Theory* (Princeton: Princeton University Press).

Bauman, Z. (1989), 'Hermeneutics and Modern Social Theory', in D. Held and J. B. Thompson (eds.), *Social Theory of Modern Sciences* (New York: Cambridge University Press).

—— (1992), *Intimations of Postmodernity* (New York: Routledge & Kegan Paul).

Becker, C. (1932), *The Heavenly City of the Eighteenth Century Philosophers* (New Haven: Yale University Press).

Bender, L. (1988), 'A Lawyer's Primer on Feminist Theory and Tort', *Journal of Legal Education* 38: 3–37.

Bentham, J. (1982), *An Introduction to the Principles of Morals and Legislation*, ed. J. H. Burns and H. L. A. Hart (London: Methuen).

Berger, P., and Luckmann, T. (1966), *The Social Construction of Reality* (Garden City, NY: Doubleday).

Berman, H. J. (1983), *Law and Revolution: The Formation of the Western Legal Tradition* (Cambridge, Mass.: Harvard University Press).

Bernstein, L. (1992), 'Opting Out of the Legal System: Extralegal Contractual Relations in the Diamond Industry', *Journal of Legal Studies* 21: 115–57.

Bianchi, A. (1997), 'Globalization of Human Rights: The Role of Non-state Actors', in G. Teuber (ed.), *Global Law Without a State* (Brookfield, Vt.: Dartmouth Publishing).

Bix, B. (1995), 'Conceptual Questions and Jurisprudence', *Legal Theory* 1: 465–79.

—— (1999a), *Jurisprudence: Theory and Context*, 2nd edn. (Durham, NC: Carolina Academic Press).

—— (1999b), 'Patrolling the Boundaries', *Canadian Journal of Law and Jurisprudence* 12: 17–33.

—— (2001), 'Natural Law Theory: The Modern Tradition', in J. L. Coleman and S. Shapiro (eds.), *Handbook of Jurisprudence and Legal Philosophy* (Oxford: Oxford University Press).

Bloch, M. (1967), 'The Feudal World', in N. Cantor and M. S. Werthman (eds.), *Medieval Society: 400–1500* (New York: Crowell).

Blumer, H. (1969), *Symbolic Interactionism* (Englewood Cliffs, NJ: Prentice Hall).

Bobbio, N. (1993), *Thomas Hobbes and the Natural Law Tradition*, trans. D. Gobetti (Chicago: University of Chicago Press).

Bodenheimer, E. (1957), 'Law as Order and Justice', *Journal of Public Law* 6: 194 ff.

—— (1973), *Power, Law and Society* (New York: Crane Russak).

Bohannan, P. (1965), 'The Differing Realms of the Law', *American Anthropologist* 67: 33 ff.

—— (1967), 'The Differing Realms of the Law', in P. Bohannan (ed.), *Law and Warfare* (Garden City, NY: Natural History Press).

Bohman, J. (1991), *New Philosophy of Social Science: Problems of Indeterminacy* (Cambridge, Mass.: MIT Press).

Bonell, M. J. (1992), 'Unification of Law by Non-Legislative Means: The UNIDROIT Draft Principles for International Commercial Contracts', *American Journal of Comparative Law* 40: 617–33.

Boorstin, D. (1996), *The Mysterious Science of the Law* (Chicago: University of Chicago Press).

Brierly, J. E. C., and David, R. (1978), *Major Legal Systems in the World Today*, 2nd edn. (New York: Free Press).

Bruhl, L. (1975), 'Sociologie du droit', trans. and quoted by L. Fuller in 'Law as an Instrument of Social Control and Law as Facilitation of Human Interaction', *Brigham Young University Law Review* 1975: 89–96.

Burman, S. B., and Harrell-Bond, B. E. (eds.) (1979), *The Imposition of Law* (New York: Academic Press).

Burton, S. (1989), 'Law as Practical Reason', *Southern California Law Review* 62: 747–93.

Cain, M., and Hunt, A. (eds.) (1979), *Marx and Engels on Law* (New York: Academic Press).

Cairns, H. (1949), *Legal Philosophy from Plato to Hegal* (Baltimore: Johns Hopkins Press).

Campbell, C. M., and Wiles, P. (eds.) (1979), *Law and Society* (New York: Barnes & Noble Books).

Cardozo, B. N. (1924), *The Growth of Law* (New Haven: Yale University Press).

Carter, J. C. (1907), *Law: Its Origin, Growth and Function* (New York: Da Capo Press).

Cassirer, E. (1951), *The Philosophy of the Enlightenment* (Princeton: Princeton University Press).

Chanock, M. (1985), *Law, Custom, and Social Order* (Cambridge: Cambridge University Press).

—— (1992), 'The Law Market: The Legal Encounter in British East and Central Asia', in W. J. Mommsen and J. A. de Morr (eds.), *European Expansion and Law* (Oxford: Berg Publishers).

Chiba, M. (1989), *Legal Pluralism: Toward a General Theory through Japanese Legal Culture* (Tokyo: Tokai University Press).

Chroust, A. (1944), 'The Philosophy of Gustav Radbruch', *Philosophical Review* 53: 23 ff.

Cicero (1998), *The Republic and The Laws*, trans. N. Rudd (Oxford: Oxford University Press).

Cohen, D. (1995), *Law, Violence and Community in Classical Athens* (Cambridge: Cambridge University Press).

Cohen, F. S. (1935), 'Transcendental Nonsense and the Functional Approach', *Columbia Law Review* 35: 809–49.

—— (1937), 'The Problems of a Functional Jurisprudence', *Modern Law Review* 1: 5–26.

—— (1960), *The Legal Conscience* (New Haven: Yale University Press).

Coleman, Janes S. (1990), *Foundations of Social Theory* (Cambridge, Mass.: Harvard University Press).

Coleman, Janet (2000a), *A History of Political Thought*, i. *From Ancient Greece to Early Christianity* (Malden, Mass.: Blackwell Publishers).

—— (2000b), *A History of Political Thought*, ii. *From the Middle Ages to the Renaissance* (Malden, Mass.: Blackwell Publishers).

Coleman, Jules (1980), 'Efficiency, Utility, and Wealth Maximization', *Hofstra Law Review* 8: 509–51.

—— (1998), 'Incorporationism, Conventionality, and the Practical Difference Thesis', *Legal Theory* 4: 381–425.

Collins, H. (1982), *Marxism and Law* (Oxford: Clarendon Press).

Collins, R., and Makowsky, M. (1972), *The Discovery of Society* (New York: Random House).

Comaroff, J. L., and Roberts, S. (1981), *Rules and Processes: The Cultural Logic of Dispute in an African Context* (Chicago: University of Chicago Press).

Cotterrell, R. (1991), 'The Durkheimian Tradition in the Sociology of Law', *Law and Society Review* 25: 923–45.

—— (1992), *The Sociology of Law* (London: Butterworths).

—— (1997), 'A Legal Concept of Community', *Canadian Journal of Law and Society* 12 (2): 75–91.

—— (1999), *Émile Durkheim: Law in a Moral Domain* (Stanford, Calif.: Stanford University Press).

Crenshaw, K., *et al.* (1995), 'Introduction', in K. Crenshaw *et al.* (eds.), *Critical Race Theory* (New York: New Press).

Daly, M. (1996), 'Thinking Globally: Will National Borders Matter to Lawyers a Century from Now?', *Journal Institute to Study Legal Ethics* 1: 297–342.

Davies, P. (1992), *The Mind of God* (New York: Simon & Schuster).

De Ly, F. (1992), *International Business Law and Lex Mercatoria* (Amsterdam: North Holland).

Dewey, J. (1941), 'John Dewey', in *My Philosophy of Law* (Boston: Boston Book Co.).

Dezalay, Y., and Garth, B. (1996), *Dealing in Virtue: International Commercial Arbitration and the Construction of a Transnational Legal Order* (Chicago: University of Chicago Press).

Doolan, A. (1954), *Order and Law* (Westminster, Md.: Newman Press).

Durkheim, É. (1972), *Émile Durkheim, Selected Writings*, ed. A. Giddens (Cambridge: Cambridge University Press).

—— (1973), 'The Division of Labour in Society', in R. Bellah (ed.), *Émile Durkheim on Morality and Society* (Chicago: University of Chicago Press).

—— (1983), 'The Division of Labour in Society', in S. Lukes and A. Scull (eds.), *Durkheim and the Law* (New York: St. Martin's Press).

—— (1993), *Ethics and the Sociology of Morals*, trans. R. T. Hall (Buffalo: Prometheus Books).

Dworkin, R. M. (1977), *Taking Rights Seriously* (Cambridge, Mass.: Harvard University Press).

—— (1986), *Law's Empire* (Cambridge, Mass.: Belknap Press).

Dyzenhaus, D. (1996), 'The Legitimacy of Legality', *University of Toronto Law Review* 46: 129–80.

Ehrlich, E. (1916), 'Montesquieu and Sociological Jurisprudence', *Harvard Law Review* 29: 582–600.

—— (1922), 'The Sociology of Law', *Harvard Law Review* 36: 130–45.

—— (1975), *The Fundamental Principles of the Sociology of Law* (New York: Arno Press).

Ellickson, R. (1989), 'A Hypothesis of Wealth-Maximizing Norms: Evidence from the Whaling Industry', *Journal of Law, Economics, and Organization* 5: 83–97.

—— (1991), *Order Without Law: How Neighbors Settle Disputes* (Cambridge, Mass.: Harvard University Press).

Elliot, E. D. (1985), 'The Evolutionary Tradition in Jurisprudence', *Columbia Law Review* 85: 38–94.

Engels, F. (1942), *The Origin of the Family, Private Property and the State, in the Light of the Researches of Lewis H. Morgan* (New York: International Publishers).

d'Entreves, A. P. (1994), *Natural Law: An Introduction to Legal Philosophy* (New Brunswick, NJ: Transaction Publishers).

Ewald, W. (1995), 'Comparative Jurisprudence (II): The Logic of Legal Transplants', *American Journal of Comparative Law* 43: 489–510.

Farber, D., and Frickey, P. (1991), *Law and Public Choice: A Critical Introduction* (Chicago: University of Chicago Press).

Fears, J. R. (2000), 'Natural Law: The Legacy of Greece and Rome', in E. B. McLean (ed.), *Common Truths: New Perspectives on Natural Law* (Wilmington, Del.: ISL Books).

Field, D. D. (1995), 'Magnitude and Importance of Legal Science', in S. B. Presser and J. S. Zainaldin (eds.), *Law and Jurisprudence* (St. Paul, Minn.: West Publishing).

Finnis, J. M. (1980), *Natural Law and Natural Rights* (Oxford: Clarendon Press).

—— (1995), 'Laws, Problems of the Philosophy of', in T. Honderich (ed.), *Oxford Companion to Philosophy* (Oxford: Oxford University Press).

—— (1996), 'The Truth in Legal Positivism', in R. George (ed.), *The Autonomy of Law: Essays on Legal Positivism* (Oxford: Clarendon Press).

—— (1998), *Aquinas: Moral, Political, and Legal Theory* (Oxford: Oxford University Press).

Fisch, J. (1992), 'Law as a Means and as an End: Some Remarks on the Function of European and Non-European Law in the Process of European Expansion', in W. J. Mommsen and J. A. de Morr (eds.), *European Expansion and Law* (Oxford: Berg Publishers).

Fish, S. E. (1989), *Doing What Comes Naturally* (Durham, NC: Duke University Press).

Foster, M. B. (1949), *Masters of Political Thought*, i. *Plato to Machiavelli* (Boston: Houghton Mifflin).

Friedman, L. (1969a), 'Legal Culture and Social Development', *Law and Society Review* 4: 29–44.

—— (1969b), 'On Legal Development', *Rutgers Law Review* 24: 11–64.

—— (1975), *The Legal System: A Social Science Perspective* (New York: Russell Sage Foundation).

—— (1994), 'Is There a Modern Legal Culture?', *Ratio Juris* 7: 117–31.

—— (1996), 'Borders: On the Emerging Sociology of Transnational Law', *Stanford Journal of International Law* 32: 65–90.

Friedmann, W. (1967), *Legal Theory*, 5th edn. (New York: Columbia University Press).

Fuller, C. (1994), 'Legal Anthropology, Legal Pluralism and Legal Thought', *Anthropology Today* 10: 9 ff.

Fuller, L. L. (1958), 'Positivism and Fidelity to Law—A Reply to Professor Hart', *Harvard Law Review* 71: 630–72.

—— (1964), *The Morality of Law* (New Haven: Yale University Press).

Fuller, L. L. (1969), *The Morality of Law* (New Haven: Yale University Press).

—— (1975), 'Law as an Instrument of Social Control and Law as a Facilitation of Human Interaction', *Brigham Young University Law Review* 1975: 89–96.

Galanter, M. (1972), 'The Aborted Restoration of "Indigenous" Law in India', *Comparative Studies in Society and History* 14: 53–70.

—— (1981), 'Justice in Many Rooms: Courts, Private Ordering, and Indigenous Law', *Journal of Legal Pluralism* 19: 1–47.

Gauchet, M. (1997), *The Disenchantment of the World: A Political History of Religion* (Princeton: Princeton University Press).

Gauthier, D. (1999), 'Why Ought One Obey God? Reflections on Hobbes and Locke', in C. W. Morris (ed.), *The Social Contract Theorists: Critical Essays on Hobbes, Locke and Rousseau* (Lanham, Md.: Rowman & Littlefield).

Gavison, R. (ed.) (1987), 'Comment', in *Issues in Contemporary Legal Philosophy: The Influence of H. L. A. Hart* (Oxford: Clarendon Press).

Geertz, C. (1983), *Local Knowledge* (New York: Basic Books).

George, R. (1992), 'Natural Law and Human Nature', in R. George (ed.), *Natural Law Theory* (Oxford: Clarendon Press).

Gessner, V. (1994), 'Global Legal Interaction and Legal Cultures', *Ratio Juris* 7: 132–45.

Giddens, A. (1990), *The Consequences of Modernity* (Stanford, Calif.: Stanford University Press).

Gleick, J. (1987), *Chaos: Making a New Science* (New York: Viking).

Goldberg, D., and Attwooll, E. (1996), 'Legal Orders, Systematic Relationships and Cultural Characteristics Towards Spectral Jurisprudence', in E. Orucu, E. Atwool, and S. Coyle (1996), *Studies in Legal Systems: Mixed and Mixing* (Boston: Kluwer Law International).

Gordon, R. (1990), 'New Developments in Legal Theory', in D. Kairys, *The Politics of Law: A Progressive Critique*, 2nd edn. (New York: Pantheon Books).

Grabes, H. (1982), *The Mutable Glass: Mirror-Imagery in Titles and Texts of the Middle Ages and English Renaissance* (Cambridge: Cambridge University Press).

Green, L. (1996), 'The Concept of Law Revisited', *Michigan Law Review* 94: 1687–1717.

Greenawalt, K. (1992), *Law and Objectivity* (New York: Oxford University Press).

Greenhouse, C. (1994), 'Democracy and Demography', *Indiana Journal of Global Legal Studies* 21: 21–9.

Greider, W. (1997), *One World, Ready or Not: The Manic Logic of Global Capitalism* (New York: Simon & Schuster).

Grey, J. (1986), *Hayek on Liberty* (Oxford: Blackwell).

Griffiths, J. (1986), 'What is Legal Pluralism?', *Journal of Legal Pluralism* 24: 1–55.

—— (1995), 'Legal Pluralism and the Theory of Legislation—With Special Reference to the Regulation of Euthanasia', in H. Petersen and H. Zahle (eds.), *Legal Polycentricity: Consequences of Pluralism in Law* (Brookfield, Vt.: Dartmouth Publishing Company).

Grosheide, F. W. (1994), 'Legal Borrowing and Drafting International Commercial Contracts', in K. Baele-Woelki, F. W. Grosheide, E. H. Hondius, and G. J. W. Steenhoff (eds.), *Comparability and Evaluation* (Norwell, Mass.: Kluwer Academic Publishers).

Habermas, J. (1996), *Between Facts and Norms* (Cambridge, Mass.: MIT Press).

—— (1999), 'Between Facts and Norms: An Author's Reflections', *Denver University Law Review* 76: 937–42.

Haglund, P. (1996), 'A Clear and Equal Glass: Reflections on the Metaphor of the Mirror', *Psychoanalytic Psychology* 13: 225–45.

Hampton, J. (1999), 'The Failure of Hobbes's Social Contract Argument', in C. W. Morris (ed.), *The Social Contract Theorists* (Lanham, Md.: Rowman & Littlefield).

Hart, H. L. A. (1958), 'Positivism and the Separation of Laws and Morals', *Harvard Law Review* 71: 593–629.

—— (1961), *The Concept of Law* (Oxford: Clarendon Press).

—— (1994), *The Concept of Law*, 2nd edn. (Oxford: Clarendon Press).

Hayek, F. A. (1973), *Law, Legislation and Liberty*, i. *Rules and Order* (London: Routledge & Kegan Paul).

Held, D. (1995), *Democracy and the Global Order* (Stanford, Calif.: Stanford University Press).

Hempel, C. (1965), *Aspects of Scientific Explanation and Other Essays in the Philosophy of Science* (New York: Free Press).

Hobbes, T. (1996), *Leviathan*, ed. J. C. A Gaskin (Oxford: Oxford University Press).

Hobsbawn, E. (1994), *The Age of Extremes: A History of the World, 1914–1991* (New York: Vintage Books).

Hoebel, A. (1954), *The Law of Primitive Man* (Cambridge, Mass.: Harvard University Press).

Hogue, A. (1966), *Origins of Common Law* (Bloomington, Ind.: Indiana University Press).

Holmes, O. W. (1897), 'The Path of the Law', *Harvard Law Review* 10: 457–78.

—— (1962), *The Occasional Speeches of Justice Oliver Wendell Holmes*, ed. M. Howe (Cambridge, Mass.: Belknap Press of Harvard University Press).

Hooker, M. B. (1975), *Legal Pluralism: An Introduction to Colonial and Neo-Colonial Laws* (Oxford: Clarendon Press).

Hovencamp, H. (1985), 'Evolutionary Models in Jurisprudence', *Texas Law Review* 64: 645–85.

Hume, D. (1966), *An Enquiry Concerning the Principles of Morals* (La Salle, Ill.: Open Court).

—— (1978), *A Treatise of Human Nature*, ed. L. A. Selby-Biggs and P. H. Nidditch (Oxford: Clarendon Press).

Hunt, A. (1978), *The Sociological Movement in Law* (Philadelphia: Temple University Press).

Jacob, H. (1996), 'Conclusion', in H. Jacob *et al.* (eds.), *Courts, Law and Politics in Comparative Perspective* (New Haven: Yale University Press).

Jaeger, W. (1944), *Paideia: The Ideals of Greek Culture*, trans. G. Highet (New York: Oxford University Press).

Jagtenberg, R., Orucu, E., and de Roo, A. (1995), 'Introduction', in Jagtenberg *et al.* (eds.), *Transfrontier Mobility of Law* (Boston: Kluwer Law International).

James, M. H. (ed.) (1973), 'Introduction', in *Bentham and Legal Theory* (Belfast: Northern Ireland Legal Quarterly).

Jay, P. (2000), *The Wealth of Man* (New York: Public Affairs).

Jenkins, I. (1980), *Social Order and the Limits of Law: A Theoretical Essay* (Princeton: Princeton University Press).

Jokela, H. (1990), 'Internationalism in Private International Law', in D. Clark (ed.), *Comparative and Private International Law* (Berlin: Duncker & Humbolt).

Jones, J. W. (1956), *The Law and Legal Theory of the Greeks* (Oxford: Clarendon Press).

Jones, C. A. (1994), 'Capitalism, Globalization and Rule of Law: An Alternative Trajectory of Legal Change in China', *Social and Legal Studies* 3: 195–221.

Kamenka, E. (1983), 'A Marxist Theory of Law?', *Law in Context* 1: 47.

Kant, I. (1991) *Kant Political Writings*, ed. H. Reiss (Cambridge: Cambridge University Press).

Kelley, D. R. (1990), *The Human Measure: Social Thought in the Western Legal Tradition* (Cambridge, Mass.: Harvard University Press).

Kelly, J. M. (1992), *A Short History of Western Legal Theory* (Oxford: Clarendon Press).

Kelsen, H. (1945), *General Theory of Law and the State* (New York: Russell & Russell).

—— (1992), *An Introduction to the Problems of Legal Theory* (Oxford: Clarendon Press).

King, M. (1993), 'The Truth about Autopoiesis', *Journal of Law and Society* 20: 218–36.

King, P. (1986), *Utilitarian Jurisprudence in America: The Influence of Bentham and Austin on American Legal Thought in the Nineteenth Century* (New York: Garland Publishing).

Kinsey, R. (1978), 'Marxism and the Law: Preliminary Analysis', *British Journal of Law and Society* 5: 202–27.

Kmiec, D. W. (1995), 'Liberty Misconceived: Hayek's Incomplete Relationship between Natural and Customary Law', *American Journal of Jurisprudence* 40: 209–27.

Kocourek, A. (1936), 'Factors in the Reception of Law', *Tulane Law Review* 10: 209–30.

Kronman, A. T. (1983), *Max Weber* (Stanford, Calif.: Stanford University Press).

Leiter, B. (1998), 'Realism, Hard Positivism, and Conceptualism Analysis', *Legal Theory* 4: 533–47.

Lempert, R. (1987), 'The Autonomy of Law: Two Visions Compared', in G. Teubner *Autopoietic law: A New Approach to Law and Society* (Berlin: W. de Gruyter).

Leue, H. J. (1992), 'Legal Expansion in the Age of the Companies: Aspects of the Administration of Justice in the English and Dutch Settlements of Maritime Asia, *c.*1600–1750', in W. J. Mommsen and J. A. de Morr (eds.), *European Expansion and Law* (Oxford: Berg Publishers).

Lind, E. A. (1998), 'Procedural Justice, Disputing and Reactions to Legal Authority', in A. Sarat *et al.* (eds.), *Everyday Practices and Trouble Cases* (Evanston, Ill.: Northwestern University Press).

Lisska, A. (1996), *Aquinas's Theory of Natural Law Revisited* (Oxford: Clarendon Press).

Llewellyn, K (1930), 'A Realistic Jurisprudence—The Next Step', *Columbia Law Review* 26: 175–228.

—— (1940), 'The Normative, the Legal, and the Law-Jobs: The Problem of Juristic Method', *Yale Law Journal* 49: 1355–1400.

—— (1962), *Jurisprudence: Realism in Theory and Practice* (Chicago: University of Chicago Press).

Locke, J. (1980), *Second Treatise of Government*, ed. C. B. Macpherson (Indianapolis: Hackett Publishing Co.).

—— (1990), *Questions Concerning the Law of Nature*, ed. and trans. R. Horowitz, J. Strauss, and D. Clay (Ithaca, NY: Cornell University Press).

Luhmann, N. (1982), *The Differentiation of Society* (New York: Columbia University Press).

—— (1985), *A Sociological Theory of Law* (Boston: Routledge & Kegan Paul).

—— (1989), 'Law as a Social System', *Northwestern University Law Review* 83: 136–50.

Lukes, S. (1973), *Émile Durkheim, His Life and Work* (Harmondsworth: Penguin).

—— and Scull, A. (1983), 'Introduction', in S. Lukes and A. Scull (eds.), *Durkheim and the Law* (New York: St Martin's Press).

Lyons, D. (1993), *Moral Aspects of Legal Theory* (Cambridge: Cambridge University Press).

Macaulay, S. (1963), 'Non-Contractual Relations in Business: A Preliminary Study', *American Sociological Review* 28: 55–67.

MacCormick, N. (1986), 'Law as an Institutional Fact', in N. MacCormick and O. Weinberger (eds.), *An Institutional Theory of Law* (Dordrecht: Kluwer Publishers.).

—— (1993), 'Law', in P. H. Scott (ed.), *Scotland: A Concise Cultural History* (Edinburgh: Mainstream Publishers.).

Macdonald, R. A., and Kleinhans, M. M. (1997), 'What is Critical Legal Pluralism?', *Canadian Journal of Law and Society* 12: 25–46.

MacIntyre, A. (1984), *After Virtue: A Study in Moral Theory* (Notre Dame: Ind.: University of Notre Dame Press).

—— (1990), *Three Rivals Versions of Moral Enquiry: Encyclopedia, Genealogy, and Tradition* (Notre Dame, Ind.: University of Notre Dame Press).

—— (1998), *A Short History of Ethics* (Notre Dame, Ind.: University of Notre Dame Press).

—— (2000), 'Theories of Natural Law in the Culture of Advanced Modernity', in E. B. McLean (ed.), *Common Truths: New Perspectives on Natural Law* (Wilmington, Del.: ISI Books).

Maine, H. S. (1986), *Ancient Law*, ed. A. Montagu (Classics of Anthropology Series; Tucson: University of Arizona Press).

Malinowski, B. (1926), *Crime and Custom in Savage Society* (New York: Harcourt, Brace & Company).

Mamut, L. S. (1993), 'Questions of Law in Marx's *Capital*', in C. Varga (ed.), *Marxian Legal Theory* (New York: New York University Press).

Manicas, Peter T. (1987), *A History and Philosophy of the Social Sciences* (Oxford: Basil Blackwell).

Marcus, G. E., and Fischer, M. M. J. (1986), *Anthropology as Cultural Critique: An Experimental Moment in the Human Sciences* (Chicago: University of Chicago Press).

Marmor, A. (1998), 'Legal Conventionalism', *Legal Theory* 4: 509–31.

Marx, K. (1954), *The Communist Manifesto*, Part II, ed. S. T. Possony (Chicago: H. Regnery Company).

—— (1970), *A Contribution to the Critique of Political Economy* (New York: International Publishers).

—— (1998), *The Communist Manifesto* (Oxford: Oxford University Press).

—— and Engels, F. (1947), *The German Ideology*, ed. R. Pascal (New York: International Publishers).

Merry, S. E. (1988), 'Legal Pluralism', *Law and Society Review* 22: 869–96.

—— (1992), 'Anthropology, Law, and Transnational Processes', *American Review of Anthropology* 21: 357–79.

Merryman, J. H. (1985), *The Civil Law Tradition*, 2nd edn. (Stanford, Calif.: Stanford University Press).

Merton, R. K. (1968), *Social Theory and Social Structure* (New York: Free Press).

Mill, J. S. (1985), *On Liberty*, ed. G. Himmelfard (London: Penguin Books).

Milovanovic, D. (1989), *Weberian and Marxian Analysis of Law* (Brookfield, Vt.: Gower Publishing Company).

Mommsen, W. J. (1992), 'Introduction', in W. J. Mommsen and J. A. de Moor (eds.), *European Expansion and Law* (New York: St Martin's Press).

—— and de Moor, J. A. (eds.) (1992), *European Expansion and Law* (New York: St Martin's Press).

Montesquieu, B. De (1991), *The Spirit of Laws*, rev. edn. trans. T. Nuget, revised by J. V. Prichard (Littleton, Colo.: Fred B. Rothman & Co.).

Moore, M. (1992), 'Law as a Functional Kind', in R. George (ed.), *Natural Law Theory* (New York: Oxford University Press).

—— (1998), 'Hart's Concluding Scientific Postscript', *Legal Theory* 4: 301–27.

Moore, S. F. (1978), *Law as Process: An Anthropological Approach* (Boston: Routledge & Kegan Paul).

—— (1986), 'Legal Systems of the World', in L. Lipson and S. Wheeler (eds.), *Law and the Social Sciences* (New York: Russell Sage Foundation).

Morrall, J. B. (1980), *Political Thought in Medieval Times* (Toronto: University of Toronto Press).

Morris, C. W. (ed.) (1999), *The Social Contract Theorists: Critical Essays on Hobbes, Locke and Rousseau* (Lanham, Md.: Rowman & Littlefield).

Morse, B., and Woodman, G. (eds.) (1987), *Indigenous Law and the State* (Dordrecht: Foris Publishers).

Mounce, H. O. (1999), *Hume's Naturalism* (New York: Routledge).

Nader, L. (1965), 'The Anthropological Study of Law', *American Anthropologist* 67: 3–32.

Nelken, D. (1981), 'The "Gap" Problem in the Sociology of Law: A Theoretical Review', *Windsor Yearbook of Access to Justice* 1: 35–61.

—— (1995), 'Disclosing/Invoking Legal Culture: An Introduction', *Social & Legal Studies* 4: 435–52.

Nielson, K. (1959), 'An Examination of the Thomistic Theory of Natural Moral Law', *Natural Law Forum* 4: 44–71.

Nonet, P., and Selznick, P. (1978), *Law and Society in Transition: Toward a Responsive Law* (New York: Octagon Books).

Orucu, E. (1996), 'Mixed and Mixing System: A Conceptual Search', in E. Orucu, E. Atwool, and S. Coyle, *Studies in Legal Systems: Mixed and Mixing* (Boston: Kluwer Law International).

Ostwald, M. (1987), *From Popular Sovereignty to Sovereignty of Law: Law, Society, and Politics in Fifth-Century Athens* (Berkeley: University of California Press).

Pardieck, A. (1996), 'Foreign Legal Consultants: The Changing Role of Lawyers in Global Economy', *Indiana Journal of Global Legal Studies* 3: 457–79.

Parsons, T. (1937), *The Structure of Social Action* (New York: McGraw-Hill Book Company).

—— (1966) *Societies: Evolutionary and Comparative Perspectives* (Englewood Cliffs, NJ: Prentice Hall).

—— (1980), 'The Law and Social Control', in W. Evan (ed.), *The Sociology of Law* (New York: Free Press).

Pashukanis, E. B. (1989), *Law and Marxism: A General Theory*, trans. B. Einhorn (Worcester, UK: Pluto Press).

Patterson, E. (1940), *Jurisprudence: Men and Ideas of Law* (Brooklyn, NY: Foundation Press).

Payne, M. A. (1982), 'Law Based on Accepted Authority', *William & Mary Law Review* 23: 501–28.

Perry, S. R. (1996), 'The Varieties of Legal Positivism', *Canadian Journal of Law and Jurisprudence* 9: 361–81.

—— (1998), 'Hart's Methodological Positivism', *Legal Theory* 4: 427–67.

Plato (1950), *The Republic* (New York: Everyman's lib. edn.).

—— (1980), *Laws*, trans. T. Pangle (New York: Basic Books).

—— (1991), *The Republic* (New York: Random House).

Polan, D. (1993), 'Toward a Theory of Law and Patriarchy', in D. K. Weisberg (ed.), *Feminist Legal Theory* (Philadelphia: Temple University Press).

Pollock, F. (1961), *Jurisprudence and Legal Essays* (New York: St Martin's Press).

Pompe, S. (1996), *The Indonesian Supreme Court: Fifty Years of Judicial Development*, on file with author.

Posner, R. (1979), 'Utilitarianism, Economics, and Legal Theory', *Journal of Legal Studies* 8: 103–40.

Posner, R. (1990), *The Problems of Jurisprudence* (Cambridge, Mass.: Harvard University Press).

—— (1992), *Economic Analysis of Law*, 4th edn. (Boston: Little Brown).

Postema, G. J. (1986), *Bentham and the Common Law Tradition* (Oxford: Clarendon Press).

Pound, R. (1908), 'Mechanical Jurisprudence', *Columbia Law Review* 8: 605–23.

—— (1911), 'The Scope and Purpose of Sociological Jurisprudence', *Harvard Law Review*, 24: 591–619.

—— (1912), 'The Scope and Purpose of Sociological Jurisprudence (II)', *Harvard Law Review* 25:140–68.

—— (1912–13), 'Theories of Law', *Yale Law Journal* 22: 114–50.

—— (1923), *Interpretations of Legal History* (New York: Macmillan Company).

—— (1938), 'Fifty Years of Jurisprudence', *Harvard Law Review* 51: 444–72.

—— (1959a), *Jurisprudence*, Vol. I (St Paul: West Publishing Company).

—— (1959b), *Jurisprudence*, Vol. II (St Paul: West Publishing Company).

Quigley, J. (1990), 'Law Reform and Soviet Courts', *Columbia Journal of Transnational Law* 28: 59–75.

Rawls, J. (1971), *A Theory of Justice* (Cambridge, Mass.: Belknap Press of Harvard University Press).

Raz, J. (1974), 'Kelsen's Theory of the Basic Norm', *American Journal of Jurisprudence* 19: 94–111.

—— (1979), *The Authority of Law: Essays on Law and Morality* (New York: Oxford University Press).

—— (1980), *Concept of a Legal System* (New York: Oxford University Press).

—— (1994), *Ethics in the Public Domain* (New York: Oxford University Press).

—— (1998), 'Two Views of the Nature of the Theory of Law', *Legal Theory* 4: 249–82.

Reimann, M. (1990), 'Nineteenth Century German Legal Science', *Boston College Law Review* 31: 837–97.

Rheinstein, M. (1954), *Max Weber on Law in Economy and Society* (New York: Simon & Schuster).

Riles, A. (1994), 'Representing the In-Between: Law, Anthropology, and the Rhetoric of Interdisciplinarity', *University of Illinois Law Review*, 1994: 597–650.

Roberts, S. (1979), *Order and Dispute: An Introduction to Legal Anthropology* (New York: St Martin's Press).

Rommen, H. (1998), *The Natural Law: A Study in Legal and Social History and Philosophy* (St Louis: B. Herder Books).

Rorty, R. (1979), *Philosophy and the Mirror of Nature* (Princeton: Princeton University Press).

Rosenblum, N. (1978), *Bentham's Theory of the Modern State* (Cambridge, Mass.: Harvard University Press).

Rousseau, J. J. (1974), 'The Social Contract', in *The Essential Rousseau*, trans. L. Blair (New York: New American Library).

Rule, J. B. (1988), *Theories of Civil Violence* (Berkeley: University of California Press).

Rule, J. B. (1997), *Theory and Progress in Social Science* (Cambridge: Cambridge University Press).

Sanders, J. (1996), 'Courts and Law in Japan', in H. Jacob *et al.* (eds.), *Courts, Law and Politics in Comparative Perspective* (New Haven: Yale University Press).

Santos, B. de Sousa (1987), 'Law: A Map of Misreading Toward a Postmodern Conception of Law', *Journal of Law and Society* 14: 279–302.

—— (1995), *Toward a New Common Sense: Law, Science and Politics in Paradigmatic Transition* (New York: Routledge).

Sassen, S. (1996), 'Towards a Feminist Analytics', *Indiana Journal of Global Legal Studies* 4: 7–41.

Schauer, F. (1994), 'Critical Notice', *Canadian Journal of Philosophy* 24: 495 ff.

Schneewind, J. B. (1998), *The Invention of Autonomy: A History of Modern Moral Philosophy* (Cambridge: Cambridge University Press).

Schofield, P. (1991), 'Jeremy Bentham and Nineteenth-Century English Jurisprudence', *Journal of Legal History* 12: 58–88.

Schur, E. M. (1968), *Law and Society: A Sociological View* (New York: Random House).

Schutz, A. (1962), *The Problem of Social Reality* (The Hague: M. Nijhoff).

—— (1967), *The Phenomenology of the Social World* (Evanston, Ill.: Northwestern University Press).

Searle, J. (1995), *The Construction of Social Reality* (New York: Free Press).

Seita, A. (1997), 'Globalization and the Convergence of Values', *Cornell International Law Journal* 30: 429–91.

Shapiro, M. (1993), 'The Globalization of Law', *Indiana Global Legal Studies* 1: 37–64.

—— (1995), 'The United States', in C. N. Tate and T. Vallinder (eds.), *The Global Expansion of Judicial Power* (New York: New York University Press).

Shiner, R. A. (1992), 'The Acceptance of a Legal System', in D. M. Patterson (ed.), *Wittgenstein and Legal Theory* (Boulder, Colo.: Westview Press).

Simmons, J. A. (1993), *On the Edge of Anarchy: Locke, Consent, and the Limits of Society* (Princeton: Princeton University Press).

Simon, Y. (1965), *The Tradition of Natural Law* (New York: Fordham University Press).

Simpson, A. W. B. (1994), *The Common Law and Legal Theory, Folk Law: Essays in the Theory and Practice of Lex Non Scripta*, ed. A. D. Rentlen and A. Dundes (New York: Garland Publishing).

Slaughter, A. M. (1997), 'The Real New World', *Foreign Affairs* 76: 183 ff.

Smith, A. (1978), *Lectures on Jurisprudence*, ed. R. L. Meek, D. D. Raphael, and P. G. Stein (Oxford: Clarendon Press).

Snyder, F. (1981), 'Colonialism and Legal Form: The Creation of "Customary Law" in Senegal', *Journal of Legal Pluralism* 19: 49–90.

Soper, P. (1998), 'Two Puzzles from the Postscript', *Legal Theory* 4: 359–80.

Stein, P. (1980), *Legal Evolution: Story of an Idea* (Cambridge: Cambridge University Press).

Stein, P. (1999), *Roman Law in European History* (Cambridge: Cambridge University Press).

Stone, A. (1985), 'The Place of Law in the Marxian Structure-Superstructure Archetype', *Law and Society Review* 19: 39–67.

Summers, R. S. (1982), *Instrumentalism and American Legal Theory* (Ithaca, NY: Cornell University Press).

—— (1984), *Lon L. Fuller* (Stanford, Calif.: Stanford University Press).

Sumner, C. (1982), 'The Ideological Nature of Law', in P. Beirne and R. Quinney (eds.), *Marxism and Law* (New York: Wiley).

Sweet, A. S. (2000), *Governing with Judges: Constitutional Politics in Europe* (Oxford: Oxford University Press).

Symposium on Globalization (1996), *Journal of Legal Education* 46: 311–41.

Tamanaha, B. Z. (1988), 'The Role of Custom and Traditional Leaders under the Yap Constitution', *University of Hawaii Law Review* 10: 81–104.

—— (1989), 'A Proposal for the Development of a System of Indigenous Jurisprudence in the Federated States of Micronesia', *Hastings International and Comparative Law Review* 13: 71–114.

—— (1993a), 'The Folly of the "Social Scientific" Concept of Legal Pluralism', *Journal of Law and Society* 20: 192–217.

—— (1993b), *Understanding Law in Micronesia: An Interpretive Approach to Transplanted Law* (Leiden: Brill Publishers).

—— (1995a), 'An Analytical Map of Social Scientific Approaches to the Concept of Law', *Oxford Journal of Legal Studies* 15: 501–35.

—— (1995b), 'The Lessons of Law and Development Studies' (Review Article) *American Journal of International Law* 89: 470–86.

—— (1996), 'The Internal/External Distinction and the Notion of a Practice in Legal Theory and Sociolegal Studies', *Law and Society Review* 30: 163–204.

—— (1997), *Realistic Socio-Legal Theory: Pragmatism and a Social Theory of Law* (Oxford: Clarendon Press).

—— (1999), 'The View of Habermas from Below: Doubts about the Centrality of Law and the Legitimation Enterprise', *Denver University Law Review* 76: 989–1008.

—— (2000), 'Conceptual Analysis, Continental Social Theory, and CLS: A Response to Bix, Rubin and Livingston', *Rutgers-Camden Law Review* 32: 281–306.

Tarnas, R. (1991), *The Passion of the Western Mind: Understanding the Ideas that have Shaped Our World View* (New York: Harmony Books).

Tate, C. N., and Vallinder, T. (1995), 'The Global Expansion of Judicial Power: The Judicialization of Politics', in C. N. Tate and T. Vallinder (eds.), *The Global Expansion of Judicial Power* (New York: New York University Press).

Taylor, G. (1994), 'U.S. Firms are Export Machines: Sale of Legal Services Abroad Soars in 90s', *National Law Journal*, 30 May 1994.

Teubner, G. (ed.) (1988), *Autopoietic Law: A New Approach to Law and Society* (New York: W. de Gruyter).

Teubner, G. (1992), 'The Two Faces of Janus: Rethinking Legal Pluralism', *Cardozo Law Review* 13: 1443–62.

—— (1997), 'Global Bukowina: Legal Pluralism in the World Society', in G. Teubner (ed.), *Global Law Without a State* (Brookfield, Vt.: Dartmouth Publishing).

Thurow, L. (1995), *The Future of Capitalism* (New York: Penguin Books).

Torti, A. (1991), *The Glass of Form: Mirroring Structures from Chaucer to Skelton* (Rochester, NY: D. S. Brewer).

Trakman, L. (1983), *The Law Merchant* (Littleton, Colo.: F. B. Rothman).

Trubek, D. (1972a), 'Max Weber on Law and the Rise of Capitalism', *Wisconsin Law Review* 1972: 720–53.

—— (1972b), 'Towards a Social Theory of Law: An Essay in the Study of Law and Development', *Yale Law Journal* 82: 1–50.

Turkel, G. (1979), 'Testing Durkheim: Some Theoretical Considerations', *Law and Society Review* 25: 721–38.

Tushnet, M. (1977), 'Perspectives on the Development of American Law: A Critical Review of Friedman's "A History of American Law" ', *Wisconsin Law Review* 1977: 81–109.

Twining, W. (1996), 'General and Particular Jurisprudence—Three Chapters in a Story', in S. Guest (ed.), *Positivism Today* (Brookfield, Vt.: Dartmouth Publishing).

—— (2000), *Globalization & Legal Theory* (London: Butterworths).

Ullmann, W. (1969), *The Medieval Idea of Law* (New York: Barnes & Noble).

Unger, R. M. (1975), *Knowledge and Politics* (New York: Free Press).

—— (1976), *Law in Modern Society: Toward a Criticism of Social Theory* (New York: Free Press).

—— (1996), *What Should Legal Analysis Become?* (New York: Verso).

Vago, S. (1981), *Law and Society* (Englewood Cliffs, NJ: Prentice Hall).

von Benda-Beckmann, F. (1992), 'Symbiosis of Indigenous and Western Law in Africa and Asia: An Essay in Pluralism', in W. J. Mommsen and J. A. de Morr (eds.), *European Expansion and Law* (Oxford: Berg Publishers).

von Ihering, R. (1915), *The Struggle for Law* (Westport, Conn.: Hyperion Press).

—— (1968), *Law as a Means to an End*, trans. I. Husik (New York: A. M. Kelley).

von Savigny, F. (1831), *Of the Vocation of Our Age for Legislation and Jurisprudence*, trans. A. Hayward, originally published in 1814 (New York: Arno Press).

Wachterhauser, B. R. (1994), 'Gadamer's Realism: The "Belongingness" of Word and Reality', in B. Wachterhauser (ed.), *Hermeneutics and Truth* (Evanston, Ill.: Northwestern University Press).

Waldron, J. (1995), 'The Dignity of Legislation', *Maryland Law Review* 54: 633–65.

—— (1996), 'Kant's Legal Positivism', *Harvard Law Review* 109: 1535–66.

Walker, G., and Fox, M. (1996) 'Globalization: An Analytical Framework', *Indiana Global Legal Studies Journal* 3: 375–411.

Watson, A. (1978), 'Comparative Law and Legal Change', *Cambridge Law Journal* 37: 313–36.

Watson, A. (1983), 'Legal Change: Sources of Law and Legal Culture', *University of Pennsylvania Law Review* 131: 1121–57.

—— (1985), *The Evolution of Law* (Baltimore: Johns Hopkins University Press).

—— (1987), 'Legal Evolution and Legislation', *Brigham Young University Law Review* 1987: 353–79.

—— (1993), *Legal Transplants: An Approach to Comparative Law*, 2nd edn. (Athens, Ga.: University of Georgia Press).

Weber, M. (1954), *Max Weber on Law in Economy and Society*, ed. M. Rheinstein (Cambridge, Mass.: Harvard University Press).

Weiner, M. (1992), 'Peoples and States in a New Ethnic Order?', *Third World Quarterly* 13: 317 ff.

Weisberg, D. K. (1993), 'Introduction', in *Feminist Legal Theory: Foundations* (Philadelphia: Temple University Press).

West, R. (1988), 'Jurisprudence and Gender', *University of Chicago Law Review* 55: 1–72.

Whitman, J. Q. (1991), 'Why Did the Revolutionary Lawyers Confuse Custom and Reason?' *University of Chicago Law Review* 58: 1321–68.

Wiegand, W. (1991), 'The Reception of American Law in Europe', *American Journal of Comparative Law* 39: 229–48.

Wilhelmsson, T. (1995), 'Legal Integration as Disintegration of National Law', in H. Petersen and H. Zahle (eds.), *Legal Polycentricity: Consequences of Pluralism in Law* (Brookfield, Vt.: Dartmouth Publishing Company).

Wilson, J. (1983), *Social Theory* (Englewood Cliffs, NJ: Prentice Hall).

Winch, P. (1958), *The Idea of a Social Science and Its Relationship to Philosophy* (Atlantic Highlands, NJ: Humanities Press).

Wittgenstein, L. (1958), *Philosophical Investigations*, 3ed edn., trans. G. E. M. Anscombe (New York: Macmillan Publishing Co.).

Wrong, D. H. (1994), *The Problem of Order: What Unites and Divides Society* (New York: Free Press).

Ziegert, K. A. (1980), 'A Sociologist's View', in E. Kamenka and A. Erh-Soon Tay (eds.), *Law and Social Control* (New York: St Martin's Press).

Zimmermann, R. (1994), 'Roman Law and European Legal Unity', in A. S. Hartkamp, M. W. Hesselink, E. H. Hondius, C. E. du Perron, and J. M. B. Vranken (eds.), *Towards a European Civil Code* (Boston: M. Nijhoff).

Zweigert, K., and Kotz, H. (1992), *Introduction to Comparative Law*, 2nd rev. edn., trans. T. Weir (Oxford: Clarendon Press).

Index

Abel, R. 131, 132, 203
Acceptance requirement 152–5
Agobard 181
Ajani, G. 110
Akers, R. 2
Albrow, M. 123, 124, 129
Allott, A. 113
Anaximenes 13
Anthropology of law xii, 45–50, 56, 59, 92, 107–9, 112–17, 175–80, 198–9, 200–5, 226, 240
Aquinas, T. 14, 16, 17, 18, 19, 20, 21
Aristotle 3, 5, 6, 7, 11, 12, 13, 14, 15, 19, 40, 52, 53, 67, 99
Atiyah, P. 105
Attwool, E. 110
Augustine 17
Austin, J. xiii, xiv, xv, 7, 11, 17, 18, 22, 24, 25, 26, 27, 143, 145, 152, 153, 233
Autopoiesis 73, 109, 186–91

Baldus 91
Barber, B. 123
Barberis, M. xv
Barnes, B. 91, 163, 168, 187, 188, 218, 223
Bartlett, R. 67
Bartolus 91
Bauman, Z. 130, 167
Becker, C. 70, 83
Behaviourism 162–3, 214–15
Bender, L. 43
Bentham, J. xiii, 24, 45, 46, 48, 49, 71, 72, 73, 94, 102
Berger, P. 142
Berman, H. 18, 19, 56, 67, 74, 98, 105, 139, 180
Bernstein, L. 207
Bianchi, A. 122
Bix, B. xv, 100, 134, 149, 150, 156, 157, 160, 169
Blackstone, W. 5, 7, 18, 46, 92, 94
Bloch, M. 89, 90
Blumer, H. 164
Bobbio, N. 57, 58, 80
Bodenheimer, E. 3
Bohannan, P. 56, 138

Bohman, J. 217
Boorstin, D. 5, 7, 18
Bourdieu, P. 206
Brierly, J. 42
Burke, E. 94
Burman, S.B. 113
Burton, S. xv

Cain, M. 87
Cairns, H. 11, 13, 23
Campbell, C. M. 41
Cardozo, B. 3
Carter, J. 5
Cassirer, E. 78, 79, 82, 84, 85, 91, 97
Chanock, M. 113, 114, 115
Chiba, M. 120, 171
Chroust, A. 8
Cicero 6, 15, 16, 17, 72
Cohen, D. 13, 50, 67
Cohen, S. 46, 47, 133, 176
Coleman, James 218
Coleman, Janet 8, 14, 21, 57, 136
Coleman, Jules 135, 156
Collins, H. 2, 41, 42
Colonization and law 112–17, 146, 226
Comaroff, J. L. 114
Common law 86, 92–5
Comparative law xiii, xvii, 107–11, 127–8, 196–7, 230–6
Concept of law xv, xvi, xviii, 16, 23, 24, 26, 31, 36, 38, 133–4, 170, 173, 175–81, 184, 192–4, 202–5
  conventionalist 135–6, 138, 142, 145, 148–56, 166–70, 172, 180, 188–9, 191, 192–4, 198, 200–5, 224–30
  Hart and 133–55
Conventionalism 135–6, 148–56, 166–70, 180, 188–9, 191, 196, 198, 200–5
Cotterrell, R. 35, 36, 61, 130, 171
Crenshaw, K. 43
Critical Feminist Theory 43
Critical Legal Studies xiii, 42–3
Critical Race Theory 43
Custom and law 4–10, 12–13, 19–22, 23–5, 26–32, 33, 35, 38, 40, 42, 44, 45, 46, 48, 52–7, 65–6, 71, 86, 89–96, 108, 113–17, 137–9, 174, 186, 227, 241

Customary law 180, 113–15, 166, 193, 195, 196, 198–9, 226–7

Daly, M. 127, 128
David, R. 42
Davies, P. 211
Dawson, J. 72
De Ly, F. 126
Democracy 49–50, 95–6, 102–4, 238–9
de Moor 112
Demosthenes 13
d'Entreves, A. 14, 17, 18, 20, 21
de Roos 110
Descartes 79
de Sousa Santos, B. 121, 123, 171, 172, 173, 174, 181, 182, 183, 184, 185, 198, 199
Dewey, J. 47, 48, 166
Dezalay, Y. 126, 127, 128
Discourse theory 64–5, 101
Doolan, A. 23
Durkheim, É. 8, 32, 34, 35, 37, 52, 55, 56, 61, 118, 137, 158, 187, 216
Dworkin, R. M. 6, 51, 105, 133, 135
Dyzenhaus, D. 102

Edgarton, R. 217
Efficacy of law 143–8
Ehrlich, E. 2, 27, 28, 30, 31, 89, 90, 116, 146, 176, 221
Elias, N. 206
Ellickson, R. 149, 207, 213, 236
Elliot, E. D. 32
Engels, F. 40, 41, 42, 44, 71, 86
Enlightenment 69–70, 78–86, 91, 93, 158
Essentialist approach to law 135, 136, 137–55, 171–2, 178, 180, 181, 188, 192–4, 204–5
Evolutionary view of law 32–6, 52–7, 58–65
Ewald, W. 51, 107, 108

Farber, D. 49
Fears, J. R. 15
Feyerabend, P. 79
Field, D. D. 2, 202
Finnis, J. xvi, 16, 17, 18, 20, 21, 51, 84, 151, 157, 160, 161, 168
Fisch, J. 112, 113
Fischer, M. xiii
Fish, S. 164
Fitzpatrick, P. 171
Force and law 65–71

Formal rationality and law 37–40, 73–4, 87, 96–106, 235, 238–9
Foster, M. B. 12, 14, 15
Fox, M. 121
Frickey, P. 49
Friedman, L. 2, 120, 126, 127, 131
Friedmann, W. 19, 20, 22
Fuller, C. 198
Fuller, L. L. 6, 18, 92, 98, 100, 101, 226
Functional view of law 135–49, 155–7, 175–81, 187, 192–4, 201
Functionalism 32, 35–6, 60–1, 109, 137, 148–9, 176–7, 178–9, 187–9, 191, 202, 209, 212, 240

Gaius 91
Galanter, M. 110, 116, 138, 171, 173, 174, 175, 178
Gap problem 131–2
Garth, B. 126, 127, 128
Gauchet, M. 58
Gauthier, D. 69
Gavison, R. xiii
Geertz, C. 195
General Jurisprudence xii–xvii, 25, 111, 133–5, 148, 151, 155–6, 168–9, 200, 230–6, 240–2
Gessner, V. 127, 130
Giddens, A. 75, 121, 122, 130
Globalization 120–2
    and law 122–5
Goffman, E. 217
Goldberg, D. 110
Gordon, R. 43
Grabes, H. 2
Gratian 18, 19
Green, L. 135
Greenawalt, K. 2
Greenhouse, C. 123
Greider, W. 124
Grey, J. 223
Griffiths, J. 115, 171, 172, 174, 175
Grosheide, F. W. 126, 128, 130
Grotius 7, 17, 21, 22, 28, 91

Habermas, J. 5, 55, 56, 60, 64, 88, 96, 97, 98, 101, 102, 214, 215
Haglund, P. 2
Hampton, J. 80
Harrell-Bond, B. E. 113
Hart, H. L. A. xiii, xiv, xvii, 2, 14, 18, 22, 25, 26, 27, 51, 52, 66, 84, 89, 133, 134, 135, 136, 137, 138, 139, 140,

141, 142, 143, 146, 148, 149, 150,
151, 152, 153, 154, 155, 156, 157,
159, 162, 165, 166, 173, 177, 178,
179, 180, 189, 195, 196, 233
Hawkins, R. 2
Hayek, F. A. 101, 214, 215, 218, 223
Held, D. 121, 123
Hobbes, T. 22, 23, 24, 26, 28, 57, 79, 80,
81, 82, 86, 208, 209, 213, 221, 223
Hobsbawn, E. 124
Hoebel, A. 61, 138, 140, 175, 177, 178,
180, 181, 196
Hogue, A. 93
Holmes, O. W. 2, 47
Homer 53
Hooker, M. B. 116
Hovenkamp, H. 32
Hume, D. 62, 79, 82, 83, 85, 86, 95, 97
Hunt, A. 35, 37, 87

Indigenous law 229
Instrumental view of law 40–1, 44–50,
94–5, 98–106, 238, 240
Instrumental view of reason 80–6, 98, 102
International law 150, 152, 162, 193–5,
196, 228
Interpretivism 32, 162–6, 214–15

Jacob, H. 106
Jaeger, W. 11, 12, 13
Jagtenberg, R. 110
James, M. H. 46
James, W. 47
Jay, P. 67
Jenkins, I. 3, 59
Jones, C. A. 115, 120
Jones, J. W. 11, 12, 16

Kamenka, E. 41
Kant, I. 62, 63, 103, 104
Kelley, D. R. 29, 53, 56, 71, 74, 90, 91,
93
Kelly, J. M. 6, 11, 16, 19, 24, 28
Kelsen, H. 2, 138, 140, 143
King, M. L. 160
King, M. 190
King, P. 46
Kinsey, R. 42
Kirgis, P. 160
Kleinhans, M. 174
Kmiec, D. W. 7
Kocourek, A. 110
Kotz, H. 6, 27

Kronman, A. T. 37, 39, 101
Kuhn, T. 79

Langdell, C. C. 94
Law and economics xiii, 44
Legal officials, identification of 138–41
Legal pluralism:
    new 115–17, 129, 138–9, 171, 172–5,
    180–1, 182
    old 115–16, 171, 199
    Santos's approach 181–5
    Teubner's approach 186–91
Legal positivism xiii, xvi, xvii, xix, 4, 11,
    14, 17–19, 22–7, 29, 31–2, 38, 44, 45,
    70–1, 80–1, 98, 103, 129, 134–5, 140,
    143–8, 152–4, 156–62
Legal profession 37, 46, 71–6, 94,
    108–10, 120, 127–8, 231, 235, 236,
    238–9
Legal Realists 45, 47–9, 94, 114, 131, 176
Legitimation of law 4–9, 14, 17–19, 32,
    39–40, 48, 56–7, 65, 67, 69–70, 94–6,
    98–106, 158, 231, 234, 240–2
Leiter, B. 156
Lempert, R. 36
Leue, H. J. 112
Levy Bruhl, L. 92
Lex mercatoria 74, 125–9, 140, 184, 229
Liebniz 79
Lind, E. A. 105
Llewellyn, K. 47, 48, 49, 131, 132
Locke, J. 20, 57, 59, 63, 64, 69, 81, 83
Luckmann, T. 142
Luhmann, N. 8, 36, 51, 52, 56, 71, 109,
    176, 177, 187, 188
Lukes, S. 34, 35
Luther, M. 72
Lyons, D. 161

Macaulay, S. 207
MacCormick, N. 110, 163, 164
Macdonald, R. A. 174
MacIntyre, A. 61, 63, 67, 70, 75, 78, 84,
    91, 164
Madonna 121
Maine, H. 27, 32, 33, 34, 37, 52, 61, 71,
    118
Maitland 93
Malebranche 79
Malinowski, B. 176, 178, 179, 187, 202
Mamut, L. S. 41, 42
Maniacs, P. T. 61, 103, 188
Marcus, G. E. xiii

Marmor, A. 136, 148, 189
Marx, K. 40, 41, 42, 44, 51, 62, 86, 213
Marxism and law 40–3
Merry, S. E. 115, 171, 173, 174, 182
Merryman, J. H. 72, 127
Merton, R. K. 137
Mill, J. S. 64, 82
Milovanovic, D. 37
Mirror thesis 1–3, 9–10, 13, 20–1, 25, 26,
    28–30, 31, 32, 35, 36, 40–4, 48, 49,
    51–2, 65, 71, 72–5, 77, 86, 92, 96,
    102–6, 107–11, 112–20, 131–2, 163,
    230–7, 239–40
Mommsen, W. J. 112, 113
Montesquieu, B. de 6, 27, 28, 29, 31, 35,
    51, 86
Moore, M. xv, 135, 137, 154, 157
Moore, S. F. 50, 173, 176, 178, 202, 203,
    206, 207
Morality and law 4–10, 13, 15, 18–19, 22,
    24, 25, 26, 28, 35, 38, 40, 42, 44, 45,
    48, 52, 71, 80–8, 137–9, 152–5,
    156–9, 174, 186, 227, 241
Morrall, J. 68, 181
Morris, C. W. 57, 65
Morse, B. 113
Mounce, H. O. 82

Nader, L. 203
Natural law 5–7, 15–22, 23, 26, 27, 28,
    29, 31–2, 45, 80–6, 97–8, 100, 105,
    136, 144, 147, 151, 156–62, 181,
    193–4, 195, 196, 198, 230, 240–1
Nelken, D. 127, 131
Nielson, K. 20
Non-essentialist approach to law 134,
    151, 172, 193–4, 200, 204–5
Nonet, P. 51, 105

Orucu, E. 110
Ostwald, M. 6, 8, 12, 13

Pardieck, A. 128
Parsons, T. 36, 54, 60, 130, 210, 211, 216
Pashukanis, E. B. 41, 62, 66, 67, 87
Patterson, E. 30
Payne, M. A. 154
Perry, S. 150, 151
Plato 7, 11, 12, 13, 14, 19, 40, 52, 67
Polan, D. 43, 44
Pollock, F. 5, 7, 22
Pompe, S. 153
Posner, R. 43, 71

Postema, G. J. 7, 19, 45, 72, 80, 92, 93
Pound, R. 6, 7, 8, 11, 14, 21, 22, 24, 29,
    30, 45, 47, 93
Primary and secondary rules 26–7, 66,
    133, 136, 137–43, 146, 148, 152–5,
    165, 173, 177
Public Choice Theory 49–50, 103
Public/private distinction 52, 54, 59–60,
    66–9, 112, 118, 140
Puchta, G. F. 30

Quigley, J. 153

Rawls, J. 57, 63
Raz, J. xv, xvi, 98, 99, 138, 139, 140, 143,
    144, 147, 151, 168
Reason and law 4–10, 13, 15, 18–19, 22,
    23, 28, 37, 38, 72, 86–8, 91, 93–4,
    96–106, 241
Reimann, M. 28, 30
Religious law 139, 140, 157–8, 162, 166,
    168, 180, 193, 199, 227–8
Riles, A. 171
Roberts, S. 50, 114, 203, 204
Rommen, H. 158
Rorty, R. 2
Rosenblum, N. 48
Rousseau. J.-J. 29, 57, 58
Rule, J. B. 208, 217, 220
Rule of law 98–106, 124, 238–9

Sanders, J. 120
Sassen, S. 126, 130
Schauer, F. 154
Schneewind, J. B. 17, 22, 80, 81, 97, 158
Schofield, P. 24
Schur, E. M. 176, 179
Schutz, A. 163, 195
Searle, J. 142, 179, 215, 224
Seita, A. 121
Selznik, P. 51, 105
Separation thesis 17–18, 24, 145, 146,
    152, 156–9, 231
Shakespeare, W. 72
Shapiro, M. 106, 122, 126
Shiner, R. A. 153
Simmons, J. A. 63
Simon, Y. 20
Simpson, A. W. B. 93
Slaughter, A. M. 124, 128
Smith, A. 40, 67, 220
Snyder, F. 115
Social arena 206–8

Social contract theory 57–8, 62–5
Social order 1–3, 8, 10, 11, 14, 16–19, 23, 24–5, 31, 34–6, 40, 42, 50, 52–8, 60–5, 69–70, 105, 107, 116–17, 135, 136–8, 140, 142–9, 157, 175–81, 187, 192–3, 203–5, 208–24, 230–6, 239–40
Social sources thesis 146, 152, 159–62
Social theory of law 162–6
Socio-legal studies xvii, 131–2, 134–5, 159, 169, 171–2, 192, 201
Sociology of law xii, xv, xviii, xix, 28, 39, 109, 115, 131–2, 140, 159, 162–6
Soper, P. 135, 136
Spinoza 79
Stein, P. 14, 28, 32, 33, 61, 91, 93, 94, 96
Stone, A. 40
Substantive view of good, away from 21–2, 23, 80–6, 96–106
Summers, R. S. 45, 48, 98, 100
Sumner, C. 42
Sweet, A. S. 105

Tamanaha, B. Z. xi, 2, 31, 48, 65, 105, 114, 115, 116, 120, 124, 145, 155, 162, 163, 165, 175, 179, 183, 215, 221, 226, 241
Tarnas, R. xiv, 78, 85, 97
Tate, C. N. 105
Taylor, G. 128
Teubner, G. 109, 171, 172, 174, 186, 187, 188, 189, 190, 191, 194
Thrasymachus 40, 67
Thurow, L. 121
Torti, A. 2
Trakman, L. 126
Transnational commercial law 128–9, 229, 237–8
Transnational law 120–30, 196, 229
Transnational legal culture 72, 74, 108–10, 127–8, 235, 238
Transplantation of law 108–20, 146, 233
Trubek, D. 37, 87, 115

Tushnet, M. 43
Twining, W. xiii, xv, xvi, 122, 125, 130, 184

Ullmann, W. 2, 5, 6, 18, 57, 99, 139, 180
Ulpian 15, 56, 72
Unger, R. M. 23, 51, 52, 55, 71, 85, 95, 105, 118, 149, 166

Vallinder, T. 105
Vago, S. 2
Vinogradoff 7
Voltaire 97
von Benda-Beckmann, F. 113
von Ihering, R. 45, 46, 48, 49, 66, 67, 68
von Savigny, F. K. 27, 28, 29, 30, 46, 48, 71, 89

Wachterhauser, B. R. 167
Waldron, J. xvi, 103, 104
Walker, G. 121
Watson, A. 5, 107, 108, 109, 110
Weber, M. 7, 32, 37, 38, 39, 51, 71, 73, 74, 75, 87, 96, 97, 98, 100, 101, 109, 115, 118, 138, 140, 158, 177, 181, 196, 209, 210, 211, 221
Weiner, M. 122, 123
Weisberg, D. K. 43
West, R. 43
Whitman, J. Q. 7
Wiegand, W. 110, 127
Wiles, P. 41
Wilhelmsson, T. 123
Wilson, J. 163
Winch, P. 185
Wittgenstein, L. 214, 215
Woodman, G. 113
Wrong, D. 23, 206, 208, 210, 211, 212, 213, 216, 222

Xenophon 11

Zimmerman, R. 74
Zweigert, K. 6, 27, 28